WOMEN OF
DISCRIMINATING
TASTE

Women of
Discriminating
Taste

WHITE SORORITIES
AND THE MAKING OF
American Ladyhood

MARGARET L. FREEMAN

THE UNIVERSITY OF
GEORGIA PRESS
ATHENS

© 2020 by the University of Georgia Press
Athens, Georgia 30602
www.ugapress.org
Designed by Kaelin Chappell Broaddus
Set in 10.5/13.5 Garamond Premier Pro by Kaelin Chappell Broaddus

Most University of Georgia Press titles are
available from popular e-book vendors.

Printed digitally

Library of Congress Cataloging-in-Publication Data

Names: Freeman, Margaret L., author.
Title: Women of discriminating taste : white sororities and the making
    of American ladyhood / Margaret L. Freeman.
Description: Athens : The University of Georgia Press, 2020. | Includes
    bibliographical references and index.
Identifiers: LCCN 2020028109 (print) | LCCN 2020028110 (ebook) |
    ISBN 9780820358154 (hardback) | ISBN 9780820358161 (paperback)
    | ISBN 9780820358147 (ebook)
Subjects: LCSH: Greek letter societies—United States—History—20th
    century. | College sorority members—United States—Conduct of
    life. | Women, White—Southern States—Conduct of life. | Racism
    in higher education—United States—History—20th century. |
    Conservatism—United States—History—20th century.
Classification: LCC LJ34 .F74 2020 (print) | LCC LJ34 (ebook) |
    DDC 371.8/5—dc23
LC record available at https://lccn.loc.gov/2020028109
LC ebook record available at https://lccn.loc.gov/2020028110

CONTENTS

—•—

ACKNOWLEDGMENTS

Well over a decade has passed since I first began this project for the American Studies Program at the College of William and Mary. Both the project and my life have taken a variety of directions since the journey began in a blank Word document. I am very grateful that I have had the opportunity to move this study from a series of chapter drafts to a completed manuscript. The issues surrounding historically white sororities and the struggle for a national culture are perhaps even more pressing for American society today than when I started my research. I am deeply indebted to Lisa Bayer and the University of Georgia Press for believing in this project and continuing to support my work as I refined the arguments and prose. Nathaniel Holly was a pleasure to work with as I readied the final draft for submission. Lori Rider provided an expert set of eyes at the editing stage and corrected my slew of grammatical and punctuation blunders. Press editor Thomas Roche kindly answered my many editorial questions and deftly guided the project to production under the added challenge of working remotely in spring 2020.

Many individuals and institutions had a hand in bringing this book to fruition. Leisa Meyer, Charles McGovern, Scott Nelson, and Maureen Fitzgerald assured me of the significance of the topic while also offering insight on ways to make the arguments stronger and more nuanced. I hope that I have built on their suggestions to make this a better work. Additional thanks to Arthur Knight for pointing out the rich material in the Margetta Hirsch Doyle diaries and to Sara Kaiser for forwarding me copies of Dean of Women Records from the University of Mississippi. Over the years I presented nascent pieces of this project at a number of conferences and workshops, including the William and Mary Graduate Research Symposium, the North Carolina State University Graduate Student History Conference, the Southern Association for Women Historians Triennial Conference, the History of Education Society Conference, the Southern History of Education Society Conference, the Southern Historical Association Annual Meeting, the Newberry Library Seminar on Gender and Sexuality, and the William and Mary American Studies Brownbag Series. Commentators, panelists, and session attendees at those events posed questions, offered encouragement, and made me think about sorority women and their world in new ways. I would particularly like to thank Katherine Charron, Kathleen Clark, Caroline Janney, Joan Johnson, Amy McCandless, Michele Nickerson, and Pamela Tyler for their comments on conference and workshop papers that helped me refine and strengthen this work. I was also motivated by conversations with historian Hilary Miller-Tomaino, an active Kappa Kappa Gamma alumna who approached me at the meeting of the Southern Historical Association to comment on the importance of my research. Additionally, several iterations of the American Studies Writing Group and the Women's History Writing Group from William and Mary's American Studies Program and its History Department, provided valuable feedback at various stages of the work. The greatest thanks goes to Libby Neidenbach, who read countless drafts over the years and provided much needed clarity to my arguments. Portions of this book have appeared in other edited collections. I wish to thank Laura J. Gifford and Daniel K. Williams for their extremely insightful comments on drafts of my chapter in their edited collection *The Right Side of the Sixties*, which forms part of chapter 6 of this work. Likewise, Christine Ogren and Marc VanOverbeke's feedback on a chapter for their edited collection *Rethinking Campus Life* helped me reconsider and reframe the introduction and main arguments of this project. The ideas in this book are much stronger as a result of these scholars' contributions. At the manuscript stage, several readers for the University of Georgia Press highlighted ways to tighten the narrative and bring forth key arguments. One of these reviewers, Nicholas L. Syrett, provided an excellent model with his exhaustively researched study of white college fraternities, *The Company He Keeps* (2009), which greatly influenced how I considered my investigation of white sororities.

Generous grants to help defray costs of research trips and photocopying along the way came from multiple sources at the College of William and Mary: the American Studies Program, the Roy E. Charles Center for Academic Excellence, and the Office of Graduate Studies, Arts and Sciences. As the 2007 Guion Griffis Johnson Visiting Scholar at the Southern Historical Collection, I benefited from the largesse of the Louis Round Wilson Library at the University of North Carolina at Chapel Hill. Many of the research trips would not have been possible without the unflagging support of my parents, who offered financial assistance as well as my old bedroom as a landing place during many research trips to the Triangle area of North Carolina.

Without archivists and reference librarians my research would have taken much longer and probably yielded much less useful material. For their interest in suggesting collections of possible use, helping track seemingly mundane details, and acquiring images and permission for the manuscript, I thank the following people at the following repositories: Dwayne Cox at Auburn University's Special Collections; Susanna Miller at the Birmingham-Southern College Archives; Amy Schindler, Kimberly Sims, and Carolyn Wilson at the College of William and Mary's Special Collections Research Center; Amy McDonald and Tom Harkins at the Duke University Archives; Jessica Roseberry and Rebecca Williams at Duke University Medical Center Archives; Judy Bolton at Louisiana State University Special Collections; Marina Klaric at the University of Alabama's Hoole Special Collections; Stephen Brown and Leigh Ann Ripley at the University of Georgia's Hargrett Library; Emilia Garvey, Lisa Renee Kemplin, Ellen Swain, and Anna Trammell at the Student Life and Culture Archives at the University of Illinois Archives; Malissa Ruffner at the University of Maryland Special Collections and University Archives; Matthew Turi and Keith Longiotti at the University of North Carolina's Wilson Library; and Elizabeth West at the University of South Carolina's South Caroliniana Library. The National Panhellenic Council, Alpha Tau Omega, Alpha Delta Pi, and Phi Mu provided great assistance and helped shape this work by granting access to portions of their records. The Interlibrary Loan departments at the College of William and Mary's Swem Library and the Portland Public Library in Portland, Maine handled my requests for obscure materials with aplomb. I particularly wish to thank the following women for their willingness to speak with me about their college experiences: Nancy Iler Burkholder, Judith Ewell, Francis Drane Inglis, Kathryn Smith Pyle, Peggy Eutemark Smith, and Melanie Wilson.

Life as a twenty-something in Williamsburg, Virginia, is not for excitement seekers. Luckily, however, the group of students in my American Studies cohort are some of the best people I've known, and I am grateful that we all randomly ended up where we did, when we did. We also had the pleasure of being guided by advisors and mentors who are real, approachable people, genuinely interested in their students' and colleagues' lives. Whether in seminars, at writing group meetings, or (way too many) nights at the Green Leafe, we kept each other going through what often can be the tedious process of procuring a humanities PhD. Thanks to Sarah Adams, Ben Anderson, Frank Cha, Evan Cordulack, Erin Krutko Devlin, Seth Feman, Mikal Gaines, Sarah

Grunder, Wendy Korwin, Kim Mann, John Miller, Libby Neidenbach, Brian Piper, and Kristen Proehl for making the 'Burg not just livable, but a place and time that I still miss.

I also wish to thank my coworkers at my nonacademic jobs since grad school, who have always been deeply interested in, supportive of, and maybe a little amazed at the book project I have been wedded to for so long. Thanks to Liam Paskvan for sharing the "dog duties" for years and reminding me that I should be proud of the work that I put into this project. After work, on weekends, and during vacation days, my furry writing companion, Nicolai the Shar-Pei husky, kept me company and took me for walks around downtown Portland, Maine, during work breaks. And last, but certainly not least, to my family: my parents, Patricia Roe Freeman and Douglas G. Freeman Jr., and my brother Doug Freeman III—all of whom really must be the most chill people ever—I very much appreciate your believing that people should do what makes them happy, and for understanding not to ask when I was going to finish this book.

ILLUSTRATIONS

REFERENCED SORORITIES
AND FRATERNITIES

——•◦•——

National Panhellenic Conference (NPC) Sororities	Greek-Letter Abbreviation
Alpha Chi Omega	ΑΧΩ
Alpha Delta Pi	ΑΔΠ
Alpha Delta Theta[1]	ΑΔΘ
Alpha Epsilon Phi[2]	ΑΕΦ
Alpha Gamma Delta	ΑΓΔ
Alpha Omicron Pi	ΑΟΠ
Alpha Phi	ΑΦ
Alpha Sigma Alpha	ΑΣΑ
Alpha Sigma Tau	ΑΣΤ
Alpha Xi Delta	ΑΞΔ
Beta Sigma Omicron[3]	ΒΣΟ
Chi Omega	ΧΩ
Delta Delta Delta	ΔΔΔ
Delta Gamma	ΔΓ
Delta Sigma Epsilon[4]	ΔΣΕ
Delta Zeta	ΔΖ
Gamma Phi Beta	ΓΦΒ
Kappa Alpha Theta	ΚΑΘ
Kappa Delta	ΚΔ
Kappa Kappa Gamma	ΚΚΓ
Pi Beta Phi	ΠΒΦ
Pi Kappa Sigma[5]	ΠΚΣ
Phi Mu	ΦΜ

National Panhellenic Conference (NPC) Sororities	Greek-Letter Abbreviation
Sigma Kappa	ΣΚ
Sigma Sigma Sigma	ΣΣΣ
Theta Sigma Upsilon[6]	ΘΣΥ
Theta Upsilon[7]	ΘΥ
Zeta Tau Alpha	ZTA

National Pan-Hellenic Council (NPHC) Sororities

Alpha Kappa Alpha	AKA
Delta Sigma Theta	ΔΣΘ

National Interfraternity Conference (NIC) Fraternities

Alpha Sigma Phi	ΑΕΦ
Alpha Tau Omega	ΑΤΩ
Kappa Alpha Order	ΚΑ
Kappa Sigma	ΚΣ
Lambda Chi Alpha	ΛΧΑ
Pi Kappa Alpha	ΠΚΑ
Phi Gamma Delta	ΦΓΔ
Sigma Alpha Epsilon	ΣΑΕ
Sigma Chi	ΣΧ
Sigma Nu	ΣΝ
Sigma Tau Gamma	ΣΤ
Theta Chi	ΘΧ
Zeta Psi	ZΨ

National Pan-Hellenic Council (NPHC) Fraternities

Alpha Phi Alpha	ΑΦΑ
Kappa Alpha Psi	ΚΑΨ
Omega Psi Phi	ΩΨΦ

1. Absorbed by Phi Mu, 1939.
2. Historically Jewish sorority.
3. Absorbed by Zeta Tau Alpha, 1964.
4. Absorbed by Delta Zeta, 1956.
5. Absorbed by Sigma Kappa, 1959.
6. Absorbed by Alpha Gamma Delta, 1959.
7. Absorbed by Delta Zeta, 1962.

*WOMEN OF
DISCRIMINATING
TASTE*

Where Y'all Does Not Mean All

*W*hite women in frilly white dresses, some hoop-skirted, some wearing wide-brimmed hats and carrying delicate parasols, framed the front portico of the Federal Revival–style Alpha Gamma Delta (ΑΓΔ) sorority house at the University of Alabama in a 1965 yearbook photo (see fig. 1). Along with the crude replicas of antebellum frocks, some of the singing and dancing sorority women appeared in pantaloons, and others wore homespun costumes indicative of yeomen farm families or, more likely, enslaved African Americans. A banner on the portico's ironwork welcomed rushees (the term for women attending sorority rush with the goal of joining a sorority) to the "ΑΓΔ Plantation." Sorority sisters enacted skits and held parties during the rush period to woo the rushees whom they wished to invite into membership. The audience for the ΑΓΔ spectacle included a group of well-coiffed rushees and behind them a group of young white men, standing casually with hands on hips, eager to gain a view of the proceedings. The layers of the rush party ritual evident in the picture were not lost on the yearbook staff, who captioned the scene with an imagined line from the ΑΓΔ sorority women: "Step right up, gents. On the inside for just one dollar . . ."[1] This double entendre—suggesting that the "show" inside the house, or perhaps a sexual experience with one of the ΑΓΔ sisters, could be had for a mere dollar—was a knowing jab at sorority women who had long relied on a heavy dose of heterosocializing to maintain their "desired" status and popularity on campuses across the country. The comment placed the supposed sexual purity of the "southern belles" on display into ques-

Step right up, gents. On the inside for just one dollar . . . .

FIGURE 1. Alpha Gamma Delta Plantation Skit. *Corolla*, 1965.
Courtesy of the W. S. Hoole Special Collections Library, the University of Alabama.

tion and upended the image of the proper white southern lady that the historically white National Panhellenic Conference (NPC) sororities sought to
present.[2] Most problematically in this incident, the writer's caption suggested
that white southern ladies were *not* in fact worthy of their vaunted position in
southern society, where they reigned as pious, genteel, feminine, and chaste yet
physically alluring paragons of womanhood. Such a proclamation could overturn the intertwined gender, race, and class hierarchies of the region, throwing
southern and national understandings of white male supremacy into disarray.

While this performance of reimagined southern ladyhood took place at a
seemingly logical location—a historically white campus in the Deep South
that was in the midst of struggles over black civil rights and racial integration—such celebrations of Old South imagery also occurred at nonsouthern colleges.[3] The plantation-themed rush party was popular among sorority
chapters across the nation from the 1920s through the 1960s and indulged in
what I term a southern aesthetic, with which sorority women were eager to associate. In sororities' quarterly journals, college members shared details about
costumes, food, and drink to make the events authentic to the South.[4] Non-

southerners too, encouraged by popular culture during these decades, adopted the southern aesthetic as they sought to connect themselves to the seemingly noble and unadulterated heritage of the South and the supposed unrivaled natural beauty of the region's women.[5] Practice of the southern aesthetic connected southern and nonsouthern women in historically white national sororities, but it also allowed nonsouthern members to distance themselves from what they, and many Americans, saw as the ugly and embarrassing history of the slaveholding and Jim Crow Souths when it was convenient to do so. Nonsouthern whites eagerly imbibed a fantasized image of the southern plantation lifestyle, from which African Americans' experiences were either largely erased or reshaped to fit the desires of the white imagination. Nonsouthern sorority leaders simultaneously desired and othered the southern aesthetic as they privately supported segregation, while also pointing to white southerners as the reason they needed to uphold their whites-only membership policies.

wow

White southern "traditions" are often invoked when Americans seek to lay blame for a national heritage of racism. I argue that we should look both to and beyond the South to map uses of a southern aesthetic. We can use the underexamined institution of the historically white Greek-letter sorority to chart a new path in the history of conservative women's activism. Over the course of the twentieth century, nonsouthern and southern sorority alumnae labored to instill values consistent with emerging conservative ideology in their members. Sororities leaned heavily on the imagery of the southern lady as the emblem of the aesthetic and as a stealthily crafted, nonthreatening image of conservative American womanhood. Their training molded white college women across the United States in the image of an imagined southern belle. *—bc men wanted them to be such*

Some scholarly treatments of the rise of modern conservatism have popularized a narrative of white racial backlash against the civil rights movement in the mid- to late 1960s as the impetus for white southerners' political realignment with the Republican Party. However, like a number of historians in recent years, I show that this realignment began much earlier, as anti–New Deal southerners of the 1930s and 1940s found commonality of ideals with white conservative Republicans outside the South. Sorority women had charted a course of "antiradical" thought in the 1910s and 1920s, and by the 1930s and 1940s they were concerned with "liberal" forces in the U.S. government and the destruction of "American democracy," which meant "white American democracy." Historians including Joseph Crespino, Kevin M. Kruse, Matthew D. Lassiter, Nancy MacLean, Elizabeth Gillespie McRae, and Jason Morgan Ward have highlighted the white, southern, grassroots networks that helped foster the modern conservative movement through support of such beliefs as sanctity of individual freedom, private property rights, and consumer choice. However, as they note, these ideals, common to conservative intellectuals and white middle-class Americans, were national in scope. To limit our investigations, or our condemnations, to southerners misses a large part of this formative story of twentieth-century American history.[6]

This book adds the history of NPC sororities to the mix of grassroots networks that have influenced the growth of the modern conservative movement in the twentieth century. By spreading a reactionary ideology through organizational communications and by maintaining segregated social spaces within institutions of higher education, NPC sororities have contributed to the shaping of generations of college women's sociopolitical thinking. This history, however, has been largely undocumented. Recent exposés and journalistic accounts of sororities' neofeminist, racist, and classist belief systems have examined contemporary situations in NPC sororities.[7] My research shows the long history of these activities that have persisted, unchecked and largely under the radar, but have directly influenced the problematic sorority behaviors of today. I argue that while the organizations may have served a valuable role as spaces of women's friendship during the early years of coeducation, they have always been conservative in nature and inherently discriminatory, whether they be selecting members according to social class, religion, race, or physical attractiveness.

The ΑΓΔ Plantation image that focused on sorority members as southern belles highlights a number of issues that NPC sororities regularly brought to bear on college campuses during the twentieth century. First, sorority rush, of which this skit was a part, typically took place concurrently with the start of the fall semester and was quite time-consuming for sorority sisters (actives) and sorority hopefuls (rushees). It emphasized social over academic pursuits and distracted many freshmen from the first few weeks of their college lives. Rush enabled sororities to engineer their membership demographic, selecting those women that met their idealized image of white women who could actively share in their conservative brand of the southern aesthetic. Second, the male bystanders in the picture represent the ever-present role of white men, and fraternity men in particular, in the function and existence of the sororities. To be a popular chapter on the Alabama campus, ΑΓΔ would need to appeal to the right type of men—those seen as the sorority women's social peers. The appeal often meant brazen displays of women's sexuality, while social convention decreed that unmarried white women remain sexually inactive. This dichotomy created an ever-present tension for sorority women who, like the belle, needed to maintain a come-hither appearance while also holding responsibility for deflecting the sexual advances of men. Third, the visual imagery of the southern belle and the Old South plantation used in this skit and others enacted by sorority chapters across the country clearly defined who would be accepted on the front steps of the "big house" and who would not. These enactments distinctly delineated sororities as powerful, private institutions reinforcing class and race divides on campuses across the country.

To understand the continuing problems of contemporary NPC sororities and their relation to a southern aesthetic, we must look to the historical role of sororities in the South and across the United States during the twentieth century. While secret societies for young women existed in the South prior to sororities, Greek-letter sororities were founded and first gained influence in nonsouthern regions of the United States in the second half of the nineteenth century. The organizations continued their spread to the South by the turn of the twentieth century, first at women-only colleges and then increasingly at what had been men-only universities, as women slowly gained entrance and acceptance at these institutions. In the South, where early sorority chapters stood to shake young, modern, white women free from the confines of proper, submissive ladyhood, they instead became critical sites for the reinforcement of southern gender prescriptions and provided a specific arena of display for the college women's femininity. This study examines NPC sororities as they affected campus life and the lives of their alumnae in the twentieth century. My analysis builds on Diana Turk's seminal work on sororities, *Bound by a Mighty Vow: Sisterhood and Women's Fraternities, 1870–1920* (2004), but moves beyond her scope to illuminate how these organizations have nationalized the image and idea of southern identity—largely emblematized by the southern lady—to support their conservative agenda across the twentieth century.

Sororities' southern aesthetic inculcated social behaviors that reinforced the white, southern lady ideal and the hegemony of the white elite in the South. While national sororities shaped class delineations and gender prescriptions for college women and alumnae all over the United States, southern-founded sororities and southern chapters of all NPC groups unofficially assumed the added duty of disseminating southern cultural values throughout the nation while producing the symbolic southern lady who had become synonymous with the region itself. White southerners repeatedly called on the image of the belle or lady to support southern racial hierarchies, but it was also a symbol easily exported for use in other areas of the United States that shared similar concerns over changing social demographics and racial unrest.[8]

The Southern Lady as the Southern Aesthetic

I began this project seeking to understand why the contemporary image of the sorority woman—often condensed to the "sorority girl"—is so readily associated with images of white southern women and the storied trope of the southern lady. Although many national sororities began at nonsouthern schools, and both southern- and nonsouthern-founded sororities maintained more chapters at nonsouthern schools, the groups and their members still conjure up ideas of physically attractive, superficially polite, and traditionally minded white women. And these are characteristics often associated with the stereotypical ideal of the white southern lady or belle, which is one of the most enduring symbols of the southern aesthetic as it continues today.[9] The lady or belle figure is a holdover from the antebellum plantation culture of the South and has remained an alluring ideal for white southerners, as well as white nonsoutherners, who have repeatedly summoned her as a symbol of a bygone yet strangely captivating era.

The southern aesthetic of early twentieth-century sorority women grew out of the Lost Cause ideology. Originally a means of honoring Confederate dead, the Lost Cause and its associated beliefs, as celebrated from 1865 to the 1920s, broadened to include the veneration of a reimagined South—the Old South—where all whites lived on slave-owning plantations, all enslaved African Americans were happy, and racial harmony reigned. This imagining provided a continuation of a supposed antebellum utopia for white southerners, which was only briefly disrupted by federal intervention during war and Reconstruction. Through the veneration and commemoration of Confederate military and political figures with statues, parades, pageants, and other public memorials, the Lost Cause also afforded white southerners a visible and tangible means of reminding black southerners that white supremacy survived the war unscathed. As the "civil religion" of the South, the Lost Cause, grounded in Old South mythology, also soothed white southerners who became increasingly fearful of emancipated African Americans in their midst by preserving the memory of a time when racial hierarchy was absolute.[10]

The image of the fragile and virtuous white southern lady loomed large in this environment, playing against the white southern male's construction of the black man as a sexual threat. The mythology of sexually dangerous black men became an integral component of white supremacy in the South in the years surrounding the turn of the twentieth century.[11] Conveniently, this trope also helped obscure the long history of white men's sexual violence against black women. Controlling sexual access to white southern women by "protecting" them from the imagined threat of black male sexuality enabled white male supremacy in the post–Civil War South.[12] For this "protection," white women were expected to pay deference to their supposedly chivalrous, white male protectors. White women's price for venerated southern womanhood was a limited social role. While they found greater freedom to enter the public sphere in the years following the Civil War—a move often made out of economic necessity—white women, Tara McPherson explains, were ultimately "unwilling to question white privilege, buying into a return to the pedestal on which southern femininity was properly situated."[13]

Around the turn of the twentieth century, young women at colleges across the nation were keen to associate themselves with these groups that offered promises of never-ending friendship and, perhaps even more significantly, a means of marking oneself as part of an elite, civilized, white society. Seeking to present themselves as social elites, middle- and upper-class white native-born Americans relied on markers of cultural refinement and education to set themselves apart from the less established, and supposedly less advanced, "new" Americans. With their faux-familial ties and selective membership, NPC sororities promised to challenge the mounting diversity of American culture by limiting those whom the members saw as undesirable from participation in the organizations and, indirectly, from important power connections in adult and professional life. Sororities, like patriotic heritage societies such as the Daughters of the American Revolution (DAR) (1890), the National Society of the Colonial Dames of America (NSCDA) (1891), and the Society of Mayflower Descendants (1897), provided further affirmation of their unadulterated, Anglo-Saxon heritage. Many of these same women joined preservation organizations such as the Association for the Preservation of Virginia Antiquities (APVA) (1889) or the Society for the Preservation of New England Antiquities (SPNEA) (1910), which sought to maintain and commemorate spaces connected to colonial forebears.[14] They also populated other organizations in the women's club movement of the late nineteenth century, such as the General Federation of Women's Clubs (GFWC) (1890), the Young Women's Christian Association (YWCA) (1858), the Woman's Christian Temperance Union (WCTU) (1873), and, in the South, the United Daughters of the Confederacy (UDC) (1894). The cultural and literal divide between the sorority "sisters" and nonmembers became another way for sorority women and alumnae to establish themselves as an elite group of all-American women.

Even as many white middle-class Americans sought connections with an imagined, aristocratic past through backward-looking aesthetic and heritage movements such as the Lost Cause and the Colonial Revival movements at the turn of the twentieth century, a populist campaign of southern and midwestern farmers launched attacks against the power of a cultured elite in these same years. Frequent targets of the populist crusade, Greek-letter organizations (GLOs) found themselves deflecting criticism that they were snobbish, divisive of the student body, and an all-around bad influence on students. Some Populist Party–led state legislatures waged war against GLOs on their state university campuses. In South Carolina and Mississippi they succeeded in banning the groups for several decades, and some private universities also decided to shutter GLOs amid the unfavorable publicity.[15] Amid this sentiment, sororities became, to their members, bulwarks of culture in a disparate sea of rabble, which sorority women saw as infiltrating American society and its college campuses.[16] The organizations viewed themselves as guardians of privilege to be conferred only to those women who met their standards. Thus, NPC groups learned to maintain vigilance in the face of what they viewed as constant criticism from those whom they believed were not GLO material in the first place—a defensive posture they continued to exert throughout the twentieth century.

Sororities' Rightward Turn

Although I argue that sororities across the United States were always havens for women who held conservative beliefs about women's activities in society, the cross-pollination of NPC sorority alumnae and groups such as the DAR and others provided an easy flow of increasingly reactionary rhetoric into sororities from the World War I years onward. Particularly in the years after World War II, when civil rights issues made headlines on the national and international stages, the organizations made a distinct rightward turn in their public-facing ideology. National Panhellenic Conference leaders felt that their rights to "freedom of association" in membership selection were endangered by "liberal" legislation and Supreme Court decisions. What others may have labeled as racism by the 1940s and 1950s, the sorority women saw as their "rights" as private, pseudo-familial organizations to "discriminate" in their membership. In this period, they allied with other conservative groups and individuals who would form the base of a new national conservative movement by the 1960s. Sorority women had sown the seeds for this relationship in their interwar-era positioning and were able to benefit from a conservative alignment by the 1970s and 1980s.

Sororities' political position and their promotion of a southern aesthetic also correlated with the growing influence of the Sunbelt states in U.S. sociopolitical realms. National sorority and NPC leaders had shown their support for the "southern way of life" as racial desegregation threatened both southern white supremacy and GLOs' white supremacy. By the 1970s, after legal segregation had been slowly dismantled on university campuses, sororities still espoused a white conservative ideology that relied on what Matthew Lassiter has called an "ethos of color-blind individualism" increasingly found among middle-class whites of the suburban South. Sororities were a converging point and training ground for white women across the country who espoused white, middle-class, suburban views on individual rights, privatization, and consumer choice.[17]

About This Book

This study is arranged thematically and moves in a roughly chronological fashion. Chapter 1 places sororities on the New South college campus in the early decades of the twentieth century. National sororities already espoused a model for American womanhood that prized domesticity and promoted the groups as a home away from home for young women attending college. Sororities could provide social training, structured activity, and often a family home in which members could live. Meanwhile, their image as a homelike space that cultivated ladylike behavior was a useful marketing tool both for sororities and for advocates of women's higher education. I argue that sororities shifted from operating as support networks for college women within the androcentric campus culture to promoters of what I term "heterosocialization" on campus by the 1920s in an attempt to ensure the public that the organizations were primarily shaping young women who sought marriage and family after graduation rather than continued education or careers. In pushing the image of nonthreatening, feminine women who sought dating interaction with male peers, sororities indirectly epitomized a conservative model of American womanhood premised on the southern lady.

Chapter 2 shows how sorority leaders worked to sell their organizations' "social education" as specialized training for ladyhood that college women would not otherwise receive from the academic curriculum. In response to critics who argued that the groups were frivolous, elitist social clubs that stratified students and diminished the scholarly environment of the campus, sorority leaders positioned the groups as an integral part of a woman's education. The ideal sorority woman, as constructed through sorority training, would be a nationalized version of the southern lady, largely concerned with physical appearances and behavioral practice as a means to convey socioeconomic status as well as sorority chapter popularity. By infiltrating their social education with the southern aesthetic, sororities designed and produced a conservative model of American womanhood.

Chapter 3 examines the southern aesthetic as practiced by both southern- and nonsouthern-founded national sororities in the first half of the twentieth century. Sorority women across the United States used popular reimaginings of the Old South and the southern belle or lady to demonstrate a supposed connection to an aristocratic past. At the same time, these nostalgic displays supported a vision of the nation premised on strict social, racial, and gender hierarchies. With national conferences organized around southern-themed locations, sorority houses modeled after southern plantation homes, rush parties featuring southern-inspired menus and costumes, and histories of aristocratic sorority founders, sororities drew on a southern aesthetic to present an image of their organizations as genteel, feminine, and racially exclusive.

Chapters 4 and 5 continue to explore the southern aesthetic in two distinct areas of national sorority practices: heterosocial interaction with fraternities and the selection of new members through rush. An examination of these sorority activities demonstrates sororities' hardening conservatism from the 1920s to the 1960s. By directing members to value and emulate characteristics of the southern lady, the most visible symbol of the southern aesthetic, sororities taught white women across the nation to connect a specific sociopolitical ideology to their gendered behavior and appearance as well as the organizations' discriminatory membership selection process.

As sororities' social activities increasingly focused on heterosocializing with fraternity men, the organizations became spaces to train women in heterosocial interactions and police their behavior to meet white, middle-class norms. While sorority chapters had been facilitating parties and dates since the late nineteenth century, chapter 4 charts these activities from the 1910s to the 1960s when sororities increasingly enforced a nonthreatening, hyperheteronormative display of belledom that aligned with the developing conservative ideal of womanhood. However, the groups' practice dating environments, including sorority mixers and formals, could become spaces of sexual danger for young women. The enduring double standard for women's sexual activity reinforced these dangers, and the growing proclivity for alcohol use within the spaces of heterosocialization only exacerbated the possibility of harmful consequences.

Chapter 5 looks at the practice of rush, when sororities selected their new members. Not merely the design of immature college students, rush was orchestrated in cooperation with, and often under the direction of, alumnae members. Heavily involved behind the scenes during rush season, sorority alumnae accepted recommendations from other alumnae and checked up on potential new members. As is practiced within the southern aesthetic, national sororities also placed an oversized importance on rushees' family background. Sororities used the visible cues of social class, primarily signaled by ladylike behavior, as well as deep research into rushees' ancestry, to gauge the likelihood that prospective members would uphold the groups' conservative image. I show how sororities shaped their organizations to support conservative ideals through their member selection and how some college women began to find fault with the rush process in the post–World War II period.

Chapter 6 continues the discussion of member selection among NPC leaders after World War II and examines alumnae members' increasing connection with the burgeoning conservative movement in the United States. The chapter focuses on the NPC's Cold War–era propaganda drive, which spread the belief among college and alumnae members that the possible loss of individual "freedoms" for white Americans would mean that Greek-letter groups could no longer select whom they wished to join their private groups. Amid growing tensions over civil rights, I show how white sorority women skillfully pioneered the use of color-blind language as they asserted their rights to freedom of association in private membership.[18]

Chapter 7 examines sororities during the 1960s and 1970s—eras that provided instances of possible change for the national organizations. Focused on chapters at southern campuses and set against the backdrop of student social movements, the chapter explores the challenges to sororities within the changing social climate of the mid- to late 1960s college campus, when some college members began to question the purpose and direction of their organizations. While sororities faced dissension within their own ranks, southern chapters also met direct challenges to their discriminatory membership policies as African American students participated in rush at recently desegregated southern universities. At this pivotal time, the image of the sorority woman as southern lady, reinvigorated as a symbol of massive resistance and conservatism, helped retrench sororities in their existing mold. The groups were able to emerge from the turbulent years of campus activism to renewed student interest in the increasingly conservative climate of the 1970s and early 1980s. By expanding to new campuses, sororities took advantage of the growing college population to build their membership for the future, while continuing their unofficial discriminatory membership practices.

Methodology

While I began this project with certain questions and assumptions, the sources available for research largely shaped the work's final form. As private organizations, Greek-letter sororities allow limited or no access to their records for outside researchers. As I initially focused on southern-founded groups and southern schools, I contacted several sororities about the possibility of research and met (polite) roadblocks from their national leadership. These initial barriers led me to rethink my research approach early on. While Alpha Delta Pi and Phi Mu allowed me limited access to their archival materials at their national headquarters, I turned my attention to university archives at various southern colleges. I visited eight southern university archives and corresponded with three more. Many examples used in the work come from the College of William and Mary, Duke University, and the University of North Carolina at Chapel Hill. There, and at other university archive collections, I found snippets of sorority-related materials in records from student organizations and the offices of deans of women, student affairs, and presidents. By reading across these collections, the story of NPC sororities began to take shape, often strengthened by accompanying information in student newspapers, yearbooks, and university archive oral history interviews. During this work, I also discovered that some NPC sororities had removed their local chapter records from student organization collections at university archives. Like the national sororities' unwillingness to share records from their headquarters, the removal of records from public archives suggested that the groups had something to hide.

While materials at individual universities allowed me to understand how sororities functioned on each southern campus I studied, the national programming and directives of the NPC helped present a large-scale picture of national sororities' agendas over the period of my study, encouraging me to connect chapters' local functions to the groups' national directions and to examine the southern/nonsouthern intersection of the organizations. The largest GLO-specific collections that I viewed for the project were the National Panhellenic Conference Archives, the Stewart S. Howe Collection, the Wilson Heller Papers, and the Alpha Tau Omega (ATΩ) Fraternity Records, all housed at the Student Life and Culture Archives at the University of Illinois Archives. I received permission from the NPC and ATΩ to use their collections for my project. These records provided some of the greatest guidance for this work.[19]

Manuscript collections and personal recollections of individuals also provided context and material for this narrative. At the University of North

Carolina at Chapel Hill's Southern Historical Collection, the Guion Griffis Johnson Papers allowed insight into alumnae officer correspondence in the tumultuous organizational period of the 1950s and 1960s. Johnson was an alumna of Chi Omega and corresponded with Mary Love Collins, Chi Omega's longtime national president, who was also heavily involved in the NPC's direction over the first seven decades of the twentieth century. The prevalence of certain sorority women in the records that I surveyed means that certain sororities are discussed more frequently than others. However, that does not mean that those sororities receiving less attention in this project were functioning any differently than the other NPC groups. They simply appeared less frequently in the records, or their national leaders were less vocal in some of the matters I discuss in the following chapters. The sorority women covered in greater detail within this work serve as archetypes for the larger network of conservative sorority women. I note the alma mater and age of the alumnae when possible to show both the growing generation gap between active and alumnae members over the course of this study and the cross-generationality and nationwide reach of sororities' conservative appeal.

I also spoke with several women who had been members of NPC sororities within the years of my study. Not all of these discussions are included in the final project, but all have influenced my thinking on the subject matter. Late in my writing and revision process, I met documentary filmmaker and former NPC sorority member Kathryn Smith Pyle, who was conducting research for a documentary on sororities. Through conversations with Pyle, I learned of additional historical instances of racially discriminatory behavior by NPC sororities. Many personal stories are yet to be uncovered, and archival digging remains to be done. This is far from an exhaustive catalog of materials describing sororities' histories, but my existing research provides a strong framework to expose a history that has been quieted, and perhaps purposely hidden, to keep public criticism at a minimum.

Considering sororities' long and continuing histories as women's organizations that valued their members' "discriminating" taste in choosing new sisters—whether outsiders saw this quality as good or bad—we can easily imagine the southern plantation–themed skit taking place during rush today.[20] Full disclosure: I was a member of an NPC sorority during my undergraduate years at a southern university. Each one of the four years I was there, our chapter performed Lynyrd Skynyrd's "Sweet Home Alabama" during rush (substituting our sorority's name in the place of "Alabama"). The message of the song, in which southern white men stand up for southern values (meaning white supremacy), lingered beneath the doctored lyrics of the modern-day sorority skit. As a college-age member of one of the sororities discussed in this book, I can attest to the continuation of the discriminatory practices I uncovered in NPC sororities' histories—both in selecting members for physical beauty or social connections and for prizing whiteness, all-Americanness, and southern belledom. Clearly, there is still much to be learned from the history of sororities that is not taught to new members along with stories of the founding chapter, founding members, and ritual songs.

While the women in my sorority chapter (and many other sorority women around the nation) would likely describe themselves as different from "*typical* sorority girls" and our chapter as "not like *most* sororities," we too were part of the larger system that I describe in this book. Most of us were there to make friends, have a social group, and for many, but not all, gain access to the fraternity dating scene. I doubt if many of us considered questioning the deeper history of the organizations or gave too much thought to problematic behaviors that the Greek system was perpetuating. Hazing was tolerated, drinking was applauded, and (heterosexual) hookups were discussed at lunch. Today, Americans take for granted that those types of behaviors are common yet derided parts of Greek life. This is not a story about my experience in a sorority, but instead, a story that resulted from my work as a historian interested in understanding the growth of these powerful national women's organizations—one of which I chose to join while in college. It is the story of how we got there that is lost or forgotten in contemporary questioning of these institutions that have become inextricably linked with universities and images of campus life in the United States.

It is a story from which sorority members and nonmembers can learn about the complexities of these groups, which we have failed to recognize as obviously connected to a grassroots conservative movement before now, and which repeatedly surface in popular and scholarly media discussions of contemporary higher education, sexual assault, alcohol abuse, and racist behaviors. These groups conjure up distinct images in the public eye, images that deserve to be examined fully and placed within the larger twentieth-century historical context in which they developed.

CHAPTER ONE

·•·

"A Very Wholesome Discipline"

FROM GIRLHOOD TO LADYHOOD IN THE
SOUTHERN SORORITY CHAPTER

*I*n her annual report of the 1922–23 school year, University of North Carolina (UNC) adviser to women Inez Koonce Stacy remarked that "the local [women's] fraternities of Beta Alpha Phi and Lambda Tau have become affiliated with the national Pi Beta Phi and Chi Omega [women's] fraternities." To this, she added her own assessment. "The existence of women's fraternities on the campus is too new for any discussion as to influence or desirability. The students involved feel keenly that fraternities will do much to make college life what it should be. The future will tell the story." Beginning her fifth year as adviser to the seventy-nine women enrolled at the university, just over half of whom were undergraduates, Stacy saw the groups as a welcome addition to the dearth of women's activities on a campus that still catered to men.[1]

At historically white, southern, coeducational colleges in the early twentieth century—an atmosphere that, to some southern whites, seemed inappropriately unfeminine—sororities stood to provide "necessary" feminine guidance for women who were living apart from their families, often for the first time. With an emphasis on femininity, domesticity, and controlled behavior, a sorority would be the perfect space to nurture the white southern lady and ensure that she remained ladylike while she attended college. A women's culture, supported by sororities, deans of women, and other women-only clubs and activities, developed on these southern campuses in the early twentieth century, but sororities would become the preeminent activity fostering traditional values of southern ladyhood. At the same time, the image of the southern lady would be ideal for sororities' national model of womanhood. As women-only clubs, national sororities saw a need to prove that their members would continue to reflect conventional understandings of white American womanhood through heterosexual marriage and motherhood. By training nonthreatening white women who would uphold conservative standards of living and be primed for marriage with their white fraternity peers, sororities enabled the perpetuation of the southern belle as sorority girl.

National Panhellenic Conference sororities existed both at white coeducational and women's colleges in the South by 1900, and they experienced massive growth, not just in the South but throughout the United States, during the 1910s and 1920s—a time when women across the nation were challenging and redefining conventional gender norms.[2] While the organizations became popular nationwide, and many college women hoped to bring chapters to their campuses, some national sororities chose to limit their expansion to campuses that they believed admitted only students of high cultural, intellectual, and financial caliber. In the early twentieth century, this practice often eliminated chapters at smaller denominational colleges, land grant institutions, or schools where coeducation was in question.[3] These restrictions would hamper national sorority expansion at schools in the South during the first quarter of the twentieth century, where coeducation remained an unsettled—and unsettling—issue.

Sororities would play a large part in the refashioning of American womanhood in the early decades of the twentieth century as they built a national brand premised on class consciousness and white Protestant Americanness. Sororities' popularity during these years was due in large part to their ability to appeal to a sizeable number of white middle- and upper-class college women through their supportive and socially geared environments. In these decades, as the organizations focused their efforts on establishing new chapters and adding to their membership, the clubs also allowed for a range of messages regarding "acceptable" sorority women's activities.[4] They made higher education for white women more palatable to the public by stressing the importance of educated women in the domestic realm and, at the same time, that of the sorority in preparing young women for homemaking and family life. Additionally, sororities provided support and role models for women who did not meet the nation's strictly domestic ideal of womanhood, either by their own choice or by dint of circumstances. The organizations included members who espoused beliefs across the political spectrum, as well as ones who did not view "politicking" as a suitable activity for "respectable" women. The common denominator among the "diverse" group of privileged women in sororities through the 1930s was their white skin, Protestant background, and middle- or upper-class status.

In the early decades of the twentieth century, sororities' membership endorsed an array of endeavors undertaken by the "college sorority girl" and her alumna counterpart as worthy and successful. Many of the college women who joined the organizations in the nineteenth century formed a generation of educated American women who fought against existing social limitations on women's behavior while placing feminine independence and career aspirations at the heart of their personal struggle. Even if these women did not become homemakers (or were slower to do so than their predecessors), they too saw the primary role of American women as mothers and caretakers. While some members in each organization clearly saw the ideal sorority woman returning to the home after graduation, other members were willing to entertain the notion of young women choosing the path that best suited their individual desires. The uniting force behind the various understandings was the members' belief that the educated sorority woman held a unique gift for social betterment, whether in her own home or in the larger community, based on her sorority experience. A sense of *noblesse oblige* enabled sorority women to claim involvement in professions or volunteer work as a duty to the "underprivileged." Their organizing and career work also reiterated the maternalist appeal that women would use their "natural" caregiving instincts to improve social conditions within the space of the female dominion.[5]

While early twentieth-century national sororities addressed a variety of contemporary, college-educated women's activities, including careers and volunteer work, they regularly promoted the message that a successful domestic life *should* be the highest goal for young women, regardless of whether it was achieved. The 1911 edition of the *Handbook of Kappa Alpha Theta* sought to describe "some distinguished members" of the sorority.

> Since the home is woman's great center of activity, it follows that the distinction of a woman's fraternity cannot be gauged by her roll of members who have gained recognition in the business or professional world. Even to name the members who, as beautiful home-makers, are fulfilling the fraternity's highest ambitions for her members is out of the question. But since such ideal positions are not occupied by all members, the fraternity would also pay tribute to her many members who are courageously and cheerfully bearing a share in more public lines of endeavor.[6]

Those members who did not reach what the sorority viewed as the epitome of womanhood still received encouragement, although the anonymous author's words suggested that the women in public were doing work to which sorority alumnae should not aspire. "Courageously and cheerfully" their sisters were "bearing a share" in public endeavors—a description seemingly designed to elicit sympathy more than admiration.

Traditionally, Americans expected girls to receive training for womanhood within the space of the family home where parents or older siblings and relatives would instill basic values of right and wrong, of moral rectitude, and of behavior befitting a lady. To replicate this domestic learning environment, universities had to recreate the image of the campus community as a family and the campus itself as a home for the young women enrolled at the institution. As a protected space for women, separate from but confined within the university campus, a women's culture at southern schools (sometimes on the completely separate coordinate campus) was dedicated to molding young ladies. Under the watchful eye of deans of women and with the grudging support of most university administrators, a women's culture began to take shape on coeducational campuses. Segregated from male students, largely ignored by male administrators, and often living away from home for the first time, female students sought out a community in the southern coeducational university. Sororities grew to dominate the women's campus culture across the nation by the 1920s as they provided a space where girls formed kinship ties outside of the traditional family and offered a means of control over women's behavior. In these previously male-homosocial spaces, sororities offered a sense of community for women while recreating the intimacy of the conventional family. The image of a protected, homelike atmosphere for young white "ladies" on college campuses lessened some of the public anxiety over women's higher education that lingered, to a greater extent, in the South. At the same time, however, the insular community of the sorority could inhibit the personal growth and individuality of members. Peer pressure, even more than national and chapter rules, could influence appearance, behavior, and beliefs.

A Home Away from Home

At universities across the United States, NPC sororities sought to reinforce the familial ideal by carving out specific domestic living spaces for their chapters and by reminding members that the ideal woman always considered first in her activities her duty to her home.[7] As Delta Delta Delta (ΔΔΔ) founder Ida Shaw Martin described in her popular guide *The Sorority Handbook*, sororities were a benefit to society. By providing a girl with "family affiliations and with the essential elements of home," she reasoned, sororities would shore up the family, the "corner stone of the social structure." The sorority chapter, she argued, was so closely patterned after the conventional family unit "that it is not difficult to see that the sorority is the expression of the college girl's belief in the power of the home." Martin supported campus sorority houses and applauded women's colleges that had instituted cottage homes instead of dormitories for their recognition of the importance of transitioning girls into young women in a space where they received "broad, liberalizing, humanizing culture" without being "weaned from home and friends, from ties of blood and kindred."[8] While a highly educated, "modern" woman of her time, Martin was hardly promoting radical ideas for women's activities. Instead, true to a conventional model of womanhood, the ideal sorority member of the early twentieth century would put her education to best use in the care of her family and household. While sorority women might expand their horizons through a variety of activities during college and in adulthood, public and sorority sentiment also advised that they reserve the greatest time and attachment to the development of a home and family. The familial atmosphere encouraged a watchfulness over members' activities that would be codified into standards of behavior, reinforcing normative gender expectations for young women. Women largely adhered to these expectations in the sorority family as the desire to "fit in" with peers—one of the main reasons women joined sororities—led members to fall in line with the chapter's demands.

By the early twentieth century, the heart of national sororities' public appeal related to the significance of sorority *houses* in the preparation of girls for womanhood.[9] Touting domesticity and family, sororities satisfied the image of refined living and protective space that southern universities proffered to the parents of prospective female students. Southern coeducational universities were slow to provide adequate living spaces for women on campus even after allowing them to enroll.[10] On these campuses, national sororities foresaw the possibility of providing a wholesome social environment that would suggest the cloistered femininity and exclusivity of women's colleges. Like sorority leaders, deans advocated the construction of living spaces that would emulate conventional domestic spaces. As deans of women pushed their university administrations to consider building appropriations designed to meet the needs for women's facilities, they relied on boardinghouses and increasingly on sorority houses to accommodate students.[11]

Sorority Houses

Sororities believed that the preparation of female students for womanhood could be more carefully monitored within a sorority house than in the typical college dormitory. The chapter house would consist of a small, close-knit group of sorority women and would be headed by a chaperone, or house-mother, who would provide wholesome guidance for the girls. In 1909 the NPC stated that chapter houses should only exist when chapters could afford to employ a chaperone that would impart "dignity and character."[12] The ability of housemothers to adequately oversee the young women in their charge may have varied depending on the situation, but their presence gave the impression of a protected environment for the sorority members.

Despite the assistance of the national organizations, not all sorority chapters could finance homes. Few universities were willing to help by offering land and financial backing for the building of new residential spaces. As of September 1923, the Epsilon Beta chapter of Chi Omega at UNC had rented an apartment that it planned to use as a chapter house during the coming year. "It is large enough to be used for social purposes also," they noted. In some instances, such as at the Woman's College of Duke University, the university would not allow the building of houses on campus, an issue that long caused friction between the NPC groups and the school's administration. However, the acquisition of a house for each sorority chapter was a goal set by the sororities' national leadership, and most deans of women seemed to support this endeavor.[13]

Chapter houses varied in style and substance, but they were clearly meant to enhance the elite image of the organizations and were important visual signifiers of affluence. During the 1920s, chapters that could afford to do so painstakingly planned, fundraised for, and constructed mansions with which to impress other students and prospective rushees. In the preface to the 1931 edition of *The Sorority Handbook*, Martin noted that "a quarter of a century ago the rented chapter house was not unusual, but rarely was it owned." By 1931 she was able to boast that "$25,000,000 would be a conservative estimate of the value of real estate held in the name of sororities today." Even as the Depression tightened finances for Greek-letter organizations (GLOs), the new home building continued.[14] Some chapter houses were very simple, resembling typical, single-family homes. As chapters grew and gained financial backing from wealthy alumnae, they were able to purchase and renovate existing structures or build new homes. Sorority houses became more spacious, comfortable, and filled with modern conveniences, and students more readily juxtaposed the cachet of living in a sorority house with that of the basic dormitory residence. The more established chapters, with greater numbers of alumnae purses to draw on, had an increased ability to construct ostentatious homes for their college members if they so desired. As many of the chapters at the southern coeducational schools were in their early years of existence, with fewer members and alumnae to supplement the coffers, chapter houses were scaled more like family homes. Most chapter houses at southern colleges in this period—indeed, most sorority houses throughout the nation—appeared modest when compared with houses such as the "typical French chateau style" manor planned by the Sigma chapter of Alpha Delta Pi (AΔΠ) at the University of Illinois in 1926. But when pitted against almost any chapter house environment, the sparsely furnished, institutional dormitories could seem downright drab and graceless, and in the minds of many students, they remained inferior living spaces.[15] Moreover, in many cases these types of houses were probably far grander than the conventional family homes where the sorority members had grown up.

The Southern Belle Goes to College

Women's matriculation at southern coeducational colleges did not occur in significant numbers until World War I, when men (and their tuition dollars) became scarce. Many newly coeducational southern colleges had few to no sorority chapters because of a lack of women on campus to sustain them. Women's college attendance continued to increase during the 1920s as a result of postwar prosperity and changing public attitudes about women's education, including an emphasis on the benefits of educating future housewives and mothers.[16] At William and Mary, for example, women's enrollment in 1919–20 doubled from the previous year to reach 32 percent of the total enrollment of 333. Alabama Polytechnic Institute (later Auburn University) enrolled 10 women a year from 1892 to 1921, but 115 by 1924. The University of Alabama enrolled 91 women in 1915–16 and 293 by 1920–21.[17]

Although sororities would become most closely associated with coeducational campuses, white women's colleges were among the first schools in the South to have chapters of national sororities.[18] However, some administrators and faculty at women's colleges opposed sororities because they felt the groups were unnecessary in the small, women-only setting, or they feared that the groups led to divisiveness among the student body. For these reasons a number of women's colleges in the South chose to end their relationships with national sororities, closing their campuses' chapters.[19] Yet the majority of white southern women attending college during the period from 1920 to 1940 went to women's colleges instead of coeducational colleges. Many parents saw the women-only college campus as a more appropriate atmosphere for their daughters. Women who hoped to complete a four-year course at the coeducational state university sometimes were turned away because of their gender or were disappointed by the limitations on curriculum for women. In some cases, when colleges admitted women as four-year undergraduates, they limited them to curricula that administrators defined as "feminine," such as home economics, education, and fine arts.[20] Colleges also found ways to physically separate students by gender through the creation of "coordinate campuses." A number of southern schools enacted the plan in the 1920s and 1930s to draw a line between the men's and women's spaces on campus, a move that would continue to segregate students by gender and curricula.[21] Educational policies followed the dictates of regional tradition.

Some southern white men of the early twentieth century remained inhospitable to the notion of higher education for their southern ladies. By taking women outside of their conventional place in the home to learn new ideas, and perhaps to challenge the gendered and racialized relations of power, higher education for women, like education for African Americans in the South, posed serious threats to elite white men's power. As concessions to the ideal of white southern womanhood guided the curricula at women's colleges in the region during the early twentieth century, the mythical ideal also was used to discourage state universities from commencing coeducation.[22] In the minds of its opponents, coeducation threatened to feminize the men's university while defeminizing its female graduates. When women were given the choice to enroll at the region's coeducational universities and began to do so, university administrators worried about the future of the region's gender and racial hierarchies.

White southern men saw the state university as the province of the white aristocratic male. Frequently the men showed open hostility toward their new classmates, barring them from campus activities and ignoring them in class. Male university administrators and professors were similarly unwelcoming to women on campus, and few faculty women were available to serve as mentors. Most women employed as university faculty held a bachelor's or master's degree in their field, while only a few held doctorates. Often employed as instructors, many taught "feminine" subjects, such as women's physical education or home economics, or in "feminine" majors, including English, fine arts, music, and education. Aside from the campuses' uncongenial atmosphere for women's scholarship, many women in these early years were discouraged by a chronic lack of suitable housing on campus.[23]

Nevertheless, young women continued to register at public universities. Nationally, by 1920 white women made up 43.7 percent of American college students; 81.3 percent of these women attended coeducational institutions. In the South matriculation rates at state universities steadily increased during the 1920s as women took advantage of the new enrollment policies.[24] Wishing to

FIGURE 2. The University of Alabama demonstrated that its campus was an "appropriate" place for women students of the 1920s with views of "sorority court" and a highly attended home economics class. *Courtesy of the W. S. Hoole Special Collections Library, the University of Alabama.*

ignore, but unable to dismiss, the persistent presence of women on campus, university administrators sought to hire women's advisers or deans of women to provide guidance and a feminizing influence, and to oversee necessary disciplinary matters. If white southern girls would continue to seek education at coeducational universities, then the universities would see to it that they became proper southern ladies while in their care (see fig. 2).

Reinforcing Southern Femininity with a Campus Women's Culture

While white southern parents increasingly saw higher education for women as an integral step between girlhood and ladyhood, in the view of some white southerners, college could pose a misstep in preparation for ladyhood. In a 1922 speech on coeducation, David C. Barrow, president of the University of Georgia (UGA), acknowledged that some of his "older friends" had "been afraid that co-education would 'take the bloom from the peach.'" Barrow assured his audience, however, that women at the university maintained their femininity, stressing the "[gentle] courtesy" they extended to their elders. He concluded that "co-education [had] a tendency to do away with a certain shyness" in women, but that it did not "affect modesty."[25] While Barrow confidently proclaimed that higher education rendered only positive effects on women, southern universities and their administrations would have to offer proof that women were welcome on their campuses and would be cared for, or sheltered, in a manner culturally acceptable to the southern populace. For southerners anxious about women's enrollment at coeducational colleges, the existence of a specialized and controlled women's culture on campus helped allay fears that the learning environment would defeminize or otherwise damage their prospective southern ladies. Sororities would play an increasing role in maintaining the image of controlled femininity on campus.

defeminize damage

University officials contended that girls needed to have the guidance and support of a mother figure at school while separated from their biological mothers or female caretakers. During the 1910s and 1920s, schools in the South hired their first deans of women to watch over the increasing number of women enrolled on campus.[26] Deans and advisers became multitaskers, acting as mother figures, serving as liaisons between the students and the university administrations, advocating for women's facilities and women's faculty appointments, and maintaining a link between their universities and professional groups such as the National Association of Deans of Women (NADW) and the Southern Association of College Women and its successor, the American Association of University Women (AAUW).[27] Deans and advisers also became unofficial sorority coordinators on their campuses, assisting with events, aiding relations between different sororities, and welcoming visiting sorority officers and alumnae. Winning the favor of their dean of women often afforded sorority chapters the stamp of approval as the premier social groups on campus and positioned their members as the cream of the crop among female students in regard to desired womanly behavior.

demeaning to deans as well!

& you get a degree to be a "mother figure"

Deans of women expressed a variety of responses to sororities on their campuses, but many were generally pleased with the moderating role the groups seemed to fulfill. At Duke University (formerly Trinity College) in 1926, president William Preston Few left Alice Mary Baldwin, the first dean of the new Woman's College of Duke University, to decide whether to allow sororities to remain on campus. National sororities had existed at Trinity since 1911 when a local sorority became the Omicron chapter of AΔΠ sorority (see fig. 3). The campus's first local sorority, Sigma Delta (1904), became a chapter of Kappa Delta (KΔ) in 1913.[28] Although not a sorority woman herself, Baldwin chose to let sororities remain. She saw the existence of sororities as a way to uphold school traditions, create ties with alumnae, and, importantly, "[encourage] them to recommend able students" to the Woman's College.[29] While

Sororities aided enrollment

FIGURE 3. Charter members of the Omicron chapter of Alpha Delta Pi
at Trinity College (later Duke University), ca. 1912.
Courtesy of Duke University Archives.

obviously appreciating the necessity of women's social education on campus,
Baldwin's approach to women's intellectual needs and abilities implied that
she kept sororities around more for their public relations potential and less for
reasons of social training.

As most deans and advisers were college alumnae, many also may have
been alumnae of Greek-letter sororities. Irene Dillard Elliott, dean of women
at the University of South Carolina, had been a member of the Nu chapter
of AΔΠ sorority at Randolph-Macon Woman's College in Lynchburg, Virginia. Following the repeal of a nearly thirty-year ban on Greek-letter organizations at South Carolina's public universities in 1927, AΔΠ was the first sorority granted a charter at the university in Columbia.[30] Although some deans
and advisers cautioned against the groups' tendency to destroy loyalties to academic class and school, others were willing to work with sororities in the
hopes that the organizations would have a positive influence on student conduct.[31] With all sorority house residents devoted to the same organization, or
family unit, the sorority could expect to receive greater accountability from its
sisters. When all members of the "family" were working toward the same goals
of upholding the image and reputation of the group, they would more readily adhere to prescribed standards to achieve these objectives.[32] For this reason, the policing of behavior that occurred *within* the sorority chapter houses
likely saw greater success than did the universities' large-scale attempts at po-

licing the behavior of dormitory women. No doubt, deans at southern universities, like their nonsouthern counterparts, saw the opportunity to use sororities to encourage proper modes of behavior.

Controlling and Promoting Sexuality among Southern Sorority Women

Although the southern belle is often depicted as surrounded by a "bevy of beaus"—like Scarlett O'Hara at the picnic at Twelve Oaks in *Gone with the Wind* (1939)—chastity was one of the most valued assets of white southern ladyhood. Southern ladies offered a tease of sexuality but supposedly abstained from sex outside of marriage and, as early twentieth-century popular understandings of women's sexuality dictated, certainly would not seek out or find physical enjoyment from sexual encounters. Just as the southern belle was pictured adeptly handling her many eligible suitors, sororities trained members to display a similar prowess in their interactions with the fraternity men or the BMOCs—the big men on campus. Although the organizations had built a reputation on providing a supportive women-only space in the often hostile, newly coeducational campus, the nationwide appearance of a dating culture by the 1920s led to a shift in public understanding of the activities and the overall purpose of sororities. No longer a sanctuary for women to bolster themselves against male students and faculty, the groups instead moved to promote heterosocial interaction with sorority women's social peers among male students.

College administrators went to great lengths to maintain control over heterosocial contact between students on campus. Women and men living on the same campus and attending classes together heightened these concerns, resulting in an ever-broadening set of rules designed to separate the sexes. Universities enacted *in loco parentis* rules, literally meaning "instead of parent," to regulate behavior of the students on their campuses, which were much more constraining for women than for men. In 1924 the University of Alabama, which had employed a dean of women for the past decade, boasted that "the social life of young women at the University is carefully guarded." Women at William and Mary recalled that in the first year of coeducation in 1918, "discipline for girls was very restrictive" and that the women's administrator, Bessie Porter Taylor, "ruled with an iron stick." While driving in cars, smoking in public, drinking, or having dates (except on weekends) was prohibited, a long list of other activities, including leaving town, going on long hikes, walking or "automobiling" with men, or visiting men's fraternity houses *all* required special ~~permission~~ from Miss Taylor. The rules of behavior for women increased in relation to their enrollment numbers.[33] *interesting!*

Sororities and fraternities claimed to offer an ordered environment for young women and men of the same social backgrounds to meet and date in preparation for choosing marriage partners. While sororities facilitated an increase in heterosocial relationships, they also created rules for heterosexual contact. Like the dormitories, sorority chapter houses issued rules of behavior for their resident members. In 1910 the *Trident* of Delta Delta Delta shared house rules from several of their chapters living in chapter homes. Beta chapter at St. Lawrence University in New York stated that "no girl shall receive more than three day or evening calls from gentlemen each week." No caller could remain past 10:00 p.m., and no girl could be on the street with a gentleman after 8:30 p.m. without special permission. The Kappa chapter at the University of Nebraska only allowed gentlemen callers (who were not male relatives) on weekend nights, and only until 10:30 at night. House parties could only be held on Friday and Saturday, lasting until midnight. Stanford University's Omega chapter called for girls to be in by 10:00 p.m. Monday through Thursday evenings. If the women did not make curfew, their names would be read at chapter meetings by the "senior critic."[34] Chapter house rules at southern campuses likely resembled those of their sister chapters but may have been even more stringent, based on the highly controlled atmosphere for young southern women.

Like ADPi date room

Additionally, such rules offered insurance for women who might be fending off the unwanted advances of male students. If pressured by a suitor, the woman could reference the "rules" on closing hours, chaperones, and the like. As sexual mores dictated, sorority women bore the brunt of the responsibility in maintaining standards of behavior in heterosocial situations. At the same time, male students faced few, if any, such regulations. A female graduate of William and Mary did not remember any rules for the men other than that they "stay on campus on Saturday night" to reduce fights between students and "townies" on the weekends. In 1930 UNC's *Carolina Handbook* listed traditions of behavior for Carolina men and made "general suggestions" for new students, such as that they "attend church at least once every Sunday," but none of these involved specific rules or required an administrator's oversight.[35]

Although sororities touted their organizations as models of domesticity replete with traditional homes, the familial ideal that sororities ascribed to their chapters did not mirror conventional, heteronormative ideals of family living. As single-sex organizations, sororities *could* be seen as a threat to heterosexuality and the status quo in gender relations. Men were conspicuously absent from the sorority-defined familial space. Sorority women would learn their socially prescribed roles as wives and caretakers in a space unlike that which they supposedly would inhabit in adulthood. As public fears over career-minded single women and same-sex relationships escalated during the 1920s and 1930s, these all-female spaces, once viewed as safe havens for young impressionable women, took on a more sinister cast.[36] What if the sorority sisters became so accustomed to their sorority "family" that they were unwilling to graduate to a heteronormative model after college? As a way to deflect attention from the possibility that sorority chapter houses could foster same-sex sexual relationships or produce "domineering," "unfeminine" women, national sororities began to publicize their greater interest in preparing members for heterosexual marriage by encouraging regular socializing with fraternity men and other men of the same social class.

insane

Some sorority women may have worried that the all-female space of the sorority, like that of cloistered groups of women at colleges and universities, could appear threatening to men and to the dominant model of the conventional family, based on heterosexual marriage and childbearing. The alumnae of the 1920s and 1930s knew the well-circulated fears of many late nineteenth- and early twentieth-century Americans in regard to women and higher education. "Experts," such as retired Harvard Medical School professor Dr. Edward C. Clarke, had promoted the belief that higher education was too strenuous for women and detrimental to their physical well-being, in particular their reproductive systems and their ability to bear healthy children. By the early twentieth century, these concerns also became intertwined with the notion of "race suicide," popularized by President Theodore Roosevelt, among others. As many of the first generation of women to attend college married later than their peers, or not at all, critics pointed to the specter of the "unsexed" or "mannish" female college graduate, who shunned conventional marriage and motherhood, thereby endangering the future population of Anglo-Americans in the United States.[37] Against this backdrop, homemaking and child-rearing became a primary duty of the white, middle- to upper-class sorority woman.

Likewise, as articles in the sororities' quarterly journals increasingly applauded white, middle-class women who desired homemaking as their primary occupation, they implicitly discouraged women-only spaces.[38] Like the college sorority chapters' increasing focus on heterosocializing, the journals' features also seemed ready to dismiss the importance of the all-female support network. This shift stood to challenge the original principle of the college social sorority. These images also stood in stark contrast to the image of a safe, women-only space, both within the college chapters and at larger gatherings, like the sororities' national biennial conventions.

National Panhellenic Conference sororities retrained their attention on domesticity and mothering in the lives of their alumnae as a reflection of the shifting public perception of women in American society during the 1930s. Although women across the board had made, and would continue to make, gains in workforce participation during the decades of the twentieth century, public concern over women's appropriate "roles" in society continued to shape their behaviors and ideals. These gains had in particular raised concerns over the femininity and the morality of white, middle-class American women. By the 1930s, sorority journals' emphasis on activities of sorority alumnae shifted from that of a cheerleader for women's vocational preparation and social activism to one that, again, reminded women of the significance of their work in the home. Amid Depression-era concerns over supposedly dominant and aggressive career women demoralizing and emasculating chronically unemployed white American men, sorority journal contributors less frequently touted vocational training as a route for feminine independence. Whereas sororities in the first quarter of the twentieth century had largely functioned as support systems, acting as boosters for young white women who sought an education on par with men and employment that offered them the opportunity to be self-supporting, sorority alumnae reshaped the NPC sorority of the 1930s to again position the ideal sorority woman as a homemaker in a conventional American family.

At the same time, however, the sororities' biennial national conventions were women-centered and designed to promote the sisterhood of the respective sororities. The events, usually held at elite resort locations such as the New Ocean House at Swampscott, Massachusetts; the Edgewater in Chicago; the Greenbrier at White Sulphur Springs, West Virginia; the Homestead at Hot Springs, Virginia; or the Grand Hotel at Mackinac Island, Michigan—just to name a few—gave generations of a sorority members the chance to meet and share experiences every other summer (see fig. 4). For many women, this likely was an exciting respite from their typical housekeeping and family management duties. It gave them an opportunity to reaffirm old friendships from their college years, as well as to make new connections with women in their sorority from all across the country. The conventions provided an environment where female leadership and authority could be displayed without question or criticism from male interlopers. They also created spaces where women who may have been in companionate or romantic relationships with other members of their sorority could mingle freely without drawing attention to themselves,

FIGURE 4. Chi Omegas Alma Menig, Ida Pace Perdue, and
Mary Love Collins pictured at the 1928 Chi Omega Convention at
the Greenbrier in White Sulphur Springs, West Virginia.
Courtesy of the University of Illinois Archives,
Stewart S. Howe Collection, Record Series (26/21/6).

and even receive tacit approval of their partnerships from the sisterhood.
From the 1910s to the 1930s, as NPC sororities promoted strong, independent women, they also seemed willing to look the other way if popular alumnae and national officers did not meet conventional standards of femininity
in dress, interests, occupation, or relationships. Again, the common denominator of acceptance—their status as white, middle- to upper-class "privileged"
women—allowed for certain transgressions from the norm to go unremarked
on.[39] These displays occurred within the private spaces of the sisterhood. The
public presentation of college sorority women, however, required heteronormative branding.

A different route to ladyhood was beginning to take shape as sororities
moved from simply promoting the sororities' somewhat nebulous nineteenth-

century ideal of true womanhood to an increasingly codified training for social education, which relied heavily on heterosocial skills and members' relationships with fraternity men. Popular representations of sorority women in
the first quarter of the twentieth century, such as those found in novels about
college life, portrayed women preoccupied by concerns of maintaining their
femininity and desirability as dates on coeducational campuses.[40] Pledge
guidebooks from national sororities in the 1920s refer to pledges' proper adjustment to college social life, which included dating men of the "appropriate" background.[41] Here the picture of the playful southern belle, not too serious about studies and ready to woo the men of her social class, *could* soften
concerns that educated white women would shun or, perhaps worse, dominate
white men. The southern lady ideal combined sororities' ideal of true womanhood, which promoted moral purity, social grace, and intellect with the image
of an ultrafeminine, sexually nonthreatening, and subordinated white, middle-
to upper-class woman. She would provide the model to train the conservative,
twentieth-century sorority woman, who would be the new epitome of white
American womanhood.

College chapters' reports to their national sororities suggested that the sisters were eager to gain access to heterosocial gatherings and dates with fraternity men. A 1914 chapter report from the Sigma Delta chapter of KΔ at
Trinity College (later, the Woman's College of Duke University) detailed a
"number of sorority affairs which have been given," as well as "a great many
functions given by the college and the fraternities." By 1924 Sigma Delta's secretary began her report by joking that "our one problem is just where shall we
cram in a bit of work," before listing a spate of social activities that chapter
members had recently attended. The KΔs had been well represented at parties held by fraternities at nearby colleges, and they hosted their own bridge
parties, as well as several dances at exclusive venues in Durham.[42] Although
the social rounds of the KΔs at the Women's College of Duke University out-
paced those of many other sorority chapters reporting in the same issue of the
Angelos, their exploits demonstrate a pronounced trend toward heterosocial
parties among sorority chapters. The focus on fashioning oneself in a manner
so as to be physically attractive and socially pleasing to young men would only
increase and would be tied to the paradigm of American beauty and femininity—the southern lady. It was this shift in emphasis from the sorority chapter
as a self-contained women's support network to a launching pad for social improvement directed at heterosocializing and marriageability that ensured sororities would function as spaces of control for women instead of challengers
to male authority.

CHAPTER TWO

⸱•⸱

"A Laboratory in
How to Get Along with People"
SELLING SORORITIES THROUGH
SOCIAL EDUCATION

*I*n March 1913 Jenn Coltrane, retiring president of Kappa Delta (KΔ), composed an article for the second issue of the monthly fraternity and sorority publication *Banta's Greek Exchange* that persuasively argued the need for sororities on college campuses. Coltrane explained that the "mission" of sororities was to "teach a girl the knowledge and value of true womanhood, and to implant in her a desire to attain it." Reiterating sorority supporters' popular argument for a home away from home for college women, Coltrane described the knowledge imparted by sororities as "the thing every true mother would teach her daughter." In the mother's stead, Coltrane contended, "the sorority merely [aimed] to supplement the home and the college," providing the necessary social education.[1]

As a useful tool and an inventive marketing ploy, national sororities adopted the public image of etiquette instructors for college women during the twentieth century. They sold themselves as effective instructors of cultural education to demonstrate their value as campus organizations and to quiet critics who questioned the need for the groups. Positioned not only as a "women's activity" on campus but also as an integral component of the curriculum by the 1920s and 1930s, sororities staked their claim in the expanding realm of higher education for women. Many university administrators bought into this logic and were pleased to find that sororities could serve as models to enforce behavioral regulations for all women on campus.

Sororities' social training programs were designed to produce and sell conservative American womanhood through a nationalized version of southern ladyhood. This model of white middle- and upper-class womanhood established the groups as socially sophisticated organizations promoting a "well-adjusted" social life, manners of gracious living, and an attractive appearance among their members. At southern coeducational campuses, sororities could add the essential components for culturally acceptable, white femininity, thereby preserving southern ladyhood among white women seeking higher education. The groups also came equipped with connections to additional "teachers" of social skills in the form of alumnae members. In this respect, the pursuits of sorority life—parties, teas, fashion shows, and dances—which appeared frivolous to some, could be exactly what university administrators at institutions across the United States sought for young women on campus. Sororities' lessons taught college women to focus greater attention on learning pleasing mannerisms than on earning academic accolades. "It is an established fact," stated Minnie Allen Hubbard, former grand president of AΔΠ, in 1939, "that a well-rounded education includes more than intellectual attainments. A charming personality and social graces should be the mark of a college bred woman."[2] Through these lessons, sororities trained members to value certain appearances and types of behavior that denoted membership in the white privileged social class, thereby establishing a foundation for the discrimination that sustained the organizations.

Sororities' social training evolved from sorority "standards," which the organizations put into practice to control member and chapter behavior, as well as to quiet critics of Greek-letter organizations (GLOs). Some of these critics saw secret societies as particularly antithetical to the atmosphere of the public university—institutions that provided education to the citizens of a state at the taxpayers' expense and supposedly created an egalitarian social and educational experience for students.[3] Greek-letter groups served to reconstitute economic class stratification that had seemed to disappear within the more democratic environment of the state university campus. In an uprising of populist sentiment around the country during the 1890s, a number of state legislatures attempted to shut down GLOs on their state university campuses.[4] Greek-letter organizations' frequent interactions with critics shaped the defensive posture sororities maintained throughout the twentieth century.

To deflect such criticisms, alumnae leaders instituted standards and initiated greater oversight of the chapters, urging college members to improve scholastic standing, reduce the amount of time and money spent on social events, and maintain cordial relationships with university administrators.[5] Already by 1908, the National Panhellenic Conference (NPC) had recommended that college sorority women limit the "number, duration, and expense of parties" as well as their "dates with men."[6] In these years, a number of sororities instituted the office of inspector (also called chapter visitor or traveling secretary), an alumna who traveled to each chapter to check on the members and the chapter procedures and report back to the national officers.[7] In 1914, as part of the NPC's increased oversight of the sorority system, the delegates suggested that each fraternity have a definite system of instructions about the NPC sent to its chapters. Although the level of supervision given each sorority chapter by their respective national organization would often vary depending on local alumnae involvement, by 1926 all NPC sororities reported an annual visit to each chapter by some official.[8]

Sororities increasingly sought to uphold their conservative behavioral standards with the development of social and educational programming for active members. Chapters molded members' behavior, appearance, and belief systems. While the peer group of the sorority chapter shaped members to fit a desired ideal, the sorority officers and alumnae were able to point to the supposed value of this endeavor for the university and for society at large. Sororities conveyed their lessons of ladyhood to college women through published handbooks, interactions with alumnae and officers, and careful monitoring by peers in the sorority chapter. Members absorbed lessons in working and living with others, good hygiene and appearance, healthy interpersonal relationships, and preparation for heteronormative womanhood through formal and informal methods. The lessons reinforced conventional notions of women's behavior—particularly in regard to women's sexuality—as well as patterns of class and racial stratification. By normalizing this structure, sorority social training primed members to enter the ranks of the white power structure and also taught them to value others with similar backgrounds and mannerisms.

Education to prepare women for heterosocial interaction and heterosexual dating with fraternity men emerged as a key point in sororities' training. Sororities' explosive growth in the early twentieth century occurred simultaneously with social changes in American courtship rituals, which moved from guarded interactions in the home to a competitive, public dating scene during the 1920s. In addition to their other purported homelike qualities, sororities and fraternities could provide a sheltered space for dating. The goal of most sorority lessons, whether explicitly stated or not, was the achievement of a physically attractive, socially pleasing group of women who would appeal to men from the same social background. American college students of the 1920s and

1930s were immersed in the emerging peer culture that increasingly valued individuals based on appearance, public performance, and personality. Membership in a Greek-letter society could help students learn the social standards to which they needed to conform, while aiding them in the cultivation of a personality that met the expectations of the popular public culture.[9]

In large part, deans of women supported sororities' educational endeavors on their campuses. Since the 1910s the NPC had attempted to cultivate a mutually beneficial relationship with the National Association of Deans of Women (NADW). With their social education programs offering assistance to the dean of women's office, sororities stood a better chance of remaining in the good graces of the NADW. By 1926 the NPC had voted to hold their biennial meetings at the same time and place as the NADW conventions to promote cooperation between the two groups, and they began holding a joint session that year.[10] At the 1935 NPC meeting, leaders reported the findings of a survey on deans of women's opinions of sororities on their campuses. Many of the deans surveyed believed that sororities' social standards were better at shaping campus social standards than were the universities' administrative rules. Sorority social standards "were the social standards which were considered valid by the students on campus."[11] By working with deans of women over the years, national sororities managed to engineer an ostensibly useful, even necessary role for the groups on campuses. While the NPC would need to constantly reassure the public of their devotion to educating students for ladyhood and good citizenship, the generally positive relationship between sorority alumnae and campus administrators created a foundation that allowed sororities to thrive on university campuses, with few detractors, through the mid-twentieth century.

While deans of women proposed to help women transition into the college environment, the reality of expanding women's enrollments hindered the deans offices' efforts at individual student attention. Sororities' firm guidance, which the organizations smartly touted as similar to the supervision administered by the young women's families back home, was intended to enable greater control over individual women than the dean's office alone. Women who were students in the 1930s recalled that campus regulations for their behavior were stricter than the rules at their families' homes. Still, most women accepted the limitations. As Audrey Moore Stewart, an Alpha Delta Theta (AΔΘ) and 1932 graduate of the University of Illinois, remembered, women generally accepted rules about closing hours. "Everyone just took it for granted. People of that era did not revolt against rules and regulations."[12] Sororities' standards required that members adhere to certain regulations for behavior and appearance, attendance at sorority events, and grades, and augmented the rules already enforced by campus authorities.

Sororities, Home Economics, and the Women's Curricula

Advertising the social training aspect of sororities could create a conundrum for the organizations. Why, some might ask, would a group supposedly formed of elite young women need to engage in social training? Did they not already possess this knowledge? As sororities strove to demonstrate the cultured status of their members, they also sought to connect the idea of "social education" with the "natural" training that a girl would receive from her mother, so that they could argue they were enhancing the personality and appearance of young women of the upper middle class, not just doling out rules of deportment to girls of any station who might be in need of basic manners. To maintain this distinction, sororities also distanced their social education from home economics and domestic science training at the university, upholding the idea that unlike a college curriculum, their lessons of ladyhood were open only to a chosen few. However, sorority social training *also* provided the groups with the added benefit of ensuring that all members were schooled in behaviors that the sororities wished to display as ideal.

In the early decades of the twentieth century, many universities actively promoted coursework designed to impart skills of normative, middle-class womanhood that included activities such as homemaking and motherhood. Classes and departments in domestic science, or the more popularly termed "home economics," became university administrators' answer to public criticism that higher education would "unsex" women and prove harmful to their perceived social duty of procreation of the white race.[13] A number of white southern universities sought to implement home economics departments during and after World War I as a way to increase women's enrollment while making the curriculum more acceptable to the families of white southern women.[14]

At campuses such as Duke that did not offer home economics courses for women, the sororities could point to their particular role in students' social education. However, the increasing popularity of vocational college curricula and the expansion of sororities to more college campuses meant that sororities' training increasingly coexisted with home economics courses. Sorority journals in the 1910s and 1920s promoted the study of home economics as practical preparation for jobs. Yet as Marie Casteen, a Kappa Delta alumna who was employed by the Statler Hotel chain as a consulting dietitian to the chef, noted, a specialization in home economics was not the only reason that she reached a successful position. She explained that a "background of good breeding and refinement" was also required. Casteen's addition of the characteristics of "good breeding and refinement" meant that she and other sorority women believed they possessed a cultural polish of ladyhood that surpassed the abilities of nonsorority women likewise trained in the domestic sciences.[15]

Some administrators, such as the University of Alabama's dean of women, Agnes Ellen Harris, saw home economics and sorority social education as two sides of the same coin. Speaking at the 1935 NPC meeting, Harris—a home economics scholar and practitioner—expressed hope that university home economics departments and sororities might find ways to work together to educate women in the future.[16] While sorority leaders may have seen promise in distinguishing sorority training from home economics courses, Harris suggested that the two entities held comparable goals for women's development, even if they relied on different methods for their achievement.

Just as home economics training could open up opportunities in young women's lives, Harris believed that the influence of sorority training could have similar benefit. At southern universities such as the University of Alabama with overall less affluent student populations, sororities could be particularly important for smoothing the rough edges of young women's etiquette. Sororities would actively create southern ladies from the southern women available on campus. While many deans simply hoped that sorority women would have a positive influence on the nonsorority women, Harris saw a specific role for sororities to play in pledging and initiating those women whom she believed had a greater need for social training as a result of their socioeconomic station. In 1935 she raised the point within a larger discussion of the cost of sorority membership during the Depression, a time when many students' families could barely make ends meet. At Duke that same year, the Gamma Epsilon chapter of Phi Mu announced chapter dues of $4.50 per month— equivalent to roughly $85 per month in 2019. At public universities parents were having difficulties paying for their daughters' room and board, let alone additional items such as sorority initiation or membership fees.[17] Harris spoke in support of making sorority dues affordable for Depression-era students in economically hard-hit southern schools. She used that platform, however, to press the idea that less wealthy young women were in even greater need of a sorority's teachings than those of upper-class backgrounds, whose families could more easily pay their membership fees. "The so-called plain man's daughter really needs more education," Harris argued, "because, after all, the ... daughter of the man of means, she is a precious young person. She has had a charming social life. [The] mother has educated the daughter and she does not need the sorority, but the plain man's daughter needs the social education."[18] For deans such as Harris, the image of the less affluent student mingled with that of the culturally inept, suggesting that they saw middle-class manners as foreign to students from working-class backgrounds. Sororities could most benefit these female students from underprivileged backgrounds, she argued, by introducing them to middle-class mores. While Harris's comments might have sounded biased against the child-rearing abilities of parents in lower socioeconomic classes, she also expressed an important and somewhat novel viewpoint that sororities at schools in the South should be vehicles by which to elevate women of lesser circumstances. Furthermore, by training working-class white women in standards of middle-class white behavior, sororities would strengthen social boundaries against racial mixing and fortify white supremacy. Sororities would provide tutelage in accepted standards of middle- and upper-class behavior—knowledge that could enable working-class women to move into a higher socioeconomic class, through either a career or, more likely, a marriage to a financially established or upwardly mobile white man.

Of course, the idea of "elevating" underprivileged women carried with it the assumption that the underprivileged individual could not, or *would* not, seek to "better" herself of her own accord. The fact that some university administrators and sorority leaders believed that the mission of national sororities should extend to "lifting" young women's class status in turn helped sorority women define their own places in the socioeconomic order. As they identified the type of women supposedly in need of their social elevation skills, the sorority women inherently defined themselves as "better than" those women they aimed to help.[19] Sororities continued to chafe at the idea of bringing the underprivileged women into membership, meaning that they wished the dividing line between "us" and "them" to remain simply those women who were and were not invited to join. Bettering the lives of the underprivileged usually fell under the purview of sorority philanthropic endeavors—projects undertaken with varying levels of interest by individual college and alumnae chapters.[20]

Even as home economics moved away from training women for specific postcollege careers and toward embracing courses that prepared them to become efficient housewives, sororities could promote their social education programs as distinctly different from the standard home economics curriculum. Instead of training women to create a household budget, mend clothing, or cook nutritious meals for their families, sororities intended their lessons in social education to impart cultural polish. Illinois AΔΘ Audrey Moore Stewart remembered that the sororities "had very stringent rules." At her chapter, "no one sat down for lunch or dinner until the house mother was seated." She described the sorority living environment as "a middle-class man's finishing school," where women were "taught quite a lot about table manners."[21] By teaching members to value other women who possessed a cultured demeanor and the ability to eschew work, both unpaid within the home as well as paid employment outside the home, the groups reinforced the conservative notion that socioeconomic class was a key indicator of both ladyhood and a woman's citizenship potential. Part of the allure of the sororities' lessons, then, was the popular perception that sorority women did not have to concern themselves with such specific and apparently mundane tasks as befell a typical white American housewife. Instead, they would learn social graces—how to conduct oneself in public, speak pleasingly, move gracefully, and interact with and date men of the same social class. As the twentieth century progressed, sororities' national leadership also promoted an increasing array of materials and programs designed to prepare their members for the "reality" of adult womanhood.

Guidebooks for "Living Beautifully"

"During the four years of a college career," a 1938 NPC publication explained, "a girl should develop social poise." The prose described how the social sorority should provide a group influence to "[correct] individual faults and [cultivate] gracious social habits." In the NPC's view, the sorority represented a microcosm of social relations in the world. More specifically, the sorority would monitor members' behavior in an environment where "social conduct [was] discussed freely, and criticism offered where it [was] due." Not only was social training a useful tool to show how sororities contributed an important service to colleges, but it also served a significant role in the groups' image maintenance. The 1936 *Pledge Manual of the Delta Gamma Fraternity* put it in stark terms: "If you fail to represent Delta Gamma with honor and achievement, disgrace and loss of prestige will be Delta Gamma's."[22] The training frequently emphasized the weight of sorority members' responsibility to maintain a ladylike image, meaning that sorority standards were no longer lofty goals for character improvement but carefully enforced rules of living. While not explicitly imbued with a southern aesthetic, the guidance for ladylike behavior built on characteristics of the southern lady.

Sorority literature, produced and distributed nationally by the groups throughout the period of this study, served to help new and veteran sorority women abide by contemporary, white middle- and upper-class gendered norms of behavior. In some ways, these guides were similar to other university rulebooks for women's behavior issued by groups such as women's student government associations or the Young Women's Christian Association (YWCA). Booklets from the 1920s and early 1930s adopted an authoritarian approach, listing dorm closing hours and rules relating to noise, attendance at fraternity parties, "motoring," and the necessity of chaperones.[23] By the late 1930s and beyond, sororities' manuals were increasingly attuned to the development of personality, attractiveness, and overall sociability of members, all while reinforcing women's heteronormativity. Sorority etiquette and pledge training books—in effect, members' lesson books—instructed the women on everything from becoming involved in campus activities and the proper application of makeup to cultivating a pleasant speaking voice and the correct way to get in and out of a chair.[24] Bodily control and attention to detail were paramount in all activities. The handbooks' exacting standards demonstrated that sororities' programs for social education could function to streamline the members' identities and morph them into the homogeneous, easily controlled groups sought by campus administrators.

Sororities saw the pledge period as the optimal time to mold the desired identity of new members. Generally, pledging lasted several months or for the entire semester following rush, leading up to the time when the sorority initiated the women into full membership. The *Kappa Alpha Theta Pledge Training Book* (1927) reported that "pledges are most impressionable, ready to follow suggestions and examples of members." The book instructed KAΘ sisters to view each pledge as "an individual problem." If she was "guided and helped rightly," the pledge would be "an asset, and if not, a liability." By shaping new members' behavior to meet accepted standards, sorority chapters sought to uphold or improve their standing on campus.[25] Delta Gamma (ΔΓ) sorority told pledges that the sorority provided a "great opportunity for developing... personality... through close association with other members." But how was personality defined? Delta Gamma suggested "morals, manners, emotions, attitudes, habits, intellect, culture and personal appearance" as elements of the "all-embracing term" and guided each pledge to "scrutinize [her]self candidly in all these respects."[26] The pledge training of KAΘ and ΔΓ in the 1920s and 1930s shows that in sororities' attempts to ensure that pledges became assets instead of liabilities, the groups often resorted to strict policing of members' behavior, appearance, and campus involvement to ensure that their chapter was well received by other students and by fraternity men in particular.

While each individual chapter's image might differ slightly, members would be expected to abide by requirements set by their own chapter as well as the national organization. By the 1920s, KAΘ's national prescriptions included participation in campus activities and heterosexual dating, attendance at social affairs, demonstration of hostessing skills, and an attention to "good grooming and proper clothes for proper occasions" to create an "attractive personal appearance." These behavioral standards, KAΘ's national leadership held, would convey the image of Thetas as "good campus citizens" who displayed a successful "adjustment to social conditions" of college life.[27]

The authors of the KAΘ pledge training book supposed that women chosen for membership could possess a variety of personality types and levels of sociability. They suggested that the most common type of girl (and the easiest to work with) was the "charming, vivacious, winning girl." The only thing the sorority members might have to teach the "winning" type of girl was how to budget her time for study so as to maintain her scholastic standing. In other words, she actually needed little of the sorority's social training and would fit right into the stylized picture of the fun, exciting, heterosocial life of a sorority woman.

"Not very uncommon," the guide stated, was the "too studious type of girl."[28] To the sororities the overly studious woman presented a problem. If too many chapter members spent an overwhelming amount of time studying, they would cut into the hours available for extracurricular involvement and heterosocializing. While sororities wanted intelligent girls among their ranks, a member who seemed *too* intent on matters of academics and earned the nickname "brain" or "grind" might appear threatening to men. Studious members could undercut the "fun" image that sororities sought to project. Women who flaunted their intellect, advice columnists warned, would be unattractive to men and would remain dateless, perhaps ending up as culturally stigmatized spinsters.[29] Ideally, sorority sisters would endeavor to help the new members adjust to college life by striking a delicate balance between the first two pledge "types," but the guidebook's language makes clear that the social butterfly who devoted less time to books was the sorority's preferred model.

Yet another but supposedly less typical type of pledge was the "timid or reticent" girl. To help these young women become a part of the group, the book proposed that "special attention" should be given to the "timid, awkward, and socially inexperienced pledges."[30] These pledges would be specifically channeled into tasks of hostessing or heterosocializing to help them overcome what their sorority sisters perceived as their social shortcomings or inabilities and train them as ladies. According to the sororities' vision, to become a "fully socialized lady," a member would follow the groups' prescriptions for her activities and behave in the manner exhibited by the elder sorority sisters and alumnae. The sororities' training booklets suggested that any woman who failed to behave as the groups prescribed, or to live up to their strictly defined standards, was at best improperly socialized and at worst *not* a "lady," the latter also a label that connoted the image of sexual impropriety.

The overwhelming attention given to the behavior of new members suggested that sororities encountered difficulties with the sociability of some of their members. If the new members needed to navigate an eighty-page pledge manual such as that produced by Delta Gamma in 1936 or an extensively detailed etiquette book such as Delta Delta Delta's *Tri Delta Hostess* in 1937, clearly there were concerns among the organizations' leadership that a number of the women being invited to membership were in need of tutelage on the finer points of ladyhood. To help members learn the behaviors that their national organization expected of them, the guidebooks offered an array of activities for the chapters to put into practice as teaching scenarios. Frequently the handbooks advised sorority chapters to stage teas, dinners, parties, and formal dances that would give members the chance to learn and exercise their skills of socializing and hostessing.

Even in the midst of the Depression, sororities' guidebooks suggested that their members and alumnae occupied the lap of luxury. Clearly sorority national officers and other sorority women were painfully aware of the strictures on family finances faced by many students at the time. Agnes Ellen Harris's comments at the NPC convention in 1935, along with reminders from the national organizations that chapters stage simple events, suggested that sorority women did adapt their activities to fit the somber tone of the time. Keeping costs down and limiting "extravagances" such as parties with fresh flowers and other expensive decorations would help sororities from being pictured as frivolous or even callous in the face of the suffering experienced by many Americans during the Depression. Yet NPC groups delivered a contradictory message as their social education guides encouraged members to prepare for an adult social life that mirrored the images of socialites portrayed in popular films of the day. At the same time, the guidebooks also made clear that the sororities expected the member of the 1930s to meet the "serious financial obligation" she undertook in joining her sisterhood. During Depression-era hardship, Delta Gamma cautioned pledges not to "neglect that duty."[31] In November 1935 the treasurer of the Gamma Epsilon chapter of Phi Mu at Duke Woman's College reminded new members that monthly chapter dues of $4.50 were due before the eleventh of each month of the school year, with a fifty-cent fine if not paid on time. On top of that, an eight-dollar national fee was due by October 15 of each school year. These costs did not include periodic collections to pay for music, event space rentals, dinners, and the like, nor the initiation fee, which was around fifty dollars. In today's money, a member was looking at nearly $945 in dues per school year.[32]

In addition to party planning, the *Tri Delta Hostess* included sections on appearance and personality, hospitality, entertaining, household routine, appearance in public, and rushing—in that order. The authors, Beverly Holtenhouse Ballard and Margaret Ward, geared these lessons toward life in the sorority house but also designed them to translate seamlessly to a woman's social life in adulthood. Although the authors put forth what they believed was a "modern" 1930s view of white women's place in contemporary society, Ballard and Ward's writing hinted at their own conformity to conventional expectations for women, as they devised their lessons to train sorority women for a distinctly white, gender-normative, upper-middle-class or elite existence. Somewhat surprisingly, Ballard and Ward were recent college graduates, not older alumnae with what might be seen as a greater wealth of cultural knowledge to share with impressionable young sorority women. Ballard was a 1932 graduate of the University of Washington; Ward had just graduated from the University of Texas in 1936.[33] The authors' youth suggested that ΔΔΔ aimed to produce a guide that presented the sorority's standards to its college members in a contemporary manner and one that pertained to the experiences of young women of the day. The fact that these sorority women, who were almost the same age as the college actives, saw these lessons as necessary indicated either that they had experienced similar training and thought it important, or that they believed women in their chapters had lacked this type of knowledge and needed tutelage. As in the case of sororities building and maintaining chapter mansions much grander than anything most members would have previously experienced, the messages of the *Hostess* helped members learn the language of a created lifestyle that would appear foreign to most young alumnae's daily existence—but which could help them learn to aspire to such living as the norm.

Still young women themselves, Ballard and Ward seemed eager to promote sorority women as modern American women. But this picture of independent white womanhood caused public alarm and could appear particularly threatening to middle- and upper-class white men. The last thing sorority women wanted to do was frighten away male students (most often fraternity men) who might become their dates or future romantic partners. The southern lady was the foil to the possibly overbearing modern woman. Popular culture was rife with portrayals of the belle in the 1930s, and although the *Hostess* did not specifically reference its trainees as such, her characteristics were reinforced by the guide's recommendations.[34] Ballard and Ward tempered their portrayal of modern womanhood with constant reminders that a "proper" sorority woman would know when to bow to convention. If a sorority sister were to become overly independent in any aspect of her life, it could spell disaster for these groups that needed cohesion and uniformity to function.

Physical appearance and personality were the primary points of instruction in the *Hostess* because of their importance to the overall image of the sorority. "A sorority's personality," the authors explained, "is expressed through the appearance and behavior of its members. There are various reasons why a sorority 'rates' on campus, but, almost invariably, the group is a leader whose members are uniformly well groomed and [possess] a good share of *savoir faire*."[35] How a sorority "rated" on campus was in direct relation to the chapter's overall popularity. Sociologist Willard Waller clinicalized the term "rating" in his 1937 article, "The Rating and Dating Complex," which described the system of popularity rankings he observed among undergraduates at Pennsylvania State College. A woman's desirability as a date relied primarily on her ability to have many dates and appear sought after by men.[36] The popularity of a sorority chapter followed the same logic. With their comments that connected rating well on campus to appearance and social fluency, Ballard and Ward basically admitted that a sorority chapter's popularity was based on superficial, "at-first-sight" assessments of the membership as a whole. Since finding a marriage partner signaled "success" for a woman during this period—and arguably still does in the present day (particularly in the southern United States)—simply gearing sororities' social training toward preparation for heterosexual dating could be perceived as beneficial to the individual woman's development.

At the root of a sorority woman's appearance was her level of conventional physical attractiveness. The *Hostess* recommended that sororities regularly dispense advice on personal grooming, fashion, and etiquette. They placed even greater emphasis on physical appearance and clothing choices than had the KAΘ leaders' guidance in the previous decade. In the South, the regional cult of beauty conditioned southern ladies-in-training to understand that physical beauty was a signifier of ladyhood and thus worth working to achieve.[37] Sororities' training, built on the model of the southern lady, exported this primary emphasis on physical beauty beyond the South. Performing ladyhood required effort on the part of the individual woman. To exact a charming bearing, the guide suggested that women "hold the head high (a good hairdo looks better that way), throw out the chest, and, by all means, pull in the abdomen."[38] Through negative reinforcement, members would learn how to conduct themselves as ladies and represent their sorority in the expected manner. Instead of a supportive group of women, working together to strengthen each member's abilities and self-image, the guidebooks painted a picture of sororities where personal criticisms stood to undermine women's confidence, perhaps even turning them against one another. Ballard and Ward did not seem concerned that a sorority chapter's routine criticism of its members might lead to group discord or teach members to forfeit tact and kindness in personal relationships in pursuit of the chapter's image goals. In fact, throughout the guidebook the two women neglect to discuss how sorority women should act toward each other. Their suggestions of how to appear and act were designed to make the women appeal to a public audience outside of the sorority chapter, and their discussions of hospitality were tailored to fit interactions with alumnae, university administrators, and other "adults"; lessons of everyday friendship and civility among the sisters are surprisingly absent.

The book's segment on entertaining, sort of a condensed version of Emily Post's *Etiquette*, explained such intricacies as how to organize a tea, dress for a tea, serve tea, create "correct forms for invitations" to teas and formal dinners, order flowers for events, set a formal dinner table, and make introductions among dinner guests. It also included menus for different meals. It should be noted that the inclusion of menus did not mean instruction on how to make the items to be served at the meal. That was left to the cook. "Household routine" covered basic "manners," including "table etiquette," advised the appropriate attire for women in public areas of the sorority house, and discussed how to address and interact with house servants.[39] While good manners and shows of courtesy to guests were essential social skills, the *Hostess*'s lessons for sorority women seemed ill prepared to supplement the basic homemaking needs of most postcollegiate women. Instead the advice might better suit the practices of a wealthy socialite. This lack of attention to the everyday issues encountered by many young housewives, such as budgeting and consumer spending, meal preparation, household cleaning, and childcare again suggests that sorority leaders did not view these topics as part of their social training program. They seemed to indicate that commonplace household duties were the purview of home economics departments, and perhaps that sorority women would not have to concern themselves with such work since it might be taken care of by servants or part-time domestic help. The guide's reference to house servants meant servants *within* the sorority house, as the houses typically employed cooks, but it also presumed that sororities expected their members to employ household help in the future and that the women should be prepared to oversee their work. With specific social training fitted to the upper-class image that sororities peddled to prospective members, the organizations left the lessons of homemaking and motherhood to home economics courses that were likely filled by many sorority women.[40]

Although Ballard and Ward adhered to the popular stereotype of the Irish female domestic workers in their discussion of "servants," the majority of domestic workers in this period were African American women.[41] When read against the guide's protocol for relations between "servants" and sorority women, the authors' examples also provide a tacit commentary on race relations in the 1930s. Relationships between the servants in the house and the sorority chapter members, Ballard and Ward noted, should remain professional, and the servants should always show deference, calling the members "by the surname prefixed by Miss." The sorority women, however, were free to refer to cooks and servants by their first name only, if they so chose. "Personal friendships between servants and chapter members" were unadvisable because they could lead to decentralization of authority in the domestic routine and by extension in the larger society.[42] By befriending the servants—likely to be African American women—the white sorority woman stood to upset the delicate balance of power in the race- and class-based social hierarchy.

The tutorials provided by the *Tri Delta Hostess* and similar sorority publications presented a lifestyle to which sorority women could aspire but in reality probably did not live. Nevertheless, this type of social education implied a level of culture and class status that the alumnae and national officers hoped to convey as their own. As they seized on the opportunity for positive publicity generated by a "school of manners" for young women, the sororities made social education and heterosocializing their primary platforms. This veneer of sophistication would become even more important for the image of the organizations in the years following World War II, as an increasing number of college students came from a variety of social backgrounds, which some sorority officers, alumnae, and active members found less than desirable.

Sororities began a more stringent policing of members' behavior at just the right time to attract the attention of the student personnel departments. Educational administrators in the second quarter of the twentieth century expressed a growing interest in shaping "well-adjusted" students who they believed would be the future upstanding leaders of the country. Universities' new student personnel departments, which included a staff specifically trained to guide students to adulthood, gradually supplanted the older model where a single dean ministered to the needs of the entire student body.[43] In a way, the dean of women's office staff, increasingly with formal training in student personnel, acted like a sorority as it kept tabs on the students and tried to identify character types or flaws that might hinder a woman in her progression to ladyhood. The personnel selection process submitted the participant, in this case the student, to a variety of tests and interviews designed to help a "trained observer" determine the participant's interests and abilities. While some personnel administrators believed that their specific training had left them better prepared to guide students than sorority alumnae and officers, it was often the college members themselves who were on the front lines of managing perceived behavioral abnormalities among their peers.

Kappa Kappa Gamma's (KKΓ) 1944 publication, *Instructions for Pledge Training for Kappa Kappa Gamma*, proposed psychological profiling of pledges as a way for chapters to "develop" desired "traits" in new members "by active means." An older sorority member would be assigned to the pledge as her "pledge mother" or "big sister," with the goal of completing a year of pledge training "with a protégé who [was] a healthy specimen of normality."[44] For a pledge to be a "specimen of normality" within her sorority, she would need to conform to the sorority's standards of middle-class behavior and dress, as well as participate enthusiastically in sorority meetings and activities. The big sisters would facilitate the work of the chapter's Personnel Committee by giving the committee "a full report on the adjustment of each pledge" to sorority behavioral standards.[45] The Delta Beta chapter at Duke used KKΓ's suggested Personnel Committee to influence desired behaviors in members. The Personnel Committee existed to "make sure that girls [were] happy" and "congenial," but it was "not necessarily" a disciplinary body.[46] One task of the personnel chairperson was to collect criticisms of members from their sorority sisters. By 1946 the committee used a seemingly awkward arrangement where the personnel chairperson would give the collected criticisms to the best friend of the member being criticized. The best friend would then have to decide how to break the news to the girl.[47] While the Personnel Committee gave members instruction on how to comport themselves at the sorority's meetings, it also counseled the membership at large on their everyday behavior, asking the women "to be conservative in action, dress, and speech." Each week, the committee would post a "watch bird" on the bulletin board "telling Kappas what not to be seen doing."[48] The Delta Beta chapter had replaced their criticism sheets with the euphemistically titled "compliment sheets" by 1949, but the basic premise of the Personnel Committee remained the same. By monitoring the appearance and behavior of the individual members, the sorority could engineer the group's image to fit southern regional standards of white ladylike propriety and extend that model to their national standards for sorority ladyhood.

Training Nonsorority Women on Campus

Although deans such as Agnes Ellen Harris suggested that broadening sororities' membership base to include lower-middle-class and working-class college women would allow sorority social training to benefit more women, sororities' national leaders did not favor this plan. Instead of inviting into membership the young women whom sorority alumnae and national officers viewed as undesirable and less "civilized," the sorority women suggested that *all* female students could benefit equally from sororities' social standards simply by following the sorority members' example. Yet the level of success of these programs depended on the status of relationships between Greeks and independents on each campus.

Sorority literature put forth the idea that unaffiliated women would have few other opportunities in which to learn ladylike graces or socialize in such an enjoyable setting as did sorority women.[49] A 1922 article in the *Adelphean* of Alpha Delta Pi by a freshman member of the Phi chapter at Hanover College in Hanover, Indiana, explained that "the college life for the non-sorority girl especially, is often very uneventful." By entertaining the independents, she noted, the sorority women would be bringing "to the other girls a little of the society side of college life."[50] Between their own chapters' events and the campus activities open to all students, members of GLOs did have more opportunities for socializing and typically more money available to fund the events.[51] Just as deans of women and sorority leaders made assumptions about young women from working-class backgrounds, college sorority women issued suppositions about the needs of nonsorority women on campus. At best, the sorority member's comments appeared to overlook other opportunities for women's campus socializing at events such as dormitory parties, teas held by the dean of women's office, campus-wide formals, sporting events, and other organizational gatherings. At worst, she simultaneously acknowledged those activities while devaluing their worth as social sites for unaffiliated women, not to mention devaluing the relationships the sites might foster.

No matter how important the appearance of friendly relations between sorority women and independents on a campus, the actual social interaction generally necessary for relationship formation did not appear to be a high priority for the sorority sisters or the independents. When required by the Duke

Woman's College administration to hold a tea for nonsorority women in 1938, the Gamma Epsilon chapter of Phi Mu decided to schedule the event during their chapter inspection.[52] Chapter inspection involved a visit from one or more regional officers, or perhaps a national officer, who would evaluate the chapter's status on campus, how it measured up to other chapters of the sorority nationally, and its ability to minister to its members. Since Gamma Epsilon chapter seemed to have a somewhat contentious relationship with the regional and national sorority leadership—they had been reprimanded for lack of pledges, lack of finances, and "deplorably low" scholarship—the chapter officers may have hoped to improve their image by holding the tea at a time when they could present themselves as superior to the nonsorority women on campus.[53] They might not be Phi Mu's best chapter, but they could at least, it seemed, try to prove themselves as "better" than women who were not in any Greek-letter group. The following year, Delta Beta chapter of Kappa Kappa Gamma at Duke had planned a picnic for the "town girls" (women who attended the college but lived with family or friends in Durham and not on campus) but ended up indefinitely postponing the affair when the original date fell through. Delta Beta had decided to fine each member seventy-five cents in the case of an unexcused absence from the picnic, suggesting that many of the sisters may have intended to skip the event.[54] In the end, the chapter may have found it easier to call the whole thing off. By creating situations through which sorority women could establish clear boundaries between themselves and the nonsorority women, they were able to reinforce their position of superiority.

A Laboratory Course in Living Beautifully

The new norm for white middle-class women in the postwar years was preparation for homemaking and motherhood. The shift away from the promotion of women's work outside of the home resulted from the American public's desire to return to a safe and steady environment in the wake of the Depression and war decades, which they equated in part with a safe and nurturing domestic existence. The change in public expectations for women's roles after college also shaped their experiences in college. University campuses catered to the returning male veterans enrolling as a result of the Servicemen's Readjustment Act (1944), also known as the G.I. Bill, meaning that, as in the early years of coeducation, college administrations were less focused on women on campus.[55] Some universities even instituted quotas limiting the number of women and nonveteran enrollees to save spaces for G.I. Bill recipients. The demotion of women's status on campuses, taken alongside the repopularized image of a woman's "place" in the home, led educators and administrators to new arguments over the most suitable curriculum for women college students. If a woman was "only" going to get married and raise a family after graduation, some wondered, was she best served by a traditional liberal arts education, or would practical courses in family life better suit her future?[56] In this environment, sororities stood at the ready, promoting their social education programs, which, their proponents maintained, would impart a "feminine culture" on the coeducational campus again filled with male students. Sororities' advertised image as centers of feminine culture could be particularly useful for deans of women and other university administrators who opposed instituting a specialized "female curriculum." Sororities, rather than the colleges, could reinforce the idea that women should prepare themselves for middle- to upper-class homemaking.

While UNC's Dean Carmichael did not approve of the social class distinctions sororities created on campus, she did find the groups useful for forming a "feminine atmosphere" and for instilling what she felt were the necessary lessons of "gracious womanhood."[57] She had pledged Alpha Chi Omega (AXΩ) at Birmingham-Southern College in the late 1920s but did not appear to remain an active alumna during her years as dean.[58] Carmichael described sorority living as a "laboratory" for socialization where women could "have a learning experience in how to live beautifully."[59] She praised the way that the sorority taught hostessing skills, having found that these small lessons helped prepare her for the many hostessing duties included in her job as an administrator.[60] Sororities' programs of character education would provide model patterns of behavior for all women on campus. Sorority leaders hoped that deans would continue to view the groups as essential tools for molding desired behaviors for the entire women's student body as sororities provided a ready means to instill traditions, produce standardization, and enforce group control.[61]

The postwar enrollment boom and development of new colleges democratized higher education and increased the U.S. college population. Speaking to a joint meeting of deans and sorority leaders in 1950, Kate Hevner Mueller, dean of women at Indiana University (IU), echoed the sentiments of Agnes Ellen Harris fifteen years prior when she suggested that "on the typical university campus, one third to one half of the students will come from the working classes rather than from the substantial business and professional or upper-middle-class." Mueller's description of a "typical university campus" primarily referred to state universities, such as her own IU. She suggested that university educators and administrators should look to Greek-letter organizations to "indoctrinate this large group of students in manners and morals with which they have never been familiar."[62] While that might mean indoctrination through membership and training, it might also include learning by example for nonsorority women.

What had begun as a way to encourage campus and public approval of sororities had become a key organizational premise by the 1930s. Sorority standards and social education, steeped in the southern aesthetic, provided the groups with malleable tools applicable to public relations work, behavioral molding, and reinforcement of "acceptable" members. Through leadership activities, planning and hostessing of social affairs, and learning, in the words of Dean Carmichael, to "get along with" others, the sorority claimed to help its members gain necessary experiences in "the art of fine living," all of which could prepare women to take on the job of a multitasking housewife while playing a leadership role in her community.[63] As the *raison d'être* of the clubs by the mid-twentieth century, social training programs and standards helped ensure sororities' transition from supportive spaces for women to yet another area of life where every aspect of their behavior would be severely critiqued.

CHAPTER THREE

·•·

Southern Belles and Sorority Girls

SORORITIES AND THE LURE OF
THE SOUTHERN AESTHETIC

*I*n the March 1915 issue of the *Aglaia* of Phi Mu (ΦM), a member identifying herself as "E.M.F." wrote, "How often have you said, and heard others say, 'Phi Mu is an old Southern fraternity,' or 'Phi Mu stands for the best in Southern womanhood?' We all say these things in rush season and at other times of enthusiasm or rapture, we know them to be true and we take a peculiar pride in our Southern ancestry." Significantly, she also noted, "this feeling for the South is not confined to Phi Mus. All Americans look upon the land of Dixie with a very real affection. . . . And all who can, say with great pride 'My family came from the South.'"[1] E.M.F. was Erna Fergusson, a well-to-do daughter of Albuquerque, a 1912 graduate of the University of New Mexico, where she was a member of the sorority's new Xi chapter, and later, a journalist and celebrated "expert" on southwestern culture.[2] While Fergusson's maternal grandfather had immigrated to Albuquerque from Germany, her father came from Alabama. Just before the turn of the century, the Fergussons spent several years living in Washington, D.C., when her father served as the congressional delegate from New Mexico Territory, and she also spent some time teaching at Chatham Hall, an exclusive girls' boarding school in Chatham, Virginia. Given her background, Erna Fergusson was not so removed from southern culture as first impressions might suggest. Yet Fergusson's article conceded her nonsouthern upbringing, explaining that her "early impressions" of the southern lady came from "books [she] read about the South" by "Thomas Nelson Page, Joel Chandler Harris, Mrs. Augusta Evans . . . and [from] the tales [she] heard southern people tell."[3] Like many members of southern-founded sororities, Fergusson suggested that she was still more southern by association than by birth. Her example sheds light on the significant cultural overlap between the southern and nonsouthern sorority women and the lure of what I term the southern aesthetic for sorority women in the early twentieth century.

As Fergusson lauded the southern heritage of Phi Mu, which became a Greek-letter organization in 1904 and was originally founded as the secretive Philomathean Society at Macon's Georgia Wesleyan College in 1852, she also articulated the early twentieth-century national preoccupation with and reverence for the South, southern people, and the southern lady in particular. Indeed, her essay appeared in the *Aglaia* concurrently with the release of Kentuckian D. W. Griffith's *The Birth of a Nation* (1915). A film based on the novel and play *The Clansman* (1905) by North Carolinian Thomas Dixon, *Birth of a Nation's* story encapsulated the themes of post–Civil War sectional reconciliation and white supremacy, while romanticizing the imagery of the Old South. The *Aglaia's* editors continued to find Fergusson's message a timely one, as they reprinted it five years later in the March 1920 issue, perhaps as a rejoinder to the ongoing race riots in northern cities and northern newspapers' new attention to the "Negro Problem" in their midst.[4] While not an overtly racial polemic, her essay evoked images of idolized and protected white womanhood of the Old South, where the *Aglaia's* audiences would understand that whites "controlled" African Americans through enslavement.

By 1915 Phi Mu and other National Panhellenic Conference (NPC) sororities were national organizations with chapters at colleges across the United States as well as some in Canada.[5] While the Philomathean Society and its counterpart, the Adelphean Society (which became Alpha Delta Phi in 1905, then Alpha Delta Pi [AΔΠ] in 1913 after complaints from an existing men's fraternity that already used those Greek letters), had existed as secret societies at Georgia Wesleyan since the mid-nineteenth century, they did not begin as Greek-letter sororities, nor did they initially have interest in becoming national organizations. Eight other sororities formed at schools in southern states between 1873 and 1919.[6] Beta Sigma Omicron (BΣO), founded in 1888 at the University of Missouri, explicitly limited expansion of chapters to southern colleges for women until 1925. While other groups initially explored a limited regional focus for expansion, only Chi Omega (XΩ), which formed at the University of Arkansas in 1895, appeared to have sought to become a national organization since its inception.[7]

At the same time, sororities founded at colleges in other regions of the United States also began placing chapters at southern schools. However, the lack of accredited colleges and the restrictions on women's enrollment at many flagship public campuses limited the southern expansion of sorority chapters, both among southern- and nonsouthern-founded groups. By 1927, of the twenty-nine NPC sororities listed in *Baird's Manual of College Fraternities*, only eight had been founded at colleges located in the southern United States. Among all twenty-nine sororities, 264 chapters were at schools in the South and 847 at schools outside the South.[8]

In the first quarter of the twentieth century, when many NPC sororities were in a great period of expansion and many southern-founded sororities were beginning to establish chapters at schools outside of the South, it was common for sororities to pay homage to their southern roots and share their version of history with their new inductees. These southern-founded national organizations conveyed a southern aesthetic to women across the United States. The southern aesthetic included a special shared history based on Lost Cause mythology, as well as an unspoken understanding that whiteness and the image of ladyhood, premised on *southern* ladyhood, provided access to an unquestionably elite status.[9] This rhetoric and imagery is recorded in the quarterly journals of NPC sororities as well as chapter newsletters, college yearbooks, and books that the sororities produced about the histories of their respective organizations. Over the years, the aesthetic broadened from the shared lore of Old South gentility found in Fergusson's piece to include such examples as national conferences themed around southern locales, sorority houses styled after southern plantation homes, carefully calculated stories of aristocratic southern sorority founders, and sorority chapter events that drew on southern belle imagery and often included white sorority sisters in blackface. While sororities' southern aesthetic provided various ways for southern and nonsouthern members to "try on" southern ladyhood, the role, like the aesthetic undergirding it, was always imbued with race and class privilege that would particularly appeal to Americans seeking to affirm their social status in a progressively rootless mass society and one in which white Americans felt increasingly threatened by African Americans' progress in attainment of education, occupational status, and civil rights.

As southern-founded sororities peddled the southern aesthetic, white college women across the country could tap into the myth to both bolster their ancestry and link themselves to the perceived "true beauty" of the southern lady.[10] In the early twentieth-century South, the association with imagery of the Old South and white privilege could help solidify the aura of gentility for aspiring middle-class whites of the New South. Likewise, for nonsoutherners the image of aristocracy associated with the mythic lady or belle of plantation tales afforded a chance to claim a piece of this heritage. Sorority women from any region of the United States who were among more recent immigrants from Europe could link themselves to a specifically Anglo-Saxon American and antebellum, if not colonial American, image to help ensure their place as "established" Americans. In addition, the ideal of an antebellum land where whites and blacks lived in "harmony"—because of the selectively disremembered fact that the African Americans had been enslaved—likely appealed to nonsouthern whites in the early twentieth century, who saw eruptions of racial discord and violence in their own communities.[11] Finally, "sisterhood" in a sorority, which was supposed to entail a greater affinity and deeper relationship than one created by general participation in Dixie-fied popular culture or membership in a women's club, literally created a kinship network among women "across the chasm" created by the Civil War. So while NPC sororities brought women throughout the nation together in a celebration of higher education, exemplary character, and "true," "civilized" womanhood, the southern-founded NPC groups also extended white southern cultural identity to their nonsouthern sisters.

While southern-founded NPC sororities imparted a particular regional difference to their national membership, the southern aesthetic also found support from nonsouthern-founded sororities. By the late nineteenth century, some nonsoutherners began to view the South and its people in a sentimental vein, as worthy of sympathy and admiration for gracefully bearing their substantial material losses while maintaining their dignity. In this understanding, the southern belle or lady appeared as the embodiment of a womanly ideal—domestic, family-inclined, and concerned with emotional rather than material concerns—that nonsoutherners found lacking in their own modern women, who sought lives outside of the private home and engaged with consumer society in ways that seemed distasteful to men who might be questioning the quality of life in America's new mass society. Nonsoutherners saw southern women maintaining strength of character in the face of their losses, which only increased their belief in the exemplary background and "good breeding" of southerners.[12] As early twentieth-century sorority women increasingly looked to the southern belle or lady as an ideal for their own life and an enhancement to their imagined family heritage, they learned of her traits through the Old South mythology promulgated by American popular culture and the references made by their own national organizations.

Like other national women's clubs and patriotic heritage societies that appeared in the late nineteenth century, such as the General Federation of Women's Clubs (GFWC), the Daughters of the American Revolution (DAR), the National Society of the Colonial Dames of America (NSCDA), and the Daughters of 1812, all founded between 1890 and 1892, sororities held the promise of reconciliation among southern and nonsouthern white women, many of whom still smarted from the "recent unpleasantness" of the Civil War and Reconstruction period. These women held the common desire to affirm their place among the most learned and enlightened white women of their generation through the identification with early American forebears—and if those ancestors also happened to be landed gentry, all the better.

White women and men from all regions of the United States concerned with rapid changes in American society participated in patriotic heritage organizations. These preservation-minded Americans attempted to connect with an idealized early America by preserving cultural traditions, symbols, and rituals. Beginning in the late nineteenth century, the Colonial Revival movement in America provided people a way to feel connected to an imagined colonial and early American past, premised on the values and "authenticity" of a largely Anglo-Saxon populace. Proponents of the Colonial Revival movement looked to preserve and recreate a way of life they believed existed prior to the Industrial Revolution in the United States. Like southerners' development of the Lost Cause mentality, Colonial Revival followers enveloped themselves in a world that looked to the past to soften the discomfort of changes in their own society. With activities that included honoring established families and their patriotic service to the nation, preserving and creating rituals used to Americanize immigrants, and preserving houses and buildings associated with old-stock American settlers, Colonial Revival adherents established norms that marked wealthy, white Anglo-Americans as "true" American citizens.[13] White sorority women also crafted their identities within this framework.

Southern-Founded Sororities and the Southern Aesthetic

Significantly, as the southern-founded NPC sororities branched out, establishing chapters at nonsouthern colleges, they continued their adherence to the southern aesthetic in their self-definition, thus carrying the regional beliefs to new audiences across North America. As Karen Cox has documented in *Dreaming of Dixie*, mass-produced images of the South in popular culture in the first half of the twentieth century helped spread an appreciation for, if not a belief in, the regional myths associated with the Lost Cause.[14] The southern-founded sorority, like other pop-culture renditions of Dixie, produced an accessible, feel-good, sanitized image of the South that leaned heavily on the "moonlight and magnolias" theme as it offered silent support for

Jim Crow. Erna Fergusson spoke to this in her essay, noting, "Girls of the far West and the North feel the same glow and show the same sparkle at the mention of the long line of Southern gentlewomen who have guarded the spirit of Phi Mu and passed it on to us."[15] No doubt Fergusson and the other new Phi Mus at the Xi chapter, the sorority's first outside the South, learned the significance of the sorority's southern heritage from Tennessean (and later Texan) Louise Monning Elliott, Phi Mu's grand president who installed the chapter in 1911. A daughter of the South, Elliott long maintained a reverence for the Lost Cause. Elliot, her daughter, and other women of the Monning family were part of the residential staff at the Forty-Fifth United Confederate Veterans (UCV) reunion, held in Amarillo, Texas, in September 1935.[16] Likewise, Georgia-born Louise Frederick Hays, who was Phi Mu's second vice president in 1911, went on to become a high-ranking officer of the Georgia Daughters of the Confederacy.[17]

The number of southern sorority women who were active in the United Daughters of the Confederacy (UDC) is unclear. However, most of the UDC's nearly hundred thousand members in 1918 were white southern women of the middle and upper-middle classes, and many of these women, as well as their daughters, were among the same demographic that entered southern institutions of higher education in the early decades of the twentieth century, which stands to reason that there may have been significant overlap between the groups.[18] Indeed, much of the early leadership of the Virginia-founded Kappa Delta (KΔ) sorority commanded authority in the UDC as well. At least three out of KΔ's first six national presidents, Genevieve Venable Holladay and Innes Randolph Harris of Virginia and Jenn Winslow Coltrane of North Carolina, were UDC members.[19] Additionally, the daughters and nieces of UDC members would have been steeped in the tradition of the Lost Cause during their childhoods. Another KΔ national president, Rebecca Washington Smith of Kentucky, was a close relative of the UDC's national president and apparently shared a house with her in Paducah.[20] So even if not directly involved with the UDC, many sorority women were figuratively, if not literally, as in Smith's case, living with the relics of the Lost Cause.

As might be expected from the interests of Phi Mu's first national officers, these sorority women closely aligned themselves with the former Confederacy. Shortly after the Civil War, during the Philomathean Society years, the group elected to bestow honorary membership on Confederate hero Gen. Robert E. Lee. Lee accepted the invitation, the organization noted, and was pleased at "thus being honored by an organization which represented the highest ideals in Southern womanhood." The group proceeded to make the late general

Thomas Jonathan "Stonewall" Jackson and the former president of the Confederacy, Jefferson Davis, honorary members as well. The practice of nominating honorary members ended in 1908, but Phi Mus of the 1980s still retold this bit of Philomathean history with great pride.[21] In 1909 the *Eleusis* carried an article on a UDC subsidiary, the United Confederate Choirs of America, which was described as "a semi-military organization for girls" with "its object . . . to revive the old-time war melodies that cheered the heart of the southern soldier during the troublous siege of the sixties." This group, like the better-known UDC auxiliary Children of the Confederacy, stood to indoctrinate the young with reverence for the Lost Cause and was apparently, to the editorial staff of the *Eleusis*, seen as an appropriate organization for young ladies and worth sharing with its national readership.[22] In 1914 two KΔs recently graduated from the Florida State College for Women attended the Confederate Reunion of the United Confederate Veterans (UCV), held in Jacksonville, as maids of honor to one of the sponsors. The following June, the alumnae of the Panhellenic of Richmond, Virginia, hosted a luncheon at the Country Club of Virginia "in honor of visiting fraternity women in town for the Confederate Reunion."[23]

Southern-founded sororities may have represented the next logical organizing space for young women of the New South who were attending college in increasing numbers and who were less directly tied to the work of honoring specific Confederate veterans and more concerned with propagating the image of the Old South that flourished alongside the Lost Cause narrative. The sorority allowed them to honor the ideals of the Old South and even share this "glorious" past with their nonsouthern sisters as the southern sororities exploded onto the national scene. And the nonsouthern women were eager to learn more about the seemingly mysterious and exotic locale of the American South. If they were still miffed about southern women's traitorous ways, they either kept it to themselves or made light of such previous disagreements.

Nonsouthern Sorority Women and the Imagined South

As sororities founded outside of the South established chapters at southern schools, the nonsouthern members who journeyed into Dixie particularly noted the "real southern atmosphere and surroundings."[24] Nonsouthern whites had been traveling to the South since the 1870s in search of an antidote to the "ills" associated with modern life in industrialized northern cities. By the 1920s and 1930s the popularity of automobile travel enabled a new generation of nonsouthern tourists to view the South at their own pace. As southern locations such as Charleston and Colonial Williamsburg increasingly marketed themselves to the automobile-owning American public as national tourist getaways, significant primarily for their historic elements, they also strengthened the connection between charming, old, historic southern houses and spaces and a sacred past of unmatched gentility to which *all* white Americans, northern and southern, should aspire.[25] Many of the sorority women who were active in their respective national organizations were highly traveled, visiting numerous college campuses to establish new chapters and check up on those extant. These nonsouthern and southern women helped bridge the sectional gap of the Civil War and Reconstruction eras as they visited one another and shared an imagined cultural history that was premised on a presumed better time in American history, when patriotic, early American settlers of Anglo-Saxon descent flourished in an agrarian-based society.

In 1913 Delta Delta Delta (ΔΔΔ) officers Hortense Imboden Hudson and Agnes Husband, recent graduates of Kansas colleges, took a southern tour to establish new chapters at Georgia Wesleyan in Macon, Judson College in Marion, Alabama, and Stetson College in DeLand, Florida. Describing the trip for the *Trident*, the women wrote, "The southern charm and hospitality were everywhere and Tri-Deltas felt that they were cordially welcomed into the Southland." She noted that during their stop at Judson, "the Birmingham papers were very generous in their accounts of the entrance of the first northern fraternity into the Old South." While they noted the many regulations for students at Wesleyan and Judson that made them quite different from the "freedom of the 'self-governed' college or the undenominational college of the North," they also mentioned that "the type of girl attending both [of] these schools is very attractive," again linking southern women with an inherent and unmatched physical beauty. On the other hand, Hudson and Husband seemed disappointed when they reached DeLand. "One hardly knows how to feel," they lamented. They noted that Stetson seemed "very much like a northern college" and that many students were from the North.[26] The two women connected the South and the southern women they encountered with an exclusive charm and attractiveness that they found lacking in northern women. While it was fine for nonsouthern women to fawn over southern culture from afar or when on tours of southern chapters, the duo seemed displeased to discover northern women "playing southern" in the South, which marred their perception of the bucolic region.

Nonsouthern sorority women seemed to prefer the manufactured image of the genteel, charming southern woman. In 1928 Cornell University's Iota chapter of Kappa Alpha Theta (KAΘ) (founded in Greencastle, Indiana, in

1870) noted the arrival of a new initiate whose "southern accent and sweet manner gives her a particular feminine charm." Sorority publications only described *southern* women in terms of their regional background, but it was always to make positive comments about their demeanor. All sororities expected new sisters to be ladylike and attractive with a pleasing personality, but southern women were popularly understood to naturally display these traits to a greater degree. In opposition to the picture of an independent and perhaps domineering woman associated with the educated, career-inclined "New Woman" of the 1910s and 1920s, the manufactured image of the southern lady was less threatening to gender relations and stood to remind college sorority women across the country of expectations for their behavior. The ideal of the southern lady became the standard by which all white *sorority* women, not just all white southern women, could judge themselves, whether they did so consciously or not.

The *reimagined* descriptions of the South increased by the late 1930s along with the appearance of Margaret Mitchell's wildly popular *Gone with the Wind* (1936) and the subsequent film version (1939), which brought the mythic imagery of the Old South to life in Technicolor and heightened the nation's popular fascination with all things plantation-themed. Young white women imagined themselves as planation belles in the mold of Scarlett O'Hara, although the sorority alumnae probably hoped young women would more closely resemble Melanie Wilkes in their character. While sorority women had been donning the belle character for several decades, *Gone with the Wind* cemented the imagery and helped popularize it among nonsouthern sorority women in both southern and nonsouthern-founded sororities.

The southern antebellum film *Jezebel* (1938), starring Bette Davis in an Oscar-winning turn as spoiled belle Julie Marsden, provided an occasion for the *Key* of Kappa Kappa Gamma (KKΓ) to note that Bette's younger sister, Barbara "Bobby" Davis Pelgram, was an alumna of KKΓ's Denison University chapter. The journal featured a picture titled "Bobby and Bette," with the sisters standing together, arms linked. Both women wore Bette's hoop-skirted costumes from the film, which was set in 1850s New Orleans. "They might be Kappa founders dressed for a party," the *Key* editors exclaimed, attempting to connect the sorority to an image of southern aristocratic finery, even though the first KKΓ chapter began in Monmouth, Illinois. The caption also noted that while visiting the East Coast, Davis had "spent some time in her native Massachusetts prowling through antique shops." Instead of highlighting Bette Davis as a Hollywood star, the *Key* underscored her association with a southern aesthetic and a colonial heritage, which were prized by the sorority women. Just as another Kappa alumna might do, Davis was seeking "an old cradle or high chair" for her dear sister Bobby, who was expecting a child.[27] By mention of "antiquing," a popular outlet for nostalgia and reimagining in the Colonial Revival movement, the *Key* further tied the Massachusetts-born Davis sisters to the supposed purity and old world charm of the colonial period, rather than the seemingly garish lives of nouveau riche film stars on the less-established West Coast.

Even as sorority women expressed themselves within the confines of acceptable ladyhood, some southern women acknowledged the falsity of their reimagined southern landscape. Apparently tired of playing the belle character that she had been saddled with as a white southern woman, one member of Kappa Kappa Gamma wrote a column specifically for the "Yankee Delegates" at the 1932 KKΓ convention at New Ocean House, Swampscott, Massachusetts, which was themed "Broadening Horizons." The satire, written in dialect, was titled "Confessions of a Southern Girl." "Of cose these lil items are gonna kinda disillusion y'all north'n and west'n gurls," she began, "but as this convention is to broad'n horizons I jus' thought I oughta set y'all straight about a heapa things." She set about to disabuse the nonsouthern Kappas of an apparent overreliance on the plantation mythology that existed prior to the popularity of such movies as *The Littlest Rebel* (1935), *Showboat* (1936), *Jezebel*, or *Gone with the Wind*, all of which featured stereotypical antebellum settings and characters. "My 'Nigger' mammy didn't chew my food for me . . . my fahthah didn't own a plantation or stable of hosses . . . I've nevah spent an evenin' in an organdy dress strummin' a guitar in a hammock on a verandah," the woman explained.[28] Whether or not the author was a daughter of the South who had tired of playing the belle, or perhaps was even a nonsoutherner alert to the national obsession with all things southern and ready to call out her peers for an unceasing belief in the mythology of the Old South, the piece stood to remind sorority women of the artifice of their womanly ideal.

"Dixie" Conventions and Belle Characters

Sororities' national conventions were also sites where southern identity could be reinscribed and celebrated by women from all regions of the country. Increasingly, these biennial events were held at exclusive resort locations, but in the first couple of decades after southern sororities' respective foundings, their conventions were usually held in cities with hotels and country club facilities suitable for business meetings, banquets, and dances that accompanied the weeklong festivities. Southern-founded sororities, whose members likely had better knowledge of and connections with southern towns, loved to welcome sisters from afar to the sunny Southland. In 1910 Chi Omega held its sixth biennial convention in Lexington, Kentucky. Announcing the event, the *Eleusis* editors gushed, "The place, Lexington, garden-spot of the world, home of real chivalry and the true southern hospitality; the [girls], dozens and scores of the noblest, truest, and best women in all the land. Now, isn't that inducement enough, even for the sisters thousands of miles distant?" The convention publicity touted the lush, green beauty of the South and the region's apparent ownership of chivalry and hospitality, popularly understood as the province of southern men and women, respectively. Mary Gayle of Chi Omega's Chi chapter at the University of Kentucky reported on "Traditions of Lexington," explaining that although "ladies no longer have their retinue of black slaves, nor do gentlemen challenge each other to a death-duel for a girl's handkerchief. . . . Chivalry and Kentucky ideals are living today, and we are making the traditions of tomorrow."[29] While unspoken, the creation of a "modern" southern wonderland with all the "virtues" of the antebellum South relied on a sturdy foundation of white supremacy.

Kappa Delta, which held more than half of its first twenty national conventions in the South, welcomed 1,400 sisters to Birmingham, Alabama's Tutwiler Hotel in 1917 with the "Birmingham Convention Song," sung to the tune of *Dixie*. Four KΔs from chapters at Florida State College for Women, Hollins College, and Louisiana State University wrote the lyrics, which seemed innocuous enough—mostly they touted what a great convention KΔ would have in Dixie—but also reiterated the strong connection between the sorority's southern birth and its national prominence. Furthermore, lines such as "In Dixie land we've made our stand . . . for the best convention ever" could not be entirely untangled from the sentiments of the actual song, an anthem of the former Confederacy and the Lost Cause where "the old times gone [were] not forgotten."[30]

Attending NPC sorority conventions in the South allowed nonsouthern sorority women to experience the "true southern hospitality" of the host city or resort while fashioning themselves as southern ladies. Sorority conventions represented a safe space for sorority women of all ages to shed the seriousness of their everyday life and return to the carefree, even silly play of college girlhood. The creation of such characters, and of the southern belle or lady in particular, helped nonsouthern women identify with the southern aesthetic of their sororities by offering a well-known visual model of feminine behavior. The 1937 KΔ convention, held at the revered Jefferson Hotel in Richmond, Virginia, was a veritable historical pageant of reimagined white antebellum southern life. For six days in the summer, 369 conference attendees (perhaps limited due to the Depression) lived out their southern fantasy, aided by costumes, themed dinners, and the sage predictions of the keynote speaker, *Richmond News-Leader* editor and Robert E. Lee biographer Douglas Southall Freeman. At the sorority council's reception a "colonial motif" reigned with twenty costumed KΔs performing "the Virginia Reel, which everyone soon joined." The banquet event featured a "real Southern Dinner" with "Confederate flags," a greedy Scarlett O'Hara character "with moneybags in her hands," and music by "a Negro quartet." The dinner menu items were all influenced by characters in *Gone with the Wind*; cocktail hour started off with a drink named the Rhett Butler, and diners could feast on foods such as Ashley Asparagus and Mammy Rolls. During the convention, KΔs also experienced 1930s heritage tourism at its finest as they took a jaunt down Route 60 to Colonial Williamsburg, Jamestown, and the College of William and Mary, where they visited the Alpha Pi chapter's house.[31]

The *Adelphean* of Alpha Delta Pi announced the sorority's June 1941 national convention location as the Homestead in Hot Springs, Virginia. As part of the various sightseeing members could do while in "Ole Virginny," one of the write-ups suggested that the authenticity of African American servers at the hotel was not to be missed. In the piece, titled "Homestead 'Darky Help' Combines Smiling Service . . . Southern Charm," the author noted that there "is a feeling of luxury and contentment when one is served by these cheerful 'darkies' with their soft southern drawls who are there to aid in every way possible."[32] By slipping into a space that seemed to defy the passage of time, where white tourists in 1941 still referred to African American bellhops and waiters as "darkies," sorority women were able to pretend that they were immersed in an antebellum southern landscape where white supremacy went unchallenged.

"In the Georgian Manner": Sorority Houses and the Southern Aesthetic

Like historic preservationists, heritage tourism boosters, and Anglo-American heritage society patrons of the interwar period, sorority women also interwove the reverence for a southern aesthetic with the Colonial Revival spirit.[33] As architectural historian Catherine Bishir notes, the "southern colonial," marked by expansive porticos and large white columns, had become a distinct style within the Colonial Revival by the 1890s. National architects and designers appreciated the appearance of the southern colonial and the imagined southern lifestyle that its style evoked.[34] By the interwar period, sorority women across the nation sought to recreate a sense of this supposed grandeur symbolized in the colonial and southern colonial styles. The 1932 *Key* introduced the Beta Tau chapter's new house as "The Glory That Is Georgian at Syracuse."[35] Six years later, Kappa heralded the opening of Boyd Hearthstone, billed as the first sorority house for alumnae in Winter Park, Florida. The house was appointed in the colonial style, from its "white columned entrance" to the "rosy color" of its living room, which, its interior designer enthusiastically proclaimed, "seems to reflect the state of the mind of the American people when the treaty was signed to end the Revolution and made the Thirteen Colonies a nation." "Dusty pink" and "Williamsburg green" dominated the palette. While the historical diorama produced by the colonial-style house and furnishings were decidedly products of the Colonial Revival movement, the designer concluded that "visiting the Boyd Hearthstone is like being entertained with traditional Southern hospitality," and its "atmosphere of gracious charm [lingered]" long after guests took their leave of the Florida manse.[36] The incorporation of large white columns and expansive porches signaled a plantation-style house that Americans had come to associate with a southern aesthetic as well as financial success and stability, if not an aristocratic pedigree. While the New England colonial also afforded an imagined connection to significant historical events, patriotic forebears, and exquisitely detailed architecture and decorative arts, it retained an air of asceticism particular to the "Yankee spirit." The southern colonial instead connoted romance, luxury, and indeed excess associated with the imagined Old South planter culture.

In 1937 alumnae of Chi Omega's Omicron chapter at the University of Illinois also displayed allegiance to the Colonial Revival movement, undertaking a renovation to enlarge and update the house (originally built as a women's dormitory, Osborne Hall) in keeping with the trendy style (see fig. 5). Gladys Hardesty Rose, a 1920 graduate of the chapter, oversaw interior decorating for the project. She described the transformation of the house, which included a new "circular stairway winding from the first to the third floor" and a "fireplace on the south" in the "Georgian" style, "very correct," she noted, "in its black and gold marble facing and hearth." All furniture in the "paneled room" was "new and colorful" with "Chippendale, Sheraton, and Duncan Phyfe reproductions being used." In addition to the decorating scheme, the newsletter story also covered at length the financing plan for the new construction. While GLOs continued buying, building, and renovating chapter houses during the Depression, the authors of the article appeared at great pains to put readers at ease that financing for the work had been obtained from "a lo-

FIGURE 5. Image of the architect's rendering of the new Chi Omega Omicron
chapter house at the University of Illinois in 1937 displays elements of the
southern colonial with an expansive veranda and large white columns.
Courtesy of the University of Illinois Archives,
Stewart S. Howe Collection, Record Series (26/21/4).

cal company backed by federal loans," which would ostensibly be more understanding should active, dues-paying membership suddenly decrease, putting
loan payments in jeopardy.[37] With the construction costs apparently squared
away, the renovation's leaders felt comfortable asking other alumnae for contributions to the furnishing fund. The financial position seemed so certain,
in fact, that the women upgraded their design plan to add a stone exterior to
the house, rather than the originally planned "brick painted white." Leaders
again requested that alumnae donate to the improvement, which would "completely change the exterior and make it an outstanding house."[38] An outstanding house meant one that was big, new, formal, and often southern colonial in
appearance. Kappa Kappa Gamma's (KKΓ) Ohio State University chapter re-
modeled their house so extensively that Colorado architect and Kappa housing chair Margaret Read, who specialized in sorority and fraternity housing,
proclaimed, "Who would ever guess this formal yet charming colonial grew
right over the near mid-Victorian at its side."[39] While the new sorority houses
included modern conveniences and space to comfortably accommodate the
thirty or forty girls that might now make up a chapter, their scale and style
were even more important for the sense of luxury and sophistication they imparted to members and those viewing the houses as "outsiders." By ensconcing
sorority chapters in colonial-style houses, NPC groups presented themselves

as cultured American women who appreciated the desired aesthetic of the moment. It also allowed the sorority woman to position herself as guardian of a sacred past and as purveyor of its lessons to the new generation of members.

The Kappa chapter of Zeta Tau Alpha (ZTA) at the University of Texas did a similar colonial overhaul in 1937, rebuilding their chapter house as an imposing colonial mansion that represented a hodgepodge of historic re-creation. The architect's plans consciously styled the overall structure after George Washington's Mount Vernon, generally considered the nation's first historic preservation project.[40] The completed interior boasted a dining room with a reproduction of "scenic wallpaper copied from the supper room at the Governor's Palace in Williamsburg" and lit by a "sparkling antique chandelier from New Orleans." The continuing plans for improvement included upcoming construction of servants' quarters in the side yard and the installation of a "low, white colonial fence" flanking the entire yard.[41]

While all of the houses exuded the Colonial Revival style, they also conveyed the familiar popular-culture imagery of the southern plantation. Sorority women from across the country could easily imagine themselves as inheritors of a "grand," *white*, southern tradition, as they lounged against the commanding columns on the wide porticos of their new chapter houses or luxuriated in the sumptuous upholstery fabrics covering their "very correct" period reproduction furnishings. With Georgian-style fanlights at the entry and cavernous interiors that mimicked the Hollywood soundstage vision of a plantation "big house" interior, it was not a huge leap of the imagination to picture the sorority girls as belles alighting the striking spiral staircases in hoop-skirted ball gowns. In fact, many accompanying pictures featured just such a display, popularized in *Gone with the Wind* and *Jezebel*. A member at the ZTA house in Austin, Texas, demonstrated how to descend the staircase in a tiered-lace, off-the-shoulder gown (a frock that seemed to signify "southern belle" in many college chapter pictures of the mid-twentieth century), her right hand languidly resting on the balustrade, her head turned demurely to the side to avert her gaze from the camera lens (see fig. 6).[42] The Austin ZTAs' fascination with creating an "appropriately" southern milieu was not limited to the purchase of antiques or the posing of college women as 1850s belles. The inclusion of a separate structure for the servants' quarters in their house plan suggested the influence of historic preservationists' zeal for a historically accurate, recreated Old South plantation, where the sorority women could imagine slave cabins might sit. Historical accuracy could be particularly useful for sorority women when used to reinforce racial divides and white supremacy.

FIGURE 6. In a 1938 image reminiscent of Hollywood depictions of
southern belles, a Zeta Tau Alpha at the University of Texas descended the
grand spiral staircase of the Kappa chapter's new house, described in the
Themis as a "Georgian colonial home, inspired by Mount Vernon."
Courtesy of the University of Illinois Archives,
Stewart S. Howe Collection, Record Series (26/21/6).

The sorority alumnae's preservationist instincts ran beyond their work on sorority house designs. Several Kappa alumnae were on the board of the Robert E. Lee Memorial Foundation, which started in 1929 to restore and preserve Lee's birthplace, Stratford Hall, an early eighteenth-century house in Westmoreland County, Virginia. The UDC and the Colonial Dames were among the original backers for the foundation, which by 1940 included on the board two University of Texas Kappas, Helen Knox of New York City and Helen Prather Davis of Waco, Texas; and a Barnard College Kappa, Elizabeth Finnegan Fain, also of New York City.

The Lee Memorial Foundation's work at Stratford Hall grew from a desire not only to venerate and share with the entire nation an excellent example of colonial American architecture connected to influential white, patriotic, colonial Americans but also to recreate an atmosphere that would instill awe in visitors. The primary reason for the preservation of the property was the establishment of a national shrine to the most celebrated Confederate hero, Gen. Robert E. Lee. It was the perfect backdrop for the foundation and its supporters to instruct patrons in a certain view of southern heritage, inextricably tied to "the cause," as they delivered reminders that it was certainly not forgotten.

In her 1940 article for the *Key*, Helen Knox subsumed some of the Lost Cause gusto within the rhetoric of "patriotism" and "liberty" palatable to Americans in the North and South who stood witness to the distressing war in Europe. Her writing contained the most direct connection between interwar sorority women's veneration of a southern aesthetic, tinged with reimagined ideals of "patriotic" colonial forebears, and certain founding principles of American government that some conservative ideologues would isolate to support their new sociopolitical worldview—a view that many sorority alumnae would support in the coming decades. She explained that the work to restore the house and gardens at Stratford represented "the highest culture of the American colonies and that from a patriotic, educational and economic point of view, it should be preserved as a symbol of the 'cause of liberty.'" The Lees of Stratford, she believed, stood for principles that "patriotic citizens of this generation" should "daily and hourly contemplate." Among those principles, Knox listed peaceful expansion, no taxation without representation, government by consent of the governed, equality of property rights and individual freedom, and human rights.[43] While the tenets are popularly considered as foundational American beliefs as established in the Bill of Rights of the U.S. Constitution, conservatives at this time began to reengineer the meanings of some of these founding principles to serve their political agenda—particularly that of the freedom to associate with people of their own choosing.

For sorority women outside the South, the thrill of visiting the "Deep South," viewing its imposing (but in some cases also crumbling) architecture, lingering in English-style gardens and cavorting with "real-life" southern belles (or, at least, costumed descendants of the southern planter and business elite who led house and garden tours), continued in the post–World War II period. In April 1947, on the occasion of Kappa's installation at the University of Mississippi, the *Key* decided to launch a full-blown southern tour issue. The Kappa leadership combined their trip to Oxford, Mississippi, with a "pilgrimage" to the famed annual month-long house and garden tour event, established in 1931, in Natchez. The *Key* proudly displayed pictures of grand old southern homes inhabited by Kappas (or once inhabited by their ancestors). During the festivities, Kappa established the Natchez Alumnae Club at the Parsonage (ca. 1852), the massive Greek Revival–style home of the Metcalfe family. Pennsylvania-born Kappa and Swarthmore College graduate Anna Rose Williams Metcalfe was pictured in the issue wearing an antebellum costume. As the tour continued, the *Key* visited Baton Rouge ("Combines the Old South with Modern Industrialism") and New Orleans ("The Mardi Gras City") in Louisiana and then wound back to Alabama and Georgia for good measure. A brief mention of the "beautiful" colonial-style buildings at the University of Alabama gave way to a discussion of Mobile's colonial splendor and fifteen-mile Azalea Trail, which the Kappas reported as dotted with magnificent gardens and fine antebellum homes and patios. The women's notes on Georgia revealed that Kappa's newly colonized Delta Upsilon chapter at the University of Georgia (UGA) was set to move into a massive southern colonial house (ca. 1899) on Athens's Prince Street.[44] In addition to the two tennis courts behind the house—mention of which would signal that the members of the new chapters were from families wealthy and sophisticated enough to partake of tennis as a pastime—the author extolled the presence of an "old dobie" house once occupied by slaves. Although she clarified her understanding that the small house had served as slave quarters "in the early days and [was] built long before the present house," the reference, whether accurate or not, served to position the new chapter's image against a backdrop of the prosperous, slaveholding Old South. At the same time, it reinforced racial separation and compartmentalization in a time when white southerners' fears of federally forced integration also had begun to take hold among white sorority women nationally. Reportedly, the small house had been used by the previous owners as a playhouse and, the author stated, "should lend itself nicely to the activities of the chapter." The housemother would be situated in "two large bedrooms" on the first floor.[45] What purpose the "dobie" house would serve in the new chapter house arrangement was yet unclear.

Southern and Nonsouthern Sorority Women Propagate the Southern Aesthetic: Sorority Histories

By the time *Gone with the Wind* was captivating the nation, southern sororities' official histories, which were purposely fashioned to link their founders to the antebellum South, had been circulating in their publications for years. But the widespread acceptance of Mitchell's story, like that conveyed in *The Birth of a Nation* more than twenty years earlier, reinvigorated the message, helping sororities successfully pass along the southern aesthetic—in reality, a thinly veiled version of the Lost Cause—to new generations of members. Although southern women had written much of the original reverent language in official sorority histories, it was adopted and promulgated wholeheartedly by nonsoutherners. As the largely nonsouthern Kappa alumnae demonstrated in 1947 with their unflagging interest in the romanticized image of the Old South, sorority women across the nation were eager to tie themselves to a history filled with Anglo-Saxon antecedents, genteel belles and dashing cavaliers, and a leisured existence where enslaved African Americans would cater to their whims.[46] Furthermore, an adherence to the southern aesthetic also established sorority women and NPC organizations on the whole as "true Americans" and members of the social elite. Southern-founded sororities may have had a greater repository of southern heritage to draw on for their tellings, but nonsouthern-founded sororities and nonsouthern women in southern sororities also proved particularly adept at mining, or embellishing, historical records to place themselves in desired relation to the southern aesthetic.

While Chi Omega had been national from its inception, its first history, written in 1928 by southerner Christelle Ferguson and other national officers, shared a selective version of southern history that aligned with that of "plantation school" authors and historians who lauded the superiority of the imagined Old South.[47] In Ferguson's telling, genteel white southerners suffered mightily during the Civil War and Reconstruction but remained "ladies and gentlemen," while "slaves were faithful to the defenseless people left behind at home." The *History* noted that "women of the South . . . cherished the glories that passed with the Civil War" but "retained their habits of gracious manner." By tying the character of 1920s sorority members to a glorified Old South, where "breeding and culture were more important than money and business," Chi Omega, like other southern-founded sororities, positioned itself both as guardian of white southern historical memory and purveyor of the modern incarnation of southern ladyhood.[48]

By the stroke of a pen, or a typewriter key, sorority alumnae could obscure any less-than-genteel backgrounds in a blur of plantation romanticism. The founders of ZTA were, according to the organization's official history, "from fine, established land-holding families that had progressed through postwar economic hardships and the Reconstruction." The author of ZTA's first history in 1928, midwesterner Shirley Kreasan Kreig, was the sorority's historian and editor of the *Themis*. Kreig joined ZTA while a student at James Milliken University in Decatur, Illinois. She was later a journalism student at the University of Illinois in Champaign, where her parents lived. Prior to her marriage and subsequent move to Toronto in 1920, she worked as the university editor of the *Champaign News-Gazette*.[49] Kreig, and other nonsouthern sorority women like her, seemed more than happy to construct an aristocratic background that connected them—through the fictive kin network of the sorority—to a southern and Anglo-American heritage. If a sorority woman was not eligible for patriotic heritage groups such as the Colonial Dames or First Families of Virginia, at least she could hint at a connection through her sorority forebears.

Sigma Sigma Sigma ($\Sigma\Sigma\Sigma$ or "Tri-Sigma"), founded at the Virginia State Normal School in 1898, began *The Years Remembered of Sigma Sigma Sigma* (1953) with a celebration of life in Virginia that detailed the aristocratic bearing of the state's colonial-era families and its ties to "English customs and habits of life." The sorority's founders were all Virginians, but the sorority's mid-twentieth-century historians were not so readily identifiable as southern belles. Authors Suzanne Stinson (of Michigan) and $\Sigma\Sigma\Sigma$ national president Mary Hastings Holloway Page (originally from Maryland and later residing in Massachusetts) quoted at length from Virginia author Thomas Nelson Page's (no known relation to Holloway Page) 1892 essay, "Social Life before the War," to describe the "Southern girl." "She was, indeed, a strange creature, that delicate, dainty, mischievous, God-fearing, Southern girl. With her fine grain, her silken hair, her musical speech, her pleasure-loving habits, and her bewitching manners, down deep in her lay the bed-rock innate virtue, piety, and womanliness on which were planted all that nature can hope, and all to which it can aspire."[50] Page's highly idealized account of the home life of whites of "aristocratic character" in Virginia before the Civil War exemplifies one of his many sentimental depictions of the Old South.[51] His sketch, like that crafted by Stinson and Page for the Tri-Sigma history sixty years later, invited readers both southern and nonsouthern to glimpse a version of life that was some-how supposedly truer, better, or more carefree for having existed in the ante-bellum South. "For all its faults," Page wrote, social life in the Old South was, he believed, "the purest, sweetest life ever lived."[52] And his description of the "Southern girl" apparently rang true for nonsoutherners writing about Tri-Sigma's founding.

By printing the Page passage in their history, the organization demon-strated a desire to remind readers of members' southern heritage while con-necting the image of the contemporary sorority woman to the powerful sym-bol of the white southern lady, ostensibly unadulterated by hard living or contact with those outside of their social and racial circle. Published on the eve of the Supreme Court's monumental ruling against public school segrega-tion in *Brown v. Board of Education of Topeka* (1954), *The Years Remembered* also served as a tacit warning that the much-heralded purity of the "delicate" and "dainty" white southern girl would be threatened by any changes in the time-honored code of racial segregation of social spaces.[53] Indeed, the book's foreword recalled Virginia's "rich heritage of deeply-rooted history, romance, sentiment, and charm" that the sisters "[cherished] and [found] more appeal-ing as the passing years [brought] into perspective the rich and abiding values written in Sigma's Book of Life."[54] Sororities' allegiance to a common white "past," drawing heavily from an imagined version of the antebellum southern white existence, which they found "more appealing," underscored the tense ra-cial landscape of the 1950s South and suggested sororities' support of contin-ued racial segregation in American society.

By connecting their respective sororities to a "deep-rooted" white heritage that they pictured as noble and genteel, sorority women hoped to solidify the image of their organizations as thoroughly American establishments of the up-per social class. In 1956, when Shirley Kresan Kreig (by then known as Shirley Kresan Strout) updated her 1928 version of ZTA's history, her laudatory take on the sorority's southern heritage remained unchanged. In fact, Strout felt that ZTA had so much southern heritage to chronicle that she began a four-part se-ries on the founders titled "Journey to Virginia," which appeared in *Themis* in 1957 and 1958. The first ten-page installment focused on Anna Bruce Houston Davis, who also was the sorority's second national president. While in her 913-page official ZTA history Strout only had time to mention that "Clifton," the Houston family home located outside of Lexington, Virginia, was a "beauti-ful, red-brick ante-bellum home with . . . brick slave quarters," in the "Journey" she was able to delve into other aspects of the deceased Davis's history to cre-ate a fanciful depiction of elite white life in Virginia during the last quarter of the nineteenth century. She believed that all Zetas would be enriched by the knowledge, "as if, someway, we, too, had some personal tie with these Virginia families," about which, Strout noted, that she actually knew "more than I do about my own family lines." Instead, like many other twentieth-century sorority women whose families arrived in the United States after the nation's founding, or even after the Civil War, she focused her attention on a tenuous connection to an embellished or completely fantasized Anglo-Saxon and southern heritage fashioned from stories of the sororities' founders.

Strout wrote adoringly of the many afternoons she imagined that the Davis family spent on their sprawling lawn, playing a spirited game of croquet. "It was a picture of a more leisurely, but abundantly full life," she explained. "In those days," Harlow reminisced, "servants were plentiful, and people had time to sit and chat." Strout envisioned that the "carpet-like expanse" of lawn was "kept velvety green by yard men who probably took their time about it all." She followed her stereotypical image of the lackadaisical black worker by reiterating the Lost Cause–propagated idea that "everyone was happy." Racial strife went unmentioned in the histories. The version of southern history portrayed in the narratives privileged white experience and virtually erased the existence of African Americans in the South, aside from the mention of "happy" figures who occasionally emerged from the shadows to offer a smile and charming service. She also constructed the supposed virtues of the Houston family and "other fine families" who had settled in the "Valley of Virginia" nearly "200 years ago" in accord with ideals commonly held by conservatives in the 1950s. Strout described the settlers as "God-fearing, upright-living, Scotch-Irish Presbyterians." She praised them for knowing "real values" and passing them along to their children. Unlike the liberal thinkers of Strout's day, whom conservatives believed susceptible to communist subversion, the descendants of established families "were not confused by fuzzy theories" and "could not be fast-talked or propagandized out of, or into, anything."[55]

Students of these history lessons included southerners and nonsoutherners born during the decades of the late nineteenth and early twentieth centuries who absorbed teachings of the Lost Cause, which stressed the importance of states' rights and white supremacy. While those outside of the South likely did not view the Civil War as a heroic cause, they were equally susceptible to a romanticized understanding of the region promoted by both southern and nonsouthern writers, including Thomas Nelson Page, Joel Chandler Harris, Julia Magruder, and John William DeForest.[56] As Karen Cox has noted, the prevailing historical narrative in white southern schools until the 1970s remained true to the myth of the Lost Cause.[57] As a result, the sororities' depictions of

the South would not appear at odds with the version of southern history understood by readers during the first three quarters of the twentieth century.
National sororities helped affirm a vaunted image of the Old South and a pro-
southern mentality, particularly as such depictions enhanced their own organizational image. While their alignment with a white southern memory may
have been designed to promote the image of the southern lady as a model for
contemporary sorority women, the regional attachment also alluded to the organizations' long-standing interest in maintaining a white, Protestant membership with suggested connections to "old stock," early American settlers.

Southern Aesthetic Practiced by College Chapters

The allegiance to a southern aesthetic was not limited to sororities' alumnae members. College actives regularly engaged in parties and skits with Old
South themes. Costumes and meals, such as those described at the Kappa
Delta convention, were popular among NPC chapters across the country. In
1934 the Iota chapter of Alpha Chi Omega (AXΩ) at the University of Illinois boasted of their successful rush parties, including a "traditional southern
breakfast" like the chapter had held in previous years. The members noted that
it was "especially fitting" because the "southern colonial house" that the chapter had moved to in 1931 made "a nice setting for the occasion." The women
decorated tables with "colored dolls and bales of cotton," as cotton and African
American slaves were two symbols readily associated with the contemporary
popular imaginary of the South. In addition to the supposedly southern-style
dishes served to rushees, the partygoers witnessed entertainment by "members
of the active chapter who dressed as Negroes and sang southern songs."[58] Minstrelsy was a popular addition to rush parties and was likely a key signifier that
rushees were attending a southern-themed event.

Chapters reported details of winning rush parties in the national journals
so that college women across the nation could adopt the themes for their own
rush events. In 1916 the Sigma Delta chapter of Kappa Delta at Trinity College
(later Duke) reported on a progressive dinner that was their "most successful"
rushing party. Although it took place in central North Carolina, the women
did not allude to the party as "southern" in style. The sisters made clear that the
excitement surrounding the event was a result of not the different dining locations but the white students in blackface playing at African American stereotypes. A "very black butler" who was "the personification of a 'flossy' butler"
met them at the first house. Before long, he revealed himself as a well-known
white friend of the women. At the next stop a "very trim negro maid" served

FIGURE 7. Tri-Delta sisters in blackface welcome rushees to a plantation-themed rush party at the University of North Carolina at Chapel Hill during the 1949 school year.
Courtesy of the North Carolina Collection, Wilson Library, University of North Carolina at Chapel Hill, University of North Carolina at Chapel Hill Photographic Laboratory Collection, 1946–1990.

the girls. Only when one of the sisters caught her "rolling her eyes" in a particular fashion that was favored by a certain white woman on campus did they guess their maid's true identity.[59] Exaggerated eye-rolling was a typical gesture from minstrelsy acts. By having "black" servants at their parties, the Sigma Delta women may have been attempting to recreate a lifestyle described by their parents and elder relatives or, more likely, one they created from their imagined, romanticized, pop-culture accounts of the pre-Emancipation Old South. Other women around the country could latch on to these ideas to ensure that they were hosting a suitably "southern" party with all of the expected activities.

The use of blackface characters in sorority skits continued into the 1940s and 1950s, apparently without eliciting negative comment from those involved.[60] In a 1949 University of North Carolina yearbook picture captioned "Plantation party at the Tri Delt house," sorority sisters costumed as "picaninnies" in pigtails and bandanas, mismatched gingham outfits, and blackened faces joyously welcomed excited rushees to their house.[61] The chapter members may have chosen to portray the "Uncle Tom's Cabin" party described in the *Tri Delta Hostess* (1937), which detailed costuming similar to that pictured in the yearbook (see fig. 7). Ballard and Ward, the *Hostess*'s authors, had described the possible party decorations in painstaking detail. "Cabin interior, tables with red checked cloths, benches, pickaninnies, Uncle Tom, cribs, etc. Tiny bales of cotton and imitation cotton bolls may be worked into a very attractive centerpiece or mantel decoration. Or, make a centerpiece of a negro cabin of construction logs, with tiny black-faced dolls dressed Aunt Jemima fashion bending over a toy tub washing and hanging up clothes while their overalled and barefooted Rastuses push wheelbarrows, hoe, etc., including at least one snoozing stretched out in the shade."[62] The authors relied on popular-culture renditions of African Americans featured in advertising—"Aunt Jemima" of Quaker Oats pancake and syrup fame and "Rastus," purveyor of Cream of Wheat cereal, both of whom had originated as stock characters in minstrel shows—to inform the sorority women on how to model their appearance for the act. By continuing to place black characters in their "southern" events, sorority women both from the South and outside of it found common ground as they reassured themselves of their own race and class superiority.[63]

Sororities' reliance on the southern aesthetic in the form of southern belles and Old South imagery continued into the 1960s. While practice of the aesthetic was always connected to the reinforcement of white supremacy, by the 1950s and 1960s it also demonstrated sororities' tacit acceptance and even support of massive resistance to the civil rights movement's momentum in these years. In 1961 the Beta Nu chapter of AΔΠ at UGA advertised the sorority's summer caravan across the state to meet potential rushees. The chapter newsletter announcement, titled "Save Your Confederate Money," described the plans for the late August event, which promised to bring "southern belles, cotton bales, pick-a-ninnies, showboat songs, a wash board band, good ole Georgia watermelons and lots of southern hospitality." The accompanying picture showed one AΔΠ in a hoop-skirted dress, holding a parasol. Another woman held a banjo while dressed in shorts, a white button-down shirt, and suspenders. The third woman wore a short satin outfit, dark tights, and black gloves. At her side she held a large, dark, painted face with exaggerated lips, presumably in preparation for Beta Nu's version of blackface entertainment. "Yes sir, the South will rise again when the Georgia AΔΠs start making their caravan rounds through the state," the announcement promised.[64] Set against the backdrop of national Civil War centennial commemorations, such displays were tangible reminders of Lost Cause ideals. They also reaffirmed NPC sororities' stance in the ongoing national dialogue on civil rights and racial equality.

Easily accessible to sorority women from a variety of backgrounds, the southern aesthetic as practiced by NPC sororities was a key mechanism through which southern and nonsouthern women could find common ground despite regional cultural differences and lingering distrust following the Civil War and Reconstruction. Southern-founded sororities drew on the aesthetic to educate the national sisterhood in the significance of their southern heritage, while sororities founded across the United States appreciated the aesthetic for its allusions to ladylike behavior, aristocratic pretense, and a time that, to them, seemed simpler and more authentic. Although sororities' southern aesthetic began as an offshoot of the Lost Cause, it also intertwined with the contemporaneous Colonial Revival movement. Yet the fear and anger over racial mixing that sat at the core of many Lost Cause commemorations carried over into NPC sororities' southern aesthetic. So every belle in costume, every southern colonial-style home, every allusion to a "better" time experienced by patriotic Anglo-American forebears in the eighteenth or nineteenth century, and every sorority party spotlighting a minstrelsy act reminded sorority members, as well as all who witnessed the performances, that NPC sororities and the members' accompanying privileges were for white women of the upper and middle class only.

As the memory and teachings of the Lost Cause shifted from a memorial to Confederate sacrifice to a celebration of a reimagined pre–Civil War South, the aesthetic was accessible to, if not appreciated by, all white sorority women. Significantly, this shared preoccupation with a southern past would continue to be an organizing force in NPC sororities after World War II, when southern- and nonsouthern-founded sororities as well as white fraternities feared the forced racial desegregation of their organizations. But the roots of the common cause had taken hold much earlier, when sorority women across the country bonded over their shared admiration of the southern aesthetic.

CHAPTER FOUR

Standardizing Sexuality

HETEROSOCIALIZING AND
SEXUAL DANGER IN SORORITY LIFE

*W*hile serving as chapter correspondent for the Zeta chapter of Kappa Delta (KΔ) sorority at the University of Alabama in spring 1914, sophomore Daphne Cunningham reported on such newsworthy items as the development of a women's student government, the appointment of the college's first dean of women, the work of President Denny in directing state funds to build a new women's dormitory, and the involvement of her fellow sorority members in campus activities. Cunningham's narrative informed readers of her sorority's journal, the *Angelos*, of the "great [steps] forward for co-education" taking place at the state university. Her final paragraph, not more than two lines long, noted, "the post-Lenten dances have just come to an end after a most enjoyable week. Many girls from all over the state attended them."[1] Cunningham's discussion of the dances seemed almost an afterthought; it provided readers with evidence that the Zeta chapter was involved in "heterosocial" activities on campus but suggested that the sisters' interest in attending parties and having "dates" with men was not as great as their hopes of making their mark as pioneering university students. Cunningham's report suggests that she understood that sorority women of the 1910s should reference a respectable amount of heterosocial activity but it should not be their main focus.

For her own part, however, Daphne Cunningham was quite the social butterfly, recording numerous engagements with a variety of men in her diaries from 1913 and 1914. By her account, male suitors accompanied Cunningham during most of her daily activities in Tuscaloosa. Of the fifty-five men with whom she socialized, at least sixteen were fraternity men. One night in 1913 she attended both the Sigma Alpha Epsilon and the Phi Kappa Epsilon dances with members of the respective organizations. Cunningham's many engagements apparently seemed acceptable to her family, friends, and prospective suitors, and her activities provide an early snapshot of the dating and youth culture that came into vogue for white middle-class adolescents and college students by the 1920s.[2] While Cunningham and her fellow coeds regularly heterosocialized (perhaps not all in the same prolific fashion as she), the Zeta chapter was not regularly planning and hosting mixed-sex social events. Cunningham mentioned just two Kappa Delta social events she attended with male suitors, while she went to twenty fraternity social events with various fraternity members over the same eighteen-month period recorded in her diaries.[3] As sorority women increasingly attended mixed-sex social events, fraternities set the boundaries of the new heterosocial environment on campuses, and their control of the spaces would only tighten as the twentieth century moved forward.

The 1920s and 1930s marked a distinct change from the first two decades of the century, as sororities became increasingly concerned that their chapters be active participants in heterosocial activities and, more specifically, that they gain and hold the attention of popular fraternity chapters on campus. Doing so was the key to the sorority chapter's popularity. While Daphne Cunningham may have believed that attracting hordes of male "callers" and being a prize "date" to the fraternity dances were not details on which she should report for the sorority's national journal in 1914, ten years later, in the midst of the exploding 1920s middle-class youth culture, the women of Kappa Delta's Sigma Delta chapter at the Woman's College of Duke University were quite happy to list their heterosocial frolics, all with fraternity men, for the sisters and alumnae across the country to read in the *Angelos*. A straightforward discussion of numerous possibly unchaperoned events among "young ladies" and "gentlemen" of the white middle class was much more permissible by the 1920s. Shifting public perceptions of acceptable sexual behavior resulted from social changes including the growing consumer culture, a new popular culture heavily influenced by mass print culture and movies, the enhanced mobility and autonomy offered by the automobile, the increased availability of birth control, the acknowledgment of female desire and sexuality, and the "companionate marriage" model.[4] Middle-class Americans began to accept casual heterosocial interaction among young men and women as preparation for heterosexual marriage.

In the South, however, white women's sexual mores held greater import as the protection of the southern belle's sexual purity was integral to the upholding of white supremacy in the region. Assertive white women, sexually or otherwise, were an aberration from the understood ideal of the demure belle. Sexually suggestive white women stood to upend southern racial boundaries, as white southerners constructed the image of the sexually pure, elite white woman in opposition to their image of the lascivious African American woman or working-class white woman. When modern sexual behavior came to southern college campuses, the lines of race and class could begin to blur.[5] In this environment, sororities sought to reinforce a conservative understanding of white women's behavior that positioned women simultaneously as pedestalized by and subservient to white males in their peer group. Appropriate heterosocial activity presupposed a hyperheteronormativity built on the southern belle model, which, in turn, reinforced the southern aesthetic and its racial hierarchy for a national sorority audience. The work of preparing women for heterosocializing became the end goal of social training as they enforced conservative gender ideals and sexual behaviors.

As socializing with fraternities became a significant part of National Panhellenic Conference (NPC) sororities' campus activities, the change in focus undermined the possibility of a supportive, women's-only space, which had operated largely separate from male students and fraternities. Sorority members increasingly discussed heterosocial events and ways to make themselves more attractive to men, and sorority chapters began to make members' attendance at these heterosocial events mandatory. Although sororities were still positioned as a helpful "home away from home" for college women, the groups' behavioral standards and educational programming shifted to support their goals to entice fraternity men.[6] Sorority chapters carefully monitored members who did not conform to normative standards of feminine appearance or seek to make themselves physically attractive to men. Likewise, sorority women who evinced too great an interest in the pursuit of men and sexual pleasure also risked critique and censure by the chapter. The organizations provided further control over the available suitors with whom women could meet on campus. For middle- and upper-class white southerners who fully expected their daughters to marry and raise families (whether after graduation or by leaving college to do so), the available yet apparently controlled dating scene held the promise of a successful marriage.

The new focus on socializing with fraternity men, often in spaces beyond the reach of university authority, expanded sorority women's awareness of and ability to experiment with their sexuality but at the same time exposed them to dangerous sexual situations where men held the upper hand. As sorority women mixed more frequently with fraternity men, chances of unwanted sexual encounters increased. Historian Nicholas Syrett has argued that fraternity men of the 1920s increasingly felt the need to prove their masculinity through heterosexual performance. The shift in standards of sexual behavior, along with the rise of the coeducational campus, meant that fraternity men more frequently sought out middle- and upper-class female classmates for their sexual conquests.[7] Gatherings of fraternity men had long involved the drinking of alcohol, oftentimes to excess. With more women from their peer group on campus, the widening array of mixed-sex events also fostered a new drinking culture on campus that would shape the tenor of fraternity-sorority interactions at universities throughout the remainder of the twentieth century. When considering the androcentric nature of the shielded, and often privately owned, spaces where fraternity and sorority gatherings typically occurred, the addition of alcohol could create highly volatile situations. Drinking became a greater concern to national sorority leaders after World War II, but that did not deter the organizations from making heterosocial popularity, rather than safety, their goal. In postwar Greek life, the practice of drinking at most heterosocial gatherings became the norm. Yet sororities ignored the physical dangers posed by the emphasis on drinking—and, in later years, drinking to the point of drunkenness. Instead, they opted to promote the southern aesthetic's model of subservient white womanhood. Sorority women related to white (fraternity) men as powerful protectors—even if they realized that the men were not always the chivalrous gents that southern mythology suggested. The postwar conservative ethos did not applaud women who shook off the control of white men.

Heterosocial Competition and Campus Status

Dating, as well as the more casual heterosocial interactions that were a fixture of university student culture by the 1920s, offered the possibility of social acceptance as well as social impropriety for young women. Through careful instruction, sororities claimed to ensure that dating was a "wholesome" experience for their members while at the same time perhaps improving the chapter's social status on campus. At southern universities, sororities formed a bridge from the segregated women's campus culture (particularly on coordinate campuses) to the world of men's activities. While many students, obviously not just members of Greek-letter organizations (GLOs), participated in heterosocializing, sororities and fraternities placed a premium on the mixed-sex social event, typically preferring it to a women's-only or men's-only activity by the 1920s onward. Regularly pairing with fraternities for social events called "mixers" or for formal dances, members were poised, even forced, to meet numerous possible dates. Like other private clubs and organizations in white southern society, sororities and fraternities acted as safeguards to protect middle- and upper-class college students from those whom GLO members saw as socially undesirable, such as African Americans, Jews, Catholics, working-class whites, or other middle-class whites who simply might be viewed as undereducated or less sophisticated. Sorority social events in controlled spaces, carefully chaperoned by college professors and their spouses or sorority alumnae, allowed women to meet with, and possibly date, the "preferred" men in respectable settings. Adolescent courtship among white southerners of the middle class in this period always occurred under heavy adult supervision. Once these young women graduated to the college campus, however, the practice of sorority dating also took place under the watchful eyes of numerous sorority sisters.[8]

Fraternity-sponsored social events were not always chaperoned to the extent that sorority parties were. This meant that sorority chapters had even greater incentive to rely on policing of members' standards to guard against any "improprieties." In this shadowed space of heterosocial interaction, young women and men were expected to abide by popular standards for ladylike and gentlemanly behavior, but public expectations continued to focus on the women as the responsible individuals who should keep the men's behavior in check. While it was now understood as natural for both women and men to have sexual desires, the persisting double standard of sexuality meant that men were free to sow their wild oats without eliciting public comment, but similar activity by women would draw widespread contempt. Dating could be a dangerous business. Although a 1922 female graduate of William and Mary recalled that there was little dating between the male and female students because the new "coeds" were still "intruders," by 1929 the practice was so prevalent at the college that the Women Students' Cooperative Government Association even printed a "black list" of men that women "should be careful" to avoid as dates (see fig. 8).[9] Sororities claimed to provide a protected social space where members would be specially guided toward appropriate male dates and away from men whom the sisters saw as social pariahs or who might be dangerous.

With a number of other young women closely observing and judging one another's dating life, the members had ample opportunity to learn the "do's" and "don'ts" of dating in their campus culture and to discuss proper dating ritu-

FIGURE 8. Kappa Kappa Gammas at William and Mary entertain
their "Kappa Dream Daddies" at the chapter house in 1929.
*Courtesy of the University Archives Photograph Collection, Special Collections
Research Center, Swem Library, College of William and Mary.*

als with their sisters. The opinions of the women around them, rather than the
rules established by the dean's office, influenced women's ideas on the respect-
ability of activities such as dancing, dating, necking, and petting with men.
Gradual shifts in white middle-class understandings of women's sexuality and
sex response influenced the sexual limits within which sorority women could
experiment by the 1920s. White middle-class college women of the 1920s were
sexually active, but their activity did not usually extend as far as sexual intercourse, which was understood to be reserved for marriage, or at least for couples engaged to be married. This scenario created a conundrum for middle-class
women for whom sexual response was now socially acknowledged but not socially accepted outside of marriage. Women had to define their own sexual limits or perhaps follow those prescribed by their sororities. For sorority sisters and
pledges, taking part in discussions about dating adventures served as a means
of group bonding (through the sharing of secrets) and as a tool for educating
the younger women about "appropriate" dating practices as well as which men
they should view as potential dates. Dating culture of the 1930s had subsumed
the earlier twentieth-century practice of "treating" that had been popularized
by working-class youth in urban spaces. Young white women of the middle and

upper classes now faced discussions with peers over how much they should "give" sexually in return for a man taking them to dinner or a movie or asking them to a fraternity dance.[10] While many sorority members received spending money from their families (as did middle-and upper-class college women not in sororities) and did not need men to pay for their entertainment, the financial setbacks of the Depression could have increased some women's willingness to repay men's ability to "treat" with sexual favors.

On each campus, sororities were in competition with one another to attract the attention of the top fraternities. A 1928 male graduate of William and Mary recalled that "fraternities pretty much controlled the social life" at the college. "They organized the dances in such a way that every girl had a card and if she didn't have a boy for every dance she was not popular."[11] Sororities wanted to pledge girls who could fill their dance cards with the right type of boys, and who would uphold or enhance their chapter's campus stature. The top-tier sororities and fraternities on a campus typically mixed socially and dated one another's members; the second-tier groups likewise mixed together and so forth on down the ratings.[12] Still, within each tier heated rivalries to establish group prominence occurred. In these power struggles, the fraternities held the upper hand. While sororities could invite fraternities to have a mixer with them, it was common to rely on a preexisting friendship or romantic relationship between a woman and a man from each group as a go-between. Social convention held that men were the active pursuers in these relationships. Women, on the other hand, were to remain passive and wait for the men to express interest, lest they appear overbearing. As a result, fraternities maintained an advantage over sororities in determining various chapters' popularity on campus. The strict control that sorority chapters sought to exercise over their members was directly influenced by their need to achieve a group image that was attractive to the men in their peer fraternities, if not the top fraternities, at their school.

While this criteria had to figure prominently in the selection of pledges during sorority rush, fraternities, who could call the shots, so to speak, in the areas of dating and mixer invitations, did not have to seek out their pledges for the express purpose of appealing to sorority women. While a fraternity chapter would *prefer* that every member be a handsome "big man on campus" (BMOC), the issue of physical appearance was not as important a factor in choosing new fraternity members as it was for sorority chapters selecting pledges. Shortcomings in physical attractiveness could be offset by sophisticated clothing, ample spending money, or an elite family background. In short, a man's physical appearance was not so explicitly linked to his social success as it was for a woman. Since public expectations for white women placed a premium on finding a husband (preferably one with financial means, or promise thereof, to support a family), women may have been less concerned with potential male partners' physical attributes than with their potential to be a good provider. For women, receiving attention from white middle- or upper-class college men, even if they were not the most desirable on campus, was better than failing to attract *any* suitable male interest.

Teaching "Appropriate" Sexuality

Sororities specifically prepared their members to display a conventionally feminine appearance and to seek attention in heterosocial spaces organized by GLOs. Sororities' pledge handbooks and etiquette manuals provided women with behavioral guidelines and were particularly important means of instructing pledges on the expectations for and limitations on their social and sexual behavior. By introducing the women to heterosocial situations, the sisters hoped to keep them from accidentally finding themselves on their own in such situations where they were unfamiliar with rules of proper social interaction. Sororities hoped to head off any behavioral "improprieties" before they might occur. Kappa Alpha Theta (KAΘ) recommended introducing pledges to "the college social world at one or more formal parties."[13] The sorority made the decision about which men on campus were supposedly worth the members' time and which ones were not. In cases where a chapter disliked their pledges' male friends, the guide suggested that the sisters could easily overcome the issue by introducing pledges to the "preferred type" of men. While the guide did not detail the characteristics of this preferred type, sororities typically expected their members to date fraternity men who were, supposedly, from the women's socioeconomic background. Introductions between pledges and potential suitors "should be frequent," the handbook's authors explained. The pledges' dating conduct would also be monitored when sisters accompanied pledges on "double dates." Sisters could use the knowledge gained during these outings to help the pledges "correct any shortcomings in social matters" or, in some cases, to decide they no longer wished to invite the girl into the sisterhood.[14]

Beyond offering friendly advice on and room for discussion of respectable dating behavior, sorority chapters also moved to control members' dating habits when they threatened to bring embarrassment to the group as a whole. The most desirable campus arrangement would allow sorority chapters to remain in close proximity to all members and keep tabs on their activities, but this was not always possible. In 1927 the Omega chapter of Alpha Delta Pi (ΑΔΠ) sorority at Louisiana State University (LSU) lamented the difficulty they had experienced in mentoring their younger members after the establishment of the coordinate campus in 1925. LSU had constructed a new university campus where junior and senior women attended class with men, while the freshman and sophomore women remained in a single-sex environment on the old campus in downtown Baton Rouge. The problems mounted for members of Omega chapter, and presumably for other sorority chapters on campus, when the school abolished sorority houses shortly after the campus division. Of the new arrangements, chapter correspondent Lucy Mercer complained, "precedent was banished and confusion reigned in its place." While the upperclassmen had been accustomed to "keeping a watchful eye on pledges during class hours," the divided campus forced ΑΔΠ senior members to "pursue their studies far away from their inexperienced freshmen." When the demise of sorority houses at LSU removed the centralized space where the junior and senior girls could instruct the newer members on campus mores, it seemed that all hell broke loose. The loss of "the center of our universe" resulted in many "unhappy occurrences," Mercer explained. Lack of scholastic supervision allowed the younger women to lose interest in their studies and resort to cheating on schoolwork. And in social matters, the "young co-eds formed the wrong ideas of association with university men" because they had not been socially introduced to men in the safety of the classroom and only met near the "soda fountain and on the dance floor." The "poor control" of the 1926–27 pledges by the chapter elders meant that many girls "failed to make the average required for initiation."[15]

Further complicating heterosocializing was the consumption of alcohol, an increasingly important component among women and men. Drinking had long been a pastime for male students but typically was not an issue for respectable female students in the 1920s who abstained by tradition, not to mention Prohibition.[16] Even with the end of Prohibition in 1933 and the glamorization of drinking as a sophisticated pastime by socialites depicted in popular 1930s films, the practice was not always a regular part of heterosocializing for sorority women.[17] A Chi Omega who attended LSU in the mid-1930s remembered that very little drinking went on among the women. "I could name on one hand the number of girls who had ever had a drink."[18] Women belonging to sororities at the University of Illinois in the late 1920s and 1930s recalled that drinking occurred at a minimum. A Theta Upsilon stated that her group of friends never drank and that she "never thought of taking a drink at any social affair on campus." An Alpha Phi noted that "there was always a small amount of drinking," but "it was very unusual" to see anyone who had enough alcohol "so that they acted odd" or were visibly drunk.[19] A Delta Zeta remembered that "girls didn't [drink] unless your date did, [otherwise it was] very frowned on." Instead, drinking was most pronounced among fraternity men.[20] However, as sorority women became more frequent guests at fraternity houses, they became accessories to the drinking culture, and eventually they too became more frequent imbibers. The Kappa Kappa Gammas at Duke required committee reports on liquor, smoking, and "relations with men" to be returned to nationals in 1934, suggesting that the leadership saw a need to monitor these behaviors. Sorority guidebooks and educational programs, however, did not appear to discuss the drinking habits of the ideal member, implying either that sorority officials believed that little drinking occurred or that they had decided to keep discussion of drinking to a minimum. Addressing the possibility that members might be found in the presence of alcohol at sorority-sanctioned events could set off alarms among educators and parents, as well as critics of GLOs.

During the 1930s a new frankness arose around sexuality as knowledge of and access to birth control helped couples achieve mutual sexual satisfaction in the new companionate marriage model. Individuals' economic concerns during the Depression also changed opinions on family planning and practical discussions of sex.[21] By 1935 "sex and sex relations" were frequent topics of conversation among sorority women, reported Ernestine Block Grigsby, Delta Delta Delta (ΔΔΔ or Tri-Delta) national president and a 1919 graduate of the University of Colorado. "Improper conduct," she noted, "[was] not censored nor considered irretrievably damning" and actually was less widespread than publicly suggested.[22] Although rather ambiguous, Grigsby's comments implied that sorority women should be viewed as modern, sexual, *and* respectable and that the characteristics could successfully coexist in individuals. Since sorority chapters required a focus on controlling their members' behavior in order to guarantee the reputation of the group, it stands to reason that sorority women may have carried on more frank discussions of sexuality than did unaffiliated college women. That national sororities regularly described their groups as "family" also helped reinforce the idea that taboo topics could be considered within the confines of the chapter without fear that they would become public knowledge. As Grigsby suggested, students were more accustomed to the openness surrounding heterosocial relations. With college dating culture less novel than it had been in the 1920s, extended discussions of dating and sexuality may have seemed blasé to students of the 1930s.[23]

They also may have become more serious-minded as a result of the financial and social challenges of the Depression years, which made some less fond of extravagance in social events. Several years into the Depression, as the financial realities began to hit university campuses and affect GLOs, the NPC and the respective national sororities addressed the issue and urged chapters to hold less frequent, less expensive social engagements.[24] Yet sororities continued to place a premium on heterosocial engagements and to strongly encourage all members and pledges to attend, even amid financial hardships.[25] In 1932 Duke's Delta Beta chapter of Kappa Kappa Gamma passed a motion that attendance at their upcoming dance be compulsory unless the president excused the member's absence. Sorority members who did not attend the heterosocial Greek-letter events missed opportunities for social instruction and for introduction to prospective dates. Additionally, if a group did not produce a large turnout for social events, it might be poorly received, or not invited, by fraternities in the future. Even while forcing members to attend social events, the Delta Beta chapter clearly realized that these were difficult times for some members and pledges.[26]

College campuses experienced further changes in the early 1940s as the United States entered World War II and many college-age men enlisted in the armed forces. While sorority women volunteered for the Red Cross and their sorority chapters voted to buy war bonds, fraternity- and sorority-sponsored dances continued but with less decoration and expense.[27] Sorority women occupied themselves with the same rush-related women-only activities that they always had, but as wartime disruptions created new spaces where couples could interact romantically and sexually, public concern about college women's morality again became a pressing topic among educators, behavioral experts, parents, and sorority alumnae. Even as campus heterosocializing was limited during the war period, sororities would continue to police female behavior in the unfamiliar landscape of the wartime home front, where women might date servicemen whom they knew little or nothing about. "There were so many blind dates during the war," recalled a woman from William and Mary's class of 1944. "None of us knew them (or they us)." A student from Waverly, Virginia, remembered that at the end of fall semester 1941, immediately following the attack on Pearl Harbor, William and Mary's campus emptied of nearly all the men from the freshman class—"a wholesale departure." The men were gone so quickly, she recalled, that the women "had to turn to the services for our escorts and boyfriends."[28] A Phi Mu at Howard College (now Samford University) in Birmingham, Alabama, noted that before the war "our parties were given so that we could ask our dates and have a good time with 'the' one."

Wartime parties were just "simple entertainment" to "keep up the morale of the Navy." No dates were made as "the" ones were already in service abroad.[29] College women's activities to "keep up the morale" of the Navy or other men in uniform included sexual behavior but generally did not extend to sexual intercourse.[30] Yet the fleeting nature of heterosocial interaction that could occur when military bases were located near college campuses made administrators increasingly wary.[31]

While student experiences suggested that women's drinking on campus was of limited importance, or at least not seen as a problem in the 1930s, the situation began to change during World War II. An example from the Woman's College of Duke University shows the evolution of college administrators' awareness of and attention to women's drinking. In 1952 Duke's dean of women, Mary Grace Wilson, detailed a history of drinking regulations at the Woman's College, as requested by Katherine Warren, dean of women at Florida State College for Women. The fact that the deans were corresponding about this issue suggested a heightened concern over drinking. Wilson reported that Duke did not have "any printed regulation with regard specifically to drinking" until the administrators were "face to face with the social problems presented by World War II and the plan to establish an Army camp near Durham." The administration feared that female students with access to alcohol and in close proximity to the army camp might make poor decisions regarding sexual behavior while under the influence. Thus, administrators "adopted a strict prohibition measure" in May 1943. Wilson noted that no regulations had been needed for years beforehand because "drinking among women was not an acceptable social custom."[32] Administrators enacted stricter rules for women during the war as a measure to protect both women *and* servicemen from coming into contact in spaces that could lead to sexual activity. They likely saw sexual activity as "dangerous" to both parties involved but also wished to safeguard the college from any criticism it might face if its female students were found to be exhibiting sexual behavior or engaging in sex with servicemen—particularly if soldiers contracted sexually transmitted diseases from women in the area.[33]

Duke students were generally receptive to the 1943 prohibition regulation until after the war "when the GIs returned to campus" and women requested a modification of the rules.[34] While on average returning veterans had drinking habits similar to those of their nonveteran collegiate peers, the war had helped change the culture of alcohol consumption.[35] American advertising had positioned beer drinking as an integral part of the national war effort and a basic right for Americans.[36] The Woman's College relaxed total prohibition in

1947. While Wilson noted that this measure probably increased the number of women drinkers, she also admitted that if the administration had left the drinking rules as strict as they had been during the war, deceitful students would have abused them regularly. Furthermore, she added that cases of intoxication were "very rare indeed," as "men and women [disapproved]" of drunkenness.[37]

The Women's Student Government Association at the University of Georgia (UGA) took a different tack in the early 1950s by writing a "no-drinking" rule into their regulations.[38] Perhaps they hoped to stem what appeared to be a popular activity on campus. "It is obvious," a UGA woman noted, "that seventy-five percent (probably an over-estimate) of the girls disobey this rule." A survey of students from one women's dormitory found that a number of women considered the no-drinking rule restrictive and out of touch with current cultural standards that endorsed moderate consumption of alcohol in social settings. "Why is drinking prohibited if you have your parents' permission? If you drink in your home?" asked one woman. Relating moderate drinking to sophistication and ladylike behavior, she continued, "Certainly if you aren't old enough to conduct yourself as a lady by the time you are in college it is a pathetic and hopeless situation." Another female student also followed this logic, suggesting that women be "allowed to indulge in a cocktail as long as [they] conducted [themselves] lady-like."[39] Drinking had become another marker of class for educated Americans by the late 1940s.[40] As a hostess in her own home, a sorority alumna would be expected to know about serving alcohol and drinking it in ladylike moderation. Like other lessons engendered by the sororities, proper drinking etiquette would also denote an air of refinement. Within the peer-monitored space of the sorority chapter, members would learn what, if any, amount of alcohol the sisterhood deemed advisable for them to imbibe.

The MRS Degree in the Postwar Era

"Everyone comes to college to achieve something different," explained a 1940s Kappa Kappa Gamma pledge training guide. "Some come to gain an intellectual education, some to build a vocational education. Many come to achieve a husband."[41] With the influx of men returning from the war and enrolling at colleges, sorority women seemed happy to return to full-time heterosocializing. Following the social upheavals and uncertainty of World War II and the preceding Depression decade, Americans in the postwar period would seek stability and security in heterosexual relationships and by reaffirming what they believed were appropriate gender characteristics in women and men.[42]

Particularly salient in the Cold War era was the idea that college women should readily conform to feminine ideals, holding heterosexual marriage and children as the primary goals after graduation and preparing themselves for that eventuality.[43] Young women arrived at college primed for sororities' conservative goals and armed with the understanding that they should make heterosocializing and dating a priority while on campus. The sorority instruction, steeped in the southern aesthetic, gave members additional training to achieve the "proper" gender characteristics, which were so clearly delineated in southern culture, and to prepare them for marriage and family living where, ideally, they would be confined to gender-specific behavior.

A 1953 study of courtship and marriage proclaimed dating to be "the center of social life in coeducational colleges" while observing that sororities and fraternities "play a lead role in dating" and that the "events sponsored by [those] organizations encourage, or even require it."[44] By providing a social skill set and an apparent entrée into the campus dating scene, sororities enticed women looking to meet the cultural expectations for heterosexual relationships and their lives as adult women. A survey of students at the Woman's College of Duke University in 1951–52, and again in 1961, showed that many women entered college with the perception that sorority women received more dates than nonsorority women.[45] Although the majority of women surveyed in 1961 did not cite the increased opportunities for dating as their deciding factor in joining a sorority, a majority did believe that membership increased dating opportunities. Significantly, the surveyed women who fell into the category "freshmen pledges" were by far the most likely to answer that sororities offered greater chances for dating (seventy-seven answering "yes," forty-nine "no").[46] It is unclear if sorority membership actually increased a woman's chance of getting a date, but it likely increased her chances of meeting men. The power of perception surrounding sorority membership and dating reveals the extent of the cultural emphasis on dating during this time and the pressure on the college woman to be an active part of the heterosocial dating scene.

In the heterosocial sorority, even the time devoted to women-only educational programming could focus on questions of female-male relationships. Sororities enlisted campus authority figures to offer parental guidance in the areas of dating and adult heterosexual relationships. The implementation of such programming in sorority chapters reflected Americans' preoccupation with the achievement of successful marriages in general, and the magnitude of interest *among* college women of this era in the preparation for marriage.[47] By giving attention to marriage preparation, sororities catered to popular demand among their membership and again demonstrated that they could fill the gaps in women's education supposedly left by the liberal arts curriculum. Sorority programming imparted conventional wisdom usually supplied by family or religious institutions. During the early 1950s, the Gamma Epsilon chapter of Phi Mu at Duke arranged a series of their educational programs to highlight these issues. Dr. James H. Phillips, director of religious activities and the first chaplain to Duke University, visited the chapter on several occasions to speak on "Catholic-Protestant Marriages" and "Problems of Marriage." They also invited Dr. James T. Cleland, dean of the Duke University Chapel and professor of preaching at the Duke University Divinity School, to speak about "Interpreting the Marriage Vows."[48] When "experts" were not available, the fraternity education chairperson might lead the program. At a 1955 meeting the chairperson facilitated discussion on the topic "What Qualities You Want in a Husband."[49] These talks, like the other forms of social education, served to impart knowledge that society believed was part of young women's necessary preparation for adult womanhood, while also establishing standards for women's behavior toward men in general and within heterosexual relationships.

Although the GLO party scene of the mid-twentieth century could pose problems for college administrators seeking to maintain control of social activities, deans of women still appreciated sororities' use of peer pressure to shape members' dating habits and attitudes toward sexual behavior.[50] In a speech to the Alpha Epsilon chapter of Alpha Chi Omega (AXΩ) sorority at the University of Alabama in 1956, UNC dean Katherine Carmichael praised sorority life for helping young women "develop wholesome attitudes, through group pressure, toward the opposite sex." Such "wholesome" attitudes also supported the sexual double standard, which proscribed women's sexual activity outside of marriage while also teaching that women should act as guardians against men's "uncontrollable" but socially acceptable sexual desires and activities. Members' sexual impulses, she suggested, could be controlled through a combination of sorority training and peer pressure. "I know that she won't sit on a young man's knee in public places," she explained, as "sorority sentiment forbids this."[51] Physical control and self-restraint were the hallmarks of a southern lady and a sorority woman. For Carmichael it was not "immoral" for a young woman to think or wonder about sex, but any behavior that publicly suggested that she was thinking about or engaging in sexual activity would cast doubt on her moral standards.

Sorority literature made clear that members should be interested in heterosexual dating as a primary component of "well-adjusted" ladyhood. *For She's an Alpha Chi!* (1961), an etiquette publication coauthored by two University of Minnesota AXΩ alumnae, revealed their opinion that "dating is one

of the concerns uppermost in every girl's mind ... throughout her college career. . . . Whether . . . a new arrival on the college scene or an upperclassman,
the main concern for girls is where to meet the dates [they] desire."[52] The book
ascribed a strong interest in dating to *all* girls, not just those in sororities. The
Social Standards Committee of the Women's Student Government Association (WSGA) at Duke published a comparable guide given to all incoming
women called *Design for a Duchess*. While college-produced etiquette guides
lacked the extreme detail on clothing, makeup, posture, and speaking voice
found in many sorority handbooks, the 1962 copy of *Design* assumed that all
women would participate in the heterosexual dating culture. The WSGA Social Standards Committee encouraged female students to get out and enjoy
Duke's spring activities, including—"oh, yes!"—men's spring athletics, which
they suggested was a great opportunity to "watch your man!" They also reminded women who "[stepped] out" to other campuses for seasonal dances
to write thank-you notes to their dates and weekend hostesses.[53] *For She's an
Alpha Chi!* also recommended extracurricular activities as excellent places to
meet "the young men who share interests similar to your own" and explained
that as Alpha Chi sisters they had "an extra special opportunity to pursue that
fellow quite undetected at [their] *open houses*." The advice seemed to suggest that sorority women were free to mingle with (and possibly date) men
who shared their interests but who were not necessarily in fraternities. Yet
they were sure to note that sorority open houses, at which most male guests
would be fraternity men, afforded the "extra special opportunity" for successful meetings. Additionally, the phrase "young men who share interests similar
to your own" reminded a woman that she should be seeking partners from her
own socioeconomic background and with compatible ideals for adult living—
aspects that may have led her back to a fraternity man—even in non-Greek
extracurriculars. Particularly as the desegregation of college campuses heightened the NPC groups' concerns over social mixing between races, the phras-
ing of "similar interests" could also be code for *white* men.

Women also had the chance to meet eligible men through blind dates, but
the authors of *For She's an Alpha Chi!* cautioned against accepting a blind date
with "someone whom none of your sisters have ever heard of or you can't seem
to place at all." In an uncharacteristically protective tone for sorority literature,
the women warned that an unknown man also had unknown "intentions,"
which meant that he might not have the same standards for respectable behavior ostensibly held by sorority women or a man known to the sisters.[54] In reality, a known man was often as likely as the unknown man to have "intentions"

of having sex with a woman, and perhaps having it against her will. It was up to the elder sorority sisters to vet possible dates and advise new members about men on campus whom the chapter perceived to be "fast" (meaning that they expected their dates to engage in sex play, and perhaps intercourse, without establishing a firm romantic commitment beforehand). By guiding the pledges and younger members away from men who would not respect the women or their need to abide by middle-class standards for sexual behavior, the elder sisters were also safeguarding the sorority's reputation. As the sororities saw it, if they failed to educate their members on the possible hazards of sexual activity, the entire group could suffer as a result. In the worst-case scenario for a sorority chapter, a member might become pregnant following a sexual encounter. While a pregnant woman would be banished from school and the sorority, others on campus could easily assume the reason for her disappearance, which would reflect poorly on others' perceptions of the chapter's standards. Sorority literature that cautioned college members' choice in dates was geared toward the protection of the sorority's image rather than the members' personal safety.

For She's an Alpha Chi!'s dating discussion culminated with the goal of many college-age women of the 1950s and 1960s: "going steady" and "being pinned." They advised that a sister give serious consideration before agreeing to this step. "Be sure you are ready to give up the dating merry-go-round for that one fellow. Going steady or being pinned brings with it a great deal of responsibility and maturity that is best to be sure you have." "But if you do choose to accept," the authors assured their readers, "the pinning ceremony can be one of the happiest and most momentous times of your college days."[55] While "going steady" did not necessarily lead to marriage, the practice of having a "steady" provided social security and allowed young couples to mimic marriage, including engaging in sexual activity, without actually being married. "Going steady" further pressed boundaries for sexual activity outside of marriage, as going steady or wearing a man's fraternity pin *suggested* a deeper commitment by the couple, even if it was not always the case.[56] The Alpha Chi Omega guidebook also seemed to acknowledge that going steady was likely a step toward increased sexual activity for both partners. By cautioning members to exercise "responsibility" and "maturity," the authors tacitly suggested that going steady was a euphemism for sexual activity, including heterosexual intercourse. For fraternity men, however, obtaining sex with conventionally desirable women on campus likely bested the emotional attachment of "going steady." As Nicholas Syrett has persuasively argued, white fraternities stringently policed their members' heterosexual identities in the postwar decades. With Americans' increasing concern over newly visible, same-sex sexual subcultures during and after World War II, fraternity men aggressively and openly pursued heterosexual sex to dispel public speculation of possible homosexual preferences.[57] Sorority women were readily available, and sorority chapters were always seeking ways to build or maintain relationships with popular campus fraternities. As sororities jockeyed for status in this increasingly permissive sexual culture, sorority women, like other women on campus, more readily responded to men's desires for sexual activity—whether the women had sought out sex for themselves or if they just went along with what their male partner wanted. Young women in the United States during the "sexual revolution" of the early to mid-1960s still lived in a culture that produced highly conflicting messages about women's sexuality. Women wrestled with public proclamations that premarital sex was immoral while also learning that sex was a normal, even enjoyable part of adult life—*and* that they should be physically appealing to men. Increasing popular attention given to women's private struggle with their sexual feelings resulted in a greater willingness to discuss sex as an individual's choice, rather than a wrong to be punished.[58]

In a time before acquaintance rape was an acknowledged reality with legal consequences, women regularly experienced sexual coercion from male dates, friends, and steady boyfriends who would, in all likelihood, meet the sororities' standards of acceptable, middle-class dates. Many attacks probably occurred without mention to friends or families, and certainly not to campus authorities. A nonsorority woman who attended the University of Illinois during the mid-1930s and lived at home in Urbana described an experience of attempted date rape while she was a student. The assault occurred in the front room of her mother's home. Luckily she was able to fight off her attacker, but she never told anyone about it at the time. Her experience led her to believe that such attacks were widespread but that other women just kept quiet, as did she. "Why would it happen to me and nobody else?" she reasoned. "I never heard anybody talk about [rape]—never. They wouldn't have reported it to [Dean] Maria Leonard under any circumstances. . . . Girls didn't even tell their best friend, I certainly didn't tell my girlfriends about it."[59] Whether a sorority member would have felt more comfortable discussing such a harrowing experience with one of her "sisters" is unknown, but it seems unlikely. Women who spoke out about sexual assault risked public shaming as women who supposedly "encouraged" their attackers. Deciding to tell anyone after their assault would not be an easy decision.[60]

Many sorority women may have viewed male sexual aggression, particularly fueled by alcohol, as a "normal" occurrence and not behavior that necessarily required a warning to their sisters.[61] Information about a potentially danger-ous man might be overlooked if he was from a top fraternity and took an in-terest in one of the sorority's members, especially if a sorority chapter hoped to secure a desirable reputation with his fraternity.[62] As fraternity men drank heavily, this regularly placed sorority women in the midst of parties where heterosocial drinking was expected. Even if women did not imbibe, they came under scrutiny simply for being in the presence of men's drinking.[63] By 1958 the Duke Woman's College Judicial Board requested that the administration re-evaluate and further relax the drinking rules to leave the choice of drinking up to the individual woman. To avoid the drinking rule, the fraternities had often held unapproved parties, and by attending the parties the women would be committing an honor code violation. The Judicial Board explained that they did not want the rules relaxed because more women wanted to drink but be-cause young women wanted to attend parties held by fraternities where drink-ing occurred. A survey of the Woman's College student body showed that, of the women who drank (503, to the 527 who did not drink), more drank at ille-gal parties (299) than at legal ones (257), and even more women (896) did not object to attending parties where others were drinking.[64]

While university administrators of the 1920s and 1930s may have chosen to conceal instances of women's drinking and public drunkenness to the best of their ability, by the 1950s and 1960s deans of women and advisory commit-tees for campus Greek life began to note the problem of increased drinking by sorority women, suggesting a concern for women's safety but perhaps an even greater concern about women's failure to maintain sororities' moral stan-dards while participating in the growing heterosocial drinking culture.[65] Of course, a relaxing of drinking rules on campus meant that more women could find themselves in situations where it reflected poorly on their chapter's social standing to say no to alcohol when offered. Greater ease of access to alcohol at fraternity parties likely meant that more women became unintentionally ine-briated in private spaces where men held the upper hand. Fraternity men's sex-ual assault of female guests could easily occur without repercussions for the perpetrators.

The fact that drinking was becoming a popular heterosocial lubricant alarmed some sorority alumnae. During the 1950s and 1960s, national soror-ity officers reminded members about regulations regarding alcohol. Deliver-ing a talk on "Techniques for Education in Standards" at the 1950 joint Na-tional Association of Deans of Women (NADW)–NPC committee meeting, Mrs. William Owen of Gamma Phi Beta (ΓΦΒ) claimed, "Our sorority de-finitively discourages the drinking of alcoholic beverages." She also noted that

ΓΦΒ recommended that members should seek out "men who respect our standards of conduct." Yet the men whom sororities generally deemed "honorable" were likely the fraternity men, who regularly outdrank their independent male peers.[66] In 1957 the Grand Council of Kappa Alpha Theta requested that Theta alumnae chapters and mothers' clubs assist them "in dealing with the greatest problem of [the] times, the problem of drinking."[67] They alluded to the problem of drinking by individual members as an issue that would reflect poorly on the entire sorority. "We all know that drinking, too frequently, is accompanied by the relaxing of normally good conduct and sometimes the abandonment of high standards, which affect the reputation of those involved far beyond their ability to realize."[68] By overindulging in alcohol, alumnae suggested, women might lose their inhibitions and engage in behavior that they, and their sorority, might regret.

The unease of university administrators and sorority alumnae was understandable. At the University of North Carolina (UNC) in 1955, and again in 1962, administrators cited concerns over instances of drinking at parties and off-campus sorority pledge dances.[69] In 1964 William and Mary's dean of women, Birdena Donaldson, reported that on one night "approximately twenty-five girls who came in from parties" required the help of the dormitory or sorority house counselors to "sober" them up. To further complicate matters, the drinking at William and Mary often took place at the apartments of young college faculty members.[70] Sharon Sullivan Mujica, a KKΓ at UNC from 1958 to 1961, remembered that women on campus "drank a lot." "Back then," she explained, "you could drink socially, but you were not supposed to get drunk." Sororities were not allowed to have alcohol in their houses, and Mujica believed that Dean Carmichael and the sorority housemothers probably "[preferred] that the women didn't drink at all."[71] Carmichael noted that "all American colleges enroll a large group of substantial young women who rapidly are metamorphosed into what [the] student generation calls the 'party girls.'" She referred to the instance of a young woman who "ran into difficulty when, after an extra drink, she considered only the lily of the field, and divorced herself from customary raiment."[72] The "difficulty" could have been a euphemism for a host of traumatic situations: loss of reputation, an unplanned pregnancy, or rape. Carmichael blamed female students who, she believed, left themselves open to unwanted male sexual advances by failing to maintain a sober awareness. She understood that women would have to answer for any socially perceived wrongdoings so far as standards of sexual propriety and, in her opinion, public drunkenness transformed a sorority woman's appearance from one that attracted male attention to one that invited sexual activity.

Fraternity Parties: A Challenge to Sorority Standards

The social events of Greek life promoted heterosocial drinking and increasingly ran contrary to drinking regulations enforced by campus administrators and suggested by national sorority leaders. Much of the drinking took place at fraternity-sponsored social events, including house parties on or near campus as well as cabin parties and beach weekends held away from the university. While the fraternity typically hosted the sorority women and provided the alcohol, the women also became accessories to party planning. A 1961 Kappa Kappa Gamma national newsletter reminded members that in planning social functions, "no chapter funds may be budgeted for alcoholic beverages."[73]

By the 1950s and 1960s, raucous fraternity parties, as well as university administrators' concerns over the activities that took place there, were on the rise, and consumption of alcohol certainly played a major role in the debauchery. Of the fraternity men's high jinks, Nicholas Syrett has noted: "When they broke the rules, most fraternity men apologized for their antics, explained that things had gotten out of hand, promised never to do it again, and claimed that the rule breaking was the result of only a few out-of-control members."[74] College administrators who saw sororities as benign or even beneficial additions to their campuses' environment typically did not extend these feelings toward fraternities. Whereas the NPC and the sororities' national leaders used a firm hand to regulate sorority members' behavior and actively cultivated working relationships with deans of women, the National Interfraternity Council (NIC) seemed less intent on controlling their member organizations or building a cooperative system with deans of students or other university officials. That left the individual university administrations to deal with the campus Interfraternity Council and the fraternity chapters largely as they saw fit.

At schools where university administrators and chapter advisers were less aggressive in monitoring fraternity activities, the groups had greater latitude in the conduct of their members. This may have been particularly true at UNC in the 1940s and 1950s, where the UNC Interfraternity Council (IFC) enjoyed what Carmichael and Dean of Students Fred Weaver believed were some of the most lenient restrictions on any university campus.[75] Of distress to both Weaver and Carmichael, the IFC fraternities seemed unwilling to abide by their own agreement regarding women's visitation in the fraternity houses. The Visiting Privileges Agreement, first put into place at UNC in the early 1930s, was a written agreement between the dean of students and the fraternity leaders to form a "basis for entertaining women in the fraternity houses without chaperones," whose presence had previously been required at par-

ties.[76] By 1940 the agreement limited women to the first floor of the houses
and placed restrictions on the men serving alcohol in the presence of their female guests and on the hours that the houses would be open to women. It
also required fraternities to apply to the IFC three days prior to the date they
wished to hold a house party and to use chaperones from a list preapproved
by the IFC.[77] The agreement simply provided a loose process for fraternities
to follow in hosting a party; the lack of outside supervision still could place
partygoers in danger. With only their own standards of gentlemanly conduct
guiding them, the fraternity members could end up seriously intoxicated, posing a physical danger to themselves as well as other guests. If female guests did
obtain alcohol, there were no guarantees that a sorority sister, or one of their
male hosts, would suggest they limit their drinking. The lack of supervision
also meant that women could end up fending off unwanted sexual advances
from fraternity members while either individual, or both, may have been ine-
briated. Overall, however, the arrangement likely suited the fraternities as it allowed for greater freedom in what activities could take place at the parties.

Up until 1947, a Visiting Committee of students routinely made rounds to
parties at UNC to report violations of the Visiting Agreement.[78] With the demise of that practice, the onus was on the guests to report any infractions of
the agreement. That put the female visitors, Carmichael contended, in a difficult position. Sorority women could issue complaints about the practices, but
seeming to protest too much could give their sorority a reputation for being
uncooperative and limit the fraternities interested in mixing with them. In addition, reporting a fraternity often meant that the women had to admit some
wrongdoing on their own part—typically that of being in the presence of men
drinking alcohol. By the late 1950s, Carmichael cited reports that fraternity
men were regularly violating nearly all of the agreed-upon "standards of good
conduct" at their events and were "gambling in the houses," allowing women
to pass "beyond social rooms" and be "present in houses at strange hours."
There were also "unchaperoned women drinking with men, [and] off-campus
parties held in questionable surroundings." All of these activities added up to
"bad publicity" for the university.[79]

The lack of resident housemothers at fraternities was also a subject of con-
tention at UNC during the postwar period. If a housemother resided in the
home, the logic went, then she could advise against parties on weeknights, ensure that women were not served alcohol, *and* guarantee that they left the preapproved parties at the prescribed times.[80] Resident housemothers at sororities and fraternities were usually older women who had been forced to take
the positions out of financial need and may have been less willing to discipline

the students for fear of losing their job and "home." Thus, a housemother's constant presence may have been as a mere figurehead if she chose to look the other way when her charges engaged in questionable or dangerous behavior or broke university rules regarding alcohol and house closing hours.[81] Still, Carmichael believed that requiring all fraternities to have resident housemothers would help control the groups' drinking and behavioral problems that had been giving the campus negative publicity.[82] Women enrolled at UNC also requested fraternity housemothers. While they acknowledged that the presence of housemothers probably would not solve the drinking problems at fraternities, they hoped that the housemothers would, as a Tri-Delta and president of the UNC Women's Government Association wrote in 1946, "create the appropriate social atmosphere in the fraternity houses."[83] The Women's Honor Council issued a recommendation that the university administration "take the immediate necessary steps to provide proper supervision in the fraternity houses, so that Carolina students can be assured of the highest standards possible."[84] Women realized that attending a party at a UNC fraternity house meant that they risked being subjected to lewd and drunken behavior by their hosts or being treated in a sexually inappropriate or aggressive manner, and that being part of these situations could jeopardize their "virtue" in the eyes of the public, so they were willing to take steps to keep the parties in check. Yet in the spring of 1958, only five of the twenty-four fraternity houses at UNC had housemothers, not all of whom were resident.[85]

The concerns over student self-policing, and among sorority women in particular, became abundantly clear following an infamous 1961 Halloween party hosted by UNC's Upsilon chapter of Zeta Psi fraternity and attended by the Alpha Sigma chapter of Delta Delta Delta ($\Delta\Delta\Delta$) sorority. At the party, Zeta Psi members wore questionable costumes: one brother dressed as a prophylactic-dispensing machine, another made "suggestive use of the end of a rubber crutch," several wore diapers, and one wore nothing at all as he streaked through the house. The men also served the Tri-Deltas a punch containing grain alcohol. Echoing the long-standing double standard of sexuality, where women should serve as moral guardians, keeping men from acting on their "natural" sexual desires, Panhellenic advisers chided the sorority women for failing to live up to their "responsibility" to make sure that partygoers conducted themselves properly. The "boys will be boys" mentality that served to excuse bad behavior by men simultaneously reinforced the social expectation that women should act as good influences to quell men's misbehaviors.[86] The advisers expressed disbelief that the women consented to be guests at the party at all. They felt that the women should have "spoken to their dates" about the "tone" of the party and left the premises.[87] While there was some dissension among the female students on the Judicial Board as to the culpability of the sorority women, the group voted to place the Tri-Deltas on social probation, ending their participation in fraternity-sorority mixers for the rest of the semester.[88] Unlike drinking and behavioral cases in the 1930s, the men of Zeta Psi also received punishment for their antics. The administration showed an increasing unwillingness to allow fraternities the leeway they had previously enjoyed, as the school placed the chapter on "indefinite general probation" for the remainder of the 1961–62 school year.[89] Much like the film depiction of the Delta Tau Chi house in *National Lampoon's Animal House* (1978), where gross and outlandish behavior lands the misfit fraternity on "double secret probation," the men of Zeta Psi likewise showed a drunken disregard for propriety.

The repercussions of the Zeta Psi–Tri Delta Halloween party certainly did not bring an end to the issue of alcohol at fraternity parties but clearly demonstrated the problematic nature of the relationship in which sororities engaged with fraternities. The desire for sorority chapters to gain and maintain popularity through heterosocial situations prized members' physical appearance and level of sexual attractiveness and expected them to accommodate fraternity men's sexual play and accept (to a limit) their sexual advances. Now that sororities had premised their organizational identities on a standard that encouraged and even required college members' constant self-monitoring and interaction with fraternities, they also operated within the dangerous spaces where excessive alcohol consumption by partygoers and women's sexual assault by fraternity men could easily occur.

Sororities and the Sexual Revolution

By the 1960s, sororities' national leaders appeared to expect that some members would choose to make drinking a regular part of socializing. Zeta Tau Alpha's (ZTA) *Ladies First* (1966), written by South Carolinian and ZTA alumna Anna Boswell McCord, explicitly addressed the fact that sorority women would face the issue of whether to drink alcohol at social gatherings. She suggested caution in these situations but left the ultimate decision up to the individual woman. McCord reminded women of the possible immediate consequences of drinking, which included "lowering of inhibitions ... in boy-girl relationships." Like Carmichael a decade earlier, she warned that "the casual, unthinking decision under such circumstances can permanently mar your life."[90] In a similarly circumspect manner, McCord referred to sororities' concerns that members' sexual activity, perhaps while inebriated, could lead to unintended pregnancy. Again, the intent of sororities' messaging around "moral standards," which encompassed sexual activity and drinking, was to keep members focused on maintaining the sorority's reputation and the woman's personal safety, in that order. Sororities required their members to participate in heterosocial situations for the good of the entire organization's image but, problematically, wanted the individual women to own responsibility for what might happen once they were there.

At the same time that McCord reminded sorority women of their duty to uphold sexual propriety, aspects of the 1960s "sexual revolution" played out on campuses. While unmarried college women were unable to obtain the birth control pill when it came on the market in 1962, the knowledge that women would have power to control the separation of sex and sexual enjoyment from the act of procreation was profound and helped reshape American attitudes toward sex in relation to marriage and family life. By the mid- to late 1960s, many college campuses also experienced student revolts against the system of campus parietals that strictly limited women's activities. Dorm and sorority house closing hours, rules about dress, permissions for leaving campus, and other minutiae that had governed women's behavior since their admission as students were called into question by women and men on campus.[91]

Sexual activity between students on campus became more commonplace. A sorority woman enrolled at William and Mary from 1969 to 1973 noted that students were having sex all over campus and that the college's rules barring dorm visitation between men and women really had no effect on campus sexual activity. "Certainly we had sex without visitation [hours]—we had sex in the Sunken Garden, in fraternity houses, in residence halls . . . it was common all over the place."[92] The eventual ability for single women to gain access to birth control also provided another means for men to pressure women into unwanted sex.[93] Of course, when sex occurred in situations where alcohol, drugs, or peer pressure from fraternity brothers and sorority sisters came into play, these interactions became increasingly risky. While alcohol had always played a large role in fraternity life, drinking slowly gained acceptance among greater numbers of sorority women through their heterosocial events with fraternities.

Much of the revolution in relation to sex surrounded a new approach to gendered roles in sexuality and sexual relationships. This change would threaten the conservative model for women and men's interaction promoted by sororities. With calls for coed living spaces and the ability for men and women to live together in off-campus housing, some of the hypocrisy was broken down surrounding Americans' "traditional" sexual practices. In 1968

Gamma Phi Beta alumna Ritajean Hartung Butterworth wrote much more candidly and positively of sex in her sorority's guide, *Ideally Speaking*. A 1953 graduate of the University of Washington, Butterworth included a four-page discussion of sex in contemporary society heavily excerpted from theologian Edward V. Stein's *The Stranger Inside You* (1965), which explained sex as a natural and valuable part of life as described in Judeo-Christian religious teachings. The discussion suggested moving away from a strict code of right or wrong in regard to sex and toward an "emphasis on integrity, responsible freedom, concern, knowledge, [and] fulfillment." Although Stein's work couched sex in religious rhetoric and clearly spoke from a male viewpoint, the openness with which *Ideally Speaking* addressed the topic was a far cry from the silence or coded language of "morals" in sorority publications from earlier decades.[94] Butterworth's treatment of sorority women's sexuality was decidedly modern when compared with most sororities' reticence to discuss anything other than an image of purity and propriety.

Yet while national sorority literature adapted to encompass the new modern thinking on sexuality, the reliance on a highly feminine, nonthreatening, physically attractive image of members persisted. Even if sorority alumnae knew that "nice girls" did have sex, most were not going to give public credence to that idea. For national sororities, the sexual revolution's challenges to conventional understandings of gendered sexuality appeared dangerous and antithetical to their models of a sorority woman's behavior. The sorority-fraternity dyad kept sorority women in a subordinate relationship to their fraternity peers. Yet like the white, southern lady, clinging to the privileges of the pedestal on which white men had placed her, sorority women were loath to relinquish their vaunted position as the most sexually desirable, yet also supposedly virginal, members of the campus community.

Women's shared experience of sexual exploitation and sexual violence helped give rise to the 1970s feminist movement, which emboldened them to speak out against unwanted sexual advances. Activists organized "Take Back the Night" marches on college campuses and in U.S. cities starting in the early 1970s. Greater attention to women's rights helped enable survivors of rape and assault feel empowered to speak out without shame or fear of blame and to gain attention from law enforcement, which often had failed to consider these attacks as crimes.[95] Just as national sorority leaders were mum on topics of women's sexuality and changing expectations of gendered behavior in sexual relationships, they also appeared to ignore the possibility of sexual assault and rape within the spaces of sorority and fraternity heterosocializing. Apparently satisfied that college actives, properly trained by their chapters, would be policing their own behavior and that of their sisters, NPC leaders did not appear ready or willing to address these crucial topics with full force or to call out the fraternities for their inability to uphold behavioral standards. The white fraternity men, presented by sororities as members' "preferred" dates, were more often than not the sexual abusers. An abundance of sociological research has shown that fraternity men are more likely than unaffiliated male students to rape women. Yet it was not until the mid-1980s that the NPC addressed the issue of sexual harassment at one of its biennial sessions.[96] The continuing reliance on an antiquated model of women's sexuality undergirded sororities' conservative approach across their organizational policies.

College sorority women, with the approval of the groups' alumnae and national officers, spearheaded the move toward mixed-sex socializing on campus, shifting sororities' purpose by the 1920s to a heterosocial focus that the organizations continue to prize today. While the boundaries of a separate women's culture still existed on coeducational campuses in the South—as evidenced by the coordinate campus ideal, the constant rules governing women's conduct, and the omnipresent myth of the southern lady—the women's culture no longer suggested a space of support for women in the male-friendly environment. Instead, the women's culture, subsumed within the sorority culture, functioned in support of and ancillary to the university men's culture of masculinity, as women understood their social value in terms of their relation to men. Ironically, while sorority women turned their attention away from women-only activities in favor of heterosocializing, the fraternity men continued to prize the "brotherhood" over the heterosocial interactions. Women were simply sexual objects used by fraternity men to prove their heterosexual masculinity; the male homosocial relationships remained of primary importance within the fraternity.[97] Framing heterosexual dating as the norm and as an integral, even mandatory part of college life channeled all women, whether they chose to participate in the dating culture or not, into an environment where male students were the arbiters of their intrinsic value. The maintenance of sororities' heterosocial appeal would play heavily into decisions about which rushees they would consider pledging as rush became the means to define the physical image of sororities.

CHAPTER FIVE

"The Chosen Are Happy,
the Rest Are Crushed"

USING RUSH TO DEFINE THE MEMBERSHIP

*I*n the college novel *I Lived This Story* (1930), a post-rush party or "scratch session" among the sisters of the fictional Gamma Theta sorority at Colossus University (a thinly veiled version of Northwestern) demonstrated the viciousness of sorority women in selecting new members. Members contributed their opinions of the rushees, typically praising the prospectives they had encountered during the quick and superficial parties. One sister, however, took apparent pride in bringing forth malicious gossip about one of the rushees. "She has a perfectly terrible reputation," the sister announced excitedly, as she explained that the rushee in question was a "wild" partier and that people from her hometown suggested that she was "fast."[1] In a moment, the rushee's name and reputation were tainted by hearsay that was, perhaps, intentionally embellished by the Gamma Theta sister.

Unsubstantiated gossip, like the rumors spread at a scratch party, could be a significant factor in rush decisions. Any detail from a woman's background, or that of her family, could be brought forth to support or deny her worthiness as a pledge and future sister. Alumnae too transmitted prospectives' histories through sorority networks, which became powerful deciders in the selection of new members. While the transfer of information both by alumnae and active members could help chapters focus attention on socially connected or conventionally attractive rushees, it also provided details about religion, race, and class and could highlight any "questionable" activities undertaken by the rushee or those close to her. The muckraking that could take place in preparation for and during rush could damage reputations far beyond the world of Greek-letter organizations (GLOs), and it was also an important practice through which sorority women could gain information to help maintain their specific membership criteria through discrimination against certain rushees. Sorority women of discriminating taste would find rush the simplest way to safeguard against prospective members who were "not like them" or "could not be considered family."

Whether selecting women by socioeconomic class, religion, race, or perceived beauty, rush was always a discriminatory practice. It also provided a way for sororities to vet women before bringing them into their conservative network. As in the southern aesthetic, an individual's background was of utmost importance. The systematized transmittance of information about rushees gave sorority women knowledge of whether prospective members would easily assimilate into the organizations' training or whether they might be good candidates to educate and incorporate into the conservative mindset.

Rushing had evolved over the years since the establishment of the first sororities. In the late nineteenth century, when newly coeducational campuses had few female students, each sorority chapter on a campus would seek out specific women to "rush." Sorority rush was less formalized; sorority chapters simply approached the new women on campus whom they viewed as desirable for membership. The term "rush" came from the actual activity of sorority women (as well as fraternity men) rushing to the train station at the start of the semester to meet the new students who were prospective Greek material. Each chapter wanted to beat out its rivals to be the first to make a good impression on the freshmen. Sorority chapters often slandered competing chapters on campus in their efforts to influence a woman to pledge their own group.[2] Hopes of controlling these "dirty" rush tactics and the bad publicity that could result were in large part what led to the creation of the National Panhellenic Conference (NPC) in 1902.[3] Still, rush remained difficult to legislate, and over the years, individual chapters continued to conduct rush in their own ways.[4] The length of rush and the number and types of parties varied from campus to campus, but rush typically ran for a period of one to two weeks at the beginning of each school year. The NPC had approved a "short early rush period" at their 1926 meeting and continued to reaffirm that choice at subsequent conferences.[5] With increasing numbers of sorority chapters competing for members, alumnae believed that enforcing some rules of engagement would make the process less contentious. The NPC sought to end the "dirty" maneuvering by adopting "open rushing," where all chapters on a campus would have the opportunity to tell new girls about their organization without any group speaking ill of another.[6] By creating an organized system of rush parties where all women interested in pledging a sorority had a chance to visit each of the national chapters on campus before making a decision, sororities believed that they would level the playing field for all groups. In cooperation with individual College Panhellenics (the local governing group of student sorority members on each campus), the nationals also began to implement a quota-limitation system on many campuses. This meant that each sorority could give bids to a set number of women based on the chapter's size and the overall number of rushees, which would help build up weaker sororities on a campus while keeping the popular groups from taking in a disproportionate number of rushees.[7]

The NPC's ideal rush system, starting with the open house round, was supposed to be more democratic, giving all women the chance to visit each sorority rather than limiting themselves, or being limited by the sisters' invitations, to only a few houses. With scientific precision, the College Panhellenic was supposed to engineer the matching of choices by rushees and sororities. Yet even when all women were allowed to go out for rush, the sororities were not required to pledge everyone. Even deans who were sorority alumnae were not always pleased. University of North Carolina dean of women and Alpha Chi Omega (AXΩ) alumna Katherine Carmichael expressed her dislike of "open rush," noting that she had "always been in disagreement with the general philosophy that a girl should 'sign up for rushing,' [or] 'go out for rushing.'" Instead, she felt that "a social woman's fraternity should seek out a girl, and that a girl should not have to seek out a fraternity." Carmichael believed that it was less painful for women to receive no rush invitations at all than for them to publicly express their desire to join a sorority only to be turned down. While she acknowledged that the open rushing system was a more "democratic [procedure]," she thought that once women had their hopes up, it was easier for them to be hurt.[8]

By the 1920s the unwritten requirement that rushees receive written recommendations from alumnae further tightened the selection process.[9] As more women from a variety of socioeconomic backgrounds attended college, the vetting system of rush enabled sororities to maintain their proclaimed "high standards" in membership. The recommendation system played a crucial role in background checks and made it much more difficult for an unknown woman to show up on campus and join a sorority. Both active and alumnae members took part in this system of recommending new girls to their sorority. The practice of recommending certain rushees, as well as passing along unfavorable reports on others, demonstrated the significant role played by alumnae in the continuing function of their sororities.

For alumnae, reading about the chapter's yearly rush successes constituted a reminder of the sorority's popularity, and by extension their own, while ensuring that the chapter was continuing to flourish at their alma mater. Sorority chapters sent in chapter reports with painstakingly detailed accounts of rush party themes and decorations, outfits worn by the sisters to each party, and names and hometowns of new pledges. Printed in the sorority journals, the reports would pique alumnae interest and pride. With well-heeled alumnae serving as important sources of financing and providers of wares for the sorority house or chapter room, it was vital to keep these women abreast of the chapter's latest rush triumphs, which suggested that their donations were going to good use. All members, actives and alumnae, were equally invested in the work of improving their chapter's image through rush successes.

Parties to Impress and Assess

Rush was a supreme performance of superficial, southern, ladylike hospitality and appeal (see fig. 9). The start of fall semester brought excitement and stress to sorority women and those who hoped to join their ranks. Rushees entered the rush period understanding that the course of the following weeks could alter the trajectory of their college experience. Sorority women knew that the image of their chapter relied on the physical appearance of the women that pledged their group. Rush parties were highly choreographed events in which both the sisters and the rushees were on display. The activities in these spaces taught women to judge and criticize one another based on superficial characteristics. Even the seemingly harmless polite introductions and small talk provided cues to a woman's level of "acceptability" as a sister.

Sorority chapters spared no expense when organizing rush events. The house (or chapter room) decorations, parties, and skits needed to impress the rushees and make a sorority stand out among a sea of similar groups, which rushees would only meet momentarily. A 1939 report of the NPC Committee for Study of Rushing revealed that chapters spent on average from $50 to $200 (roughly $945 to $3,700 in 2019) preparing for rush.[10] Years of rush-inspired competition had pushed sororities toward ever more elaborate parties in increasingly ostentatious houses by the 1930s. While the Depression somewhat dampened the enthusiasm for spending, the national organizations continued to send mixed messages as they constructed and decorated new chapter

MAHOUT GOES TO 1956
SORORITY RUSH

Photo by Little Woods
The Mahout catches the Phi Mu show boat to sorority rush. The old south never looked better.

FIGURE 9. The University of Alabama student humor magazine, the *Mahout*,
caught a glimpse of 1956 rush and the "Phi Mu Showboat." Small Confederate
battle flags were rooted by the entrance to the mock gangplank, where white
sorority women stood guard. Ironically, the plot of the musical *Show Boat*
(1936) dealt with difficult themes of racial "passing" and miscegenation.
Courtesy of the W. S. Hoole Special Collections Library, the University of Alabama.

houses and stressed the finer points of hostessing without so much as an acknowledgment of the financial difficulties faced by many Americans.

For aspiring sorority women, their education in acceptable behavior began
even as they prepared for rush. To succeed, rushees needed to be attuned to
the kinds of behaviors, attitudes, and appearances exhibited by sorority members and be working to emulate these practices. College Panhellenic councils often provided incoming students with booklets telling them what to expect during sorority rush and answering the all-important question of "what
to wear?" The Eta chapter of Alpha Delta Pi (AΔΠ) at the University of Alabama suggested appropriate wardrobe choices for each round of rush parties

in 1961. While "a cool summer dress with a comfortable pair of flats" was suitable for the first day of rush, the final night's parties required the women to wear a "fancy cocktail dress."[11] Women who lacked knowledge of or failed to follow the wardrobe rules for each event would surely be criticized by the sisters in the postparty discussions.

Likewise, the sisters also followed definite rules of engagement during rush. The chapters' control of members' behavior and appearance during this period of first impressions was crucial to the image that a chapter wished to present to potential new members. Specific rush rules about what to wear, how to sit and stand, how to serve refreshments to guests, and how to create seemingly natural conversation with strangers were all extensions of the social education that sororities conveyed to their members throughout the year. The groups hoped that these requirements for behavior would become second nature to members and would exemplify for rushees the type of personality that sororities desired in pledges. Through their demonstration of the "correct" behaviors, sororities trained rushees, some of whom would be their future pledges, to perform these same actions. Successful rushees would normalize and internalize the behaviors that sororities deemed acceptable and would come to value and highlight these same qualities in themselves, as well as expect them of others.

Rushees and sorority sisters saw only glimpses of one another during the hurried and highly choreographed parties and teas. These brief meetings were not conducive to making well-reasoned decisions about others' personalities or qualities desirable for deep and lasting friendships. Unless a woman was joining a sorority chapter whose members included a relative or close friend from home, she was making a decision that rested on a surface assessment of the sorority as a whole. The sorority sisters chose their pledges based on a combination of superficial appearances and alumnae recommendations, while the rushees picked sororities based on friends' and relatives' comments, the rumored popularity of the group on campus, and the physical and stylistic appearance of the sisters. This is why such detailed directives on proper self-grooming and what to wear appeared for women on both sides of rush. Appearing in the correct outfit dictated by rush conventions, and by literal prescriptions on the sorority side, signaled that a woman was willing to convey the image of the sorority and, perhaps more importantly, could afford to purchase the latest styles of clothing. A 1944 article in the *Aglaia* suggested that Phi Mu (ΦM) women were not "worth their while" if they were not attending to their looks.[12] That same year, the Phi Mus at the Woman's College of Duke University directed that sisters visit the prospective rushees they had contacted over the summer "as soon as possible" so that they could "eliminate goons" from their rush list.[13] Rushees who were conventionally unattractive or whose appearance evinced a lack of effort would be objectionable to most chapters.

At William and Mary in November 1942 Kappa Delta (KΔ) member Margetta Hirsch recorded the year's rush activities in her diary. Hirsch's rendering provides an insider's view of rush from the perspective of a sorority sister. Based on her comments, it seemed that William and Mary did not yet follow all of the NPC's preferred methods for "open rush." The college held rush late in the fall semester, rather than at the start of the year, as the NPC recommended. The chapters also appeared to target specific women to invite to the rush events, rather than holding an open house round at the start of the rush period, where all interested rushees had the ability to visit every sorority. Hirsch and two of her KΔ sisters had "rushed the town girls in Rexall's [drugstore]." The sisters invited eight of the nine girls from Rexall's to the KΔ house for the evening, after which they held a "scratch meeting" to cut those rushees they no longer wanted to entertain as possible pledges. Two more days of rushing that included playing games and singing, as well as more scratching of rushees, led up to the theme parties on Sunday and Monday. On the sixth day of rush, Hirsch noted that the KΔs were up until 2:00 a.m. decorating the house. By the seventh day, she still said that rush "was lots of fun," but this time she added that she "[couldn't] take much more of it."[14]

After each round of parties, the sororities would hold meetings to decide which women to invite back and which women they wished to cut from their invitation list. The rushees also chose which sororities they did not want to visit again as well as the ones from which they wished to continue to accept party invites, in the hopes that they would receive a bid, or an invitation, to pledge the group that they had most liked. Problems arose when the sororities' choices of whom to invite back for the next round and the rushees' choices of which sororities they wanted to pledge did not match up. While hurt feelings were possible on both sides, the process left rushees most vulnerable to outright rejection from groups, which was often made worse by the fact that members had erected a facade of friendliness during rush. Both sorority sisters and rushees, who might present themselves as polite when face to face, were eager to gossip about the other women when out of earshot.

An April 1945 article by Mrs. Glenn Frank, Pi Beta Phi (ΠΒΦ) alumna, in the mass monthly *Woman's Home Companion* urged the abolition of GLOs. As a graduate of the University of Missouri and the widow of the former president of the University of Wisconsin, she spoke with the experience of both a sorority member and a contemporary campus insider when she described the hurt of students not selected for membership. She criticized her fellow Americans for allowing such a system to "flourish in our public schools" and was distressed that parents had become more concerned that their daughters gain membership in top sororities than get a good education.[15] Another exposé, "College Sororities: They Pose a Social Problem," followed in *LIFE* magazine in December 1945. The article charted the experience of one rushee, "Shirley Smith," who was accepted as a sorority member at the end of the seventeen-day-long rush process at the University of Colorado (CU). But the article also purported to show the supposed "dark side" of the sorority system as it exclaimed, "The Chosen Are Happy, the Rest Are Crushed." The article focused on the fact that 259 of 802 total women at CU would join sororities, but it was unclear from their telling how many of the 802 went out for rush in the first place.[16] If a woman's favored sorority did not ask her back to the next round of parties or withheld their bid for pledgeship at the end of rush, she would either have to accept the bid of another group that sought to pledge her or forego joining a sorority that year—or at all. Even when the scientific process of rush appeared successful and nearly all women were pledged, it did not mean that everyone was happy.

The Trouble with Duke:
The Sorority System Debate

In fall of 1945, a number of Duke women voiced their dissatisfaction with sororities and the tendency of the groups to hurt women's feelings during rush. The administration of the Woman's College sought to allow a healthy discussion of the issues among students with the hope of bringing the campus sorority system more in line with what the majority of students desired.[17] At the college's open discussion on sororities, women debated sororities' positive and negative effects on the student body and whether the removal of sororities from campus would remedy these problems. Both sorority and independent women spoke out on each side of the issue. Many of the concerns expressed by those speaking against sororities related to women's emotional distress resulting from rush outcomes. A Delta Delta Delta ($\Delta\Delta\Delta$ or Tri-Delta) from Suffolk, Virginia, noted that she had seen women arrive at Duke "thinking that they could and would be accepted [by a sorority]," but when they were not, they "were hurt for years to come." With more and more women enrolling at Duke, the Tri-Delta believed that it was "wise to eliminate a system that . . . hurt so many girls." "We have had fifteen years [since the establishment of the Woman's College] to reach the high ideal which each sorority has sought to gain," she explained. "Each one 'strives' for character, but still it takes only those who have looks or money, with few exceptions." The reinforcement of socioeconomic status and physical attractiveness as the measures of a woman's popularity and ability to succeed in the campus community, she argued, led to the emotional stress and even social maladjustment of many female students.[18] A former KΔ from Salisbury, North Carolina, explained that the "whole question" about sororities at the college "started out from the point of view of personal hurt.... I looked around my freshman group and saw girls that would never be members of sororities, and then I asked myself why. They were ordinary girls and eager to enter into the college life." She hoped to make the campus more inclusive by removing the social divisions created by sororities. "If one more freshman on my hall feels better by my taking off my pin—if she will realize that being just a 'good 'ol girl' is all that is required to make friends, I shall feel much better." She believed that sororities had good ideals, but she doubted that the sorority women lived up to those ideals in their meetings. Also speaking against sororities was a member of the Jewish sorority Alpha Epsilon Phi (ΑΕΦ) from Jersey City, New Jersey, who felt that "sororities [diverted] interest away from other campus activities that would be more beneficial." Unlike other organizations on campus that were "interested in something bigger than the campus itself" and helped students "to be conscious of world events," she argued that sororities kept them "too wrapped up in college activities" and "[narrowed their] view even more." Other speakers maintained that women could make friends and have an active social life on campus without being a member of a sorority. "I have not been in a sorority," stated a female student from Cincinnati, Ohio. "You can get along without them and you can have just as much fun."[19]

Alumnae advisers and national leaders of sororities at Duke found the antifraternity action on campus disconcerting. On October 9, 1945, following a scramble for information among the ΑΔΠ alumnae network, Grand President Caralee Stanard penned a letter to members of the sorority's Grand Council detailing the situation at Duke. She had contacted the nationals of other sororities and had heard that campus chapter advisers were asking local alumnae groups to assist in quelling the uprising. Kappa Kappa Gamma (KKΓ) planned to send an officer to campus to assess the situation, and they advised ΑΔΠ to do likewise. Stanard explained that she had heard from an alumna who currently worked on campus that "an Alpha Delta Pi had been one of the most convincing antifraternity speakers and had aired her views in a general campus meeting." That one of their own "sisters" was portraying the organization in a negative light represented a failure of the sorority to educate members about proper behavior and conformity to group norms. When the Duke alumna reporting to Stanard noted that the "arguments presented for sororities at the meeting had been very weak," Stanard responded that "evidently none of the girls had been coached by experts" before the meeting on how to respond to critics.[20] Like other national officers, Stanard recognized that the lack of communication between alumnae and actives could prove disastrous to the future of sororities. In instances where chapters or entire campuses sought to overhaul the sorority system, national leaders would find it necessary to step in to reindoctrinate the college members who were straying from the path.

Although sororities' national officers believed that providing appropriate "guidance" to the chapters at Duke would bring an end to sorority women's agitation against the groups on campus, the issue cropped up year after year. In 1951 the antisorority feeling reached a "fever pitch," and the Panhellenic president "had gotten so upset" that she called the NPC. Mary Grace Wilson, dean of students at the Woman's College, worked with the Order of the White Duchy, a women's honorary society on campus, to quell the unrest at that time.[21] They established a Sorority Evaluation Committee to administer a questionnaire designed to determine the perceived benefits and detriments of sororities on campus. A total of 769 women returned the survey. Of those, 511 were sorority members and 258 were independents. Among the respondents, 45 percent were in favor of "improving sororities," while 23 percent favored the current system; 17 percent wanted "complete abolition" and 15 percent were for "gradual de-emphasis." Some of the suggestions from respondents on how to change the current system included delaying rushing, holding sophomore rushing, eliminating pledging and abolishing sororities painlessly, giving sororities more responsible work, organizing independents, and ensuring the campus had enough sororities so that everyone wishing to join would have the opportunity.[22] However, the report of the Sorority Evaluation Committee only gave the Panhellenic Council and college administration suggestions on how to improve the acceptance of sororities at Duke, which sounded much like the ones that college women repeatedly voiced when criticizing sororities. They failed to fully explain how the campus and the sororities would *enact* alternative methods. Changes to the scheduling of rush or the elimination of a pledge quota would not find favor with the NPC and national sorority leaders who seemed to believe that they had been perfecting the rush process for the past half century. In reality, the desires of women on a handful of campuses were not going to cause the nationals to overhaul their rush systems.

Administrators' Concerns about Rush

Some deans at southern universities expressed more serious misgivings about the groups. Deans were often wary of campus divisions between sorority and independent women. They also disliked the possible adverse effects of the often insensitive rush system on first-year female students. Arney Robinson Childs, dean of women (1935–57) and professor of history at the University of South Carolina, felt that the sorority system on her campus led to a number of troubles.[23] She referred to rush as an attendant "evil" of the system.[24] At the university, Childs continually dealt with the issue of a "top-heavy" sorority system where three of the sororities dominated the campus. The smaller sororities "steadily" decreased in size as the "choice" groups "practically [divided] the desirable material among [themselves]."[25]

Childs advocated for the quota system at South Carolina to help newer chapters gain a foothold on campus. Even with quotas, however, it was often an uphill climb for less established sorority chapters. With minor effort, all incoming students could ascertain the popular groups on campus, but the cream of the incoming rush crop were primed by friends, family, and alumnae to know the "choice" campus sororities. So the "top" rushee picks would know to express interest in the popular chapters and vice versa, thus leaving the "less desirable material" to take a spot in one of the struggling upstart groups. If a campus followed the quota-limitation system and continued to welcome a healthy number of women interested in Greek life, over time the former "upstart" chapter could build status, but it could take years for such change to occur.

Childs was aware of the displeasure of women who were left out of sorority membership and of small sorority chapters that were driven off of campus by the competition. Yet her description of certain students at the university as "desirable material" suggested that Childs herself viewed some of the women as unsuited for membership in a self-proclaimed elite, heterosocially popular club. The smaller groups, Childs explained, were often left with pledges who "for scholastic or financial reasons would probably never be initiated."[26] Though not a sorority alumna herself, Childs appeared to have adopted the sororities' belief that some women were not fit for sorority membership and not just by their own choosing. Additionally, the sororities' regular use of the term "material" to describe possible new members set a dangerous precedent, teaching members to view rushees as physical objects to be acquired for the benefit of the group.

Private student groups at public universities such as the University of South Carolina presented another conundrum for administrators. At UNC, Dean

Carmichael acknowledged that even "with all [of] their good points," sororities "illustrate a fundamental conflict" in that they were "pseudo-aristocratic
[bodies] superimposed on a democratic campus."[27] She believed that sororities
stratified students by financial status and popularity, and she was troubled by
their influence on public and supposedly democratic university campuses. The
pecking order that sororities and fraternities helped establish on both public and private campuses resulted in a class-conscious environment, separat-
ing the "haves" from the "have nots." Despite her trepidation, however, she was
against doing away with the sorority system at UNC.[28] Her belief in sorority
social education as a way to teach young women "proper" behaviors and "morals" seemed to have outweighed her concerns about the socioeconomic class
divisions often caused by GLOs.

A primary concern of administrators and sorority advisory committees was
the "exhaustive and time-consuming" schedule of rush. As Margetta Hirsch's
diary entries revealed, rush involved a whirlwind of activity and often became
overwhelming for both sisters and rushees. The late-night decorating, the
repetitive practicing of skits and songs, the tense meetings to decide which
rushees to ask back to the next party, and the constant need to be looking and
acting their best could quickly wear on the sisters. Needless to say, the commitment to rush left little time for other activities, let alone schoolwork. Particularly for freshman rushees, the trend toward socializing at the expense of
studying could create a confusing environment. New students would learn that
parties and schoolwork were both integral parts of the collegiate culture, but
striking a balance between the two could be tough when social events seemed
all-encompassing. By the time the excitement (or anguish) of rush was over, a
first-year student might find herself impossibly behind in her coursework. At
the meetings of the UNC Sorority Advisory Committee, Anne Queen, director of the Campus Y, "expressed a vital concern over the conflict between en-
ergy and time expended on rush, during classes, and the temporary relinquish-
ing of responsibility to academic life during [the] period." Yet the committee's
only response seemed to be congratulating the groups that had shortened their
postparty discussions.[29] At Duke, the Panhellenic Council attempted to improve matters of scheduling by moving to a deferred rush system in 1947. That
meant that the four-day rush program would take place during the third week
of spring semester rather than the start of the fall. The plan seemed beneficial. By pushing rush back, the freshmen would have an entire semester to adjust to "the total campus before entering into group affiliation." This also allowed women to learn more about the different chapters and get to know the
groups' members outside of the artificial rush environment. Of course, delay-

ing rush could work against some chapters if their members displayed unattractive character traits over the course of the fall semester. To the sororities' benefit, they would have access to rushees' first-semester grades when making decisions about membership. Women who had completed a minimum of twelve semester hours and maintained a 2.0 grade point average during the fall would be eligible to participate in rush.[30]

An analysis of the system following two years of deferred rushing suggested that the benefits were not as great as they had first appeared. Rather than more easily adjusting to life on campus, the prospective rushees waited for rush to occur before "[settling] into the year's activity." The "attitude of suspended excitement and the hovering expectancy" during the entire fall semester put women into a precarious position as they tried to adjust to college life. Moreover, the report argued that once women had an entire semester to learn about the sororities and get to know their members, they would suffer greater disappointment if they did not get a bid from their group of choice. The study also noted that a disappointed rushee's emotional injury was more publicly visible in the deferred system; after a semester, it would have become evident which group a prospective pledge preferred. While many women apparently arrived at Duke without an idea of which sorority they would like to join, the deferred rush system allowed time for favorites to develop and for rumors to be spread. With this process, "there [was] an inevitable perpetuation of the groups long established on the campus resulting from their accrued prestige."[31]

Choosing New "Material"

Rush increasingly caused headaches for deans at southern universities as sorority chapters on their campuses reached their second and third generations of rushees. Chapters often guaranteed pledge slots to daughters and other female relatives of the chapters' alumnae, known as legacies. Alumnae networks returned the required recommendation blanks, reporting diligently on the desirability of incoming students as new "material." This ensured that the selection process was increasingly mediated by a woman's family connections, making it more difficult for the lower middle-class or socially up-and-coming women to break into the ranks. The Chi Omega rush policies for 1952 listed the "standards emphasized in choosing members." Background counted 35 percent; scholarship and reputation, 20 percent each; appearance and personality, 10 percent each; and physique, 5 percent.[32] The breakdown clearly showed that "who you knew" played a major role in the sorority's decisions. Also, a full 35 percent of each decision came down to a rushee's superficial characteristics.

With little time for the sorority to really get to know the rushees as individual women, sorority members' discussion about prospective members had the potential to become highly critical and quite mean-spirited.

Recommendation blanks allowed for detailed reports on incoming rushees. Beyond ascertaining the prospective's name and address, Tri-Delta's two-page form from 1939 quickly moved into questions about her father's occupation, her parents' college and fraternity affiliations, their "church preference" (signaling they sought Protestants), and the ability of the family to "meet college or fraternity financial obligations." The sorority wished to know if the "girl's environment has been as such to promote high ideals and refinement," again showing that the groups had no intention of offering social lessons to women who were not already imbued with social abilities, and that a woman's family situation could prove detail enough for the sorority to classify her character, sight unseen. The second page assisted with physical appearance, whether "attractive or unattractive," and her social manner: "diffident, congenial, or impressive."[33]

During discussion of rushee evaluations at the inaugural meeting of UNC's Advisory Committee on Sororities, which included faculty women and staff and local sorority alumnae, the president of the student Panhellenic stated that "chapters tried not to have unpleasant facts brought out about a girl, lest [her] reputation be damaged."[34] Yet the recommendation blanks specifically requested such material be brought to the attention of the rush chairperson. This meant that the sorority women had to find a way to present their opinions about rushees—as negative as they might be—without straying into scandalous territory that would mar a woman for her entire college career. On one hand, if only one or two sisters had a significant issue with a rushee, she still might be given a bid by their sorority—particularly if the rushee was a legacy or came from a powerful family in the region. If the woman in question then pledged the sorority, members would have to pretend that they had not heard other sisters disparaging the woman behind her back during rush. On the other hand, if the rushee was cut during rush and the sisters' scratch-session discussions about her moved beyond the walls of the sorority house, the damaging rumors could be spread to students on campus, both Greek-letter and independent. The committee members "suggested that the chapters investigate their present systems of evaluating girls, with a view toward making discussion in chapter meetings more objective," and they seemed to believe that the actives were capable of instituting these changes themselves.[35] The committee's apparent unwillingness to press the Panhellenic president about the situation may have stemmed from the fact that the sorority alumnae resorted to similar tactics themselves.

FIGURE 10. Guion Johnson (far right), Chi Omega Epsilon Beta chapter
adviser and a member of the Committee on Special Sorority Problems with
UNC chancellor R. B. House and students (left to right) Judy King (ΔΔΔ)
and Catherine Pharr (ΧΩ pledge) in the *Daily Tar Heel*, October 1, 1953.
*Courtesy Southern Historical Collection, Wilson Library, the University
of North Carolina at Chapel Hill, Guion Griffis Johnson Papers.*

Alumnae dutifully wrote to national officers and chapter advisers explaining why a chapter should or should *not* pledge specific rushees. Correspondence between Dr. Guion Griffis Johnson, a Chi Omega (ΧΩ) traveling secretary in the early 1950s and an adviser for the Epsilon Beta chapter at UNC, and
other alumnae illustrates the types of conversations traded by these women as
they sought to limit ΧΩ membership to those who met their exacting social
standards (see fig. 10). Johnson was a primary recipient of rush recommendations, many coming in the form of personal notes or letters from friends or acquaintances throughout the state. The confidential letters between alumnae
show the harsh reality of gossip and malicious words bandied about as a routine part of rush. It is unclear how Johnson felt about her part in this practice.
Typically she was on the receiving end of correspondence from a concerned
alumna, but she did not hesitate to pass information along to ΧΩ's national

leaders, Mary Love Collins and Elizabeth Dyer, and include some of her own opinions.[36]

Johnson was a noted historian who worked alongside her sociologist husband, Dr. Guy Benton Johnson, a professor at UNC.[37] She had joined XΩ while at the University of Missouri, yet it was not until the early 1950s that she took an active role in the sorority's local and national alumnae network. During this same period, UNC trustees and administrators had become highly critical of Guy Johnson, whose controversial research on African American culture in the South had led to his involvement in racial justice issues. Guion Johnson's increased civic work and activities with XΩ may have been designed to mediate the tension from her husband's work.[38] A strong affiliation with an NPC sorority—most of which, at this time, were espousing shrill warnings against communism and formulating plans to maintain whites-only membership policies—would help ease southern criticism that the Johnsons were too friendly with radical elements.

Chapters relied heavily on information from alumnae located in the communities where prospective members resided. The subjective nature of their comments, however, shows how the rush process could easily devolve into a muckraking exercise before the college sorority members ever met the rushees. Late summer was a busy time for sorority alumnae as they filled out recommendations for the upcoming fall rush season. One of Guion Johnson's close friends and a XΩ alumna, "Pinky," sent a hurried letter with a list of subjective observations about Sally Thompson,[39] a prospective rushee from Salisbury, North Carolina. Pinky had already turned in an official recommendation form for Thompson, but as an added measure, she wanted to include a "personal note" to Johnson with details that she may have felt were inappropriate for the official record. "Thompson's parents," she wrote, "are new-rich . . . like to make a splash . . . but not the type to endow Chi Omega." Pinky continued, "Her mother is very pretty and a charming personality . . . [and] belongs to a family that has risen in the world considerably in the last generation." While finances were important in securing a sorority bid, the family's history and when and where they came into their wealth was even more significant. Pinky's words cautioned that the family was not an established member of the state's elite. Painting the mother as of questionable background immediately tainted the daughter as well, though Pinky's description of Sally herself was even more damning. "I understand that Sally has blossomed," Pinky wrote. "She was an original little girl but very homely. She did well at Stephens [College], but is not too good a student, according to the information I have received." Although Pinky's informants suggested that Sally had come into her own, Pinky made sure to remind Johnson that Sally *had* been unattractive and still was not an outstanding scholar. In her estimation, Sally would not add much to the Epsilon Beta chapter. While the social education and improvement of their members was a goal of sororities, there were obvious limits to the women the groups would deign to "pick up" and refine. Ironically, at a time when many families had moved up the social ladder by relocating from rural areas to larger towns and through achievement of a college education, these Chi Omega alumnae (and their counterparts in other national sororities) sought to separate themselves from families that were, perhaps, one generation behind their own in the quest for upper-middle-class status.

In spring of 1951 Johnson reported being invited to attend a chapter meeting where Epsilon Beta discussed a girl who had not received a bid from the chapter the previous fall. Johnson believed that she had been purposely invited to the meeting by the chapter president, who was a very close friend of the girl, so as to give "support to the candidacy for membership." She was able to tell the members that the girl in question was "from a good family in the state and should make a desirable member as far as scholarship and personal adjustment to the group [were] concerned." Following the discussion, four girls from Goldsboro, North Carolina, who had pledged the chapter in the fall "also presented the name of one of their life-long friends" who, like the president's friend, had not received a bid. As Johnson explained to Mary Love Collins, the woman was "the only one of six attractive girls of excellent families from Goldsboro who had not been pledged." Never failing to insert status and tradition into the background of favored rushees, Johnson described Goldsboro as "an old and aristocratic town in Eastern Carolina." The girls' parents were major players in the state, and some of the fathers were university trustees. She claimed that the men were so upset by the snub that they were "threatening to try to outlaw fraternities." Johnson recalled a party at the Goldsboro Country Club she had attended several months earlier where the parents "could talk of nothing else." Their conversation, she reported, "centered about 'the evils of a system which would permit a beautiful and gifted girl to be so cruelly hurt.'"

Johnson stated that she was "never able to determine just why [the] two girls were not pledged in the fall," but after the meeting she heard from one of the opponents of the Goldsboro woman who said, "I have never seen her do anything unladylike but she sometimes looks to me as if she would like to." Johnson was careful to preface the opponent's statement with the aside that she was "a girl who [did] not often have dates."[40] By portraying the opposing member as a poorly adjusted and perhaps jealous woman, Johnson seemed willing to overlook the comment (admittedly, also subjective) about the Goldsboro woman's potential propensity toward some sort of "unladylike" behavior. The larger point of this particular membership vote was to safeguard the sorority against critics and not to appease the whim of one sister. The outcome of the meeting pleased Collins. She wrote to Johnson that "the chapter was quite wise it seems to me in deciding to ask the Goldsboro student. I am glad you were present at the meeting."[41] In a time when GLOs faced criticism about their membership policies, Chi Omega did not need an obvious scandal to its name. Just as important as keeping the "wrong" people out was allowing the "right" people *in* to the organization.

Later in summer 1951, Johnson received another letter from Collins, who reported a recent letter from a young woman named Alice Miller in Wilmington, North Carolina, expressing great interest in XΩ. Miller was "very much interested ... and would like to belong to [the sorority]" when she entered college. She wanted to know about the "qualifications" for membership and "how she should go about planning to be pledged." Collins seemed suspicious of Miller's overture and had not yet responded. Before making a reply, she hoped that Johnson could write to any Epsilon Beta alums in Wilmington to gain information about the girl. "In this day and age," Collins confided, "one never knows what individuals may really have in mind."[42] Collins was a staunch conservative who encouraged XΩ and other national sororities to pursue a vehemently reactionary ideology in the name of anticommunism. Evidently she saw the letter not as a legitimate request for information from a conscientious high school student but instead as an attempt to discern the membership policies of the private and secretive social organization. Collins regularly advocated vigilance in her crusades against communist infiltration, urging sorority alumnae to trust no one. Johnson responded to Collins, saying that the letter from Wilmington "amaze[d]" her and that she was "starting inquiry concerning [the young woman]." Again networking across the state, Johnson spoke with the athletic director of the New Hanover High School at a party, and he confirmed that he knew the Millers and that they were "very fine people." Still, Johnson explained to Collins that she was writing to one of the recent Epsilon Beta members from Wilmington "for a further check on the name, address, family, etcetera."[43] The background of a woman and her family must be double-checked prior to rush in order to ensure that a sorority chapter did not inadvertently pledge an undesirable or disreputable woman or, by the 1950s, a possible political radical who might subvert the organization once she was a sister.

Unlike fraternities, where men were judged on their individual character and personality, or on the standing of the chapter's university, sororities sought firmly to establish the unimpeachable reputation of prospective sisters prior to rush.[44] Whereas men's reputations were largely made by their heterosexual conquests, women's reputations were upheld by their lack of sexual experience coupled with a sexually desirable appearance and family background that supported the ladylike image she promised to provide to the sorority chapter.

"Desirable" Members and Rush Success: Alpha Gamma Delta at UNC

Sororities continued to engage in these types of conversations about rushees because of the power of prospective members to positively or negatively affect the sorority's appearance and performance during rush in future years. Presenting women who met (or exceeded) white middle-class standards of physical beauty would attract attention and admiration from fraternities, solidifying a chapter's desirability among men and women. Along with greater emphasis on heterosocializing, sororities' focus on members' physical beauty also increased. To continue to gain "attractive" pledges that would ensure the chapter's campus popularity, the chapter always needed to have desirable sisters on display. If a sorority began to have difficulties attracting desirable members during rush—or if it was a newer chapter on campus that never got its footing—the problem often compounded each year, making it increasingly unlikely each successive season that the "hot" rushees would want to join their group.[45]

The case of the Gamma Epsilon chapter of Alpha Gamma Delta (ΑΓΔ) at UNC offers a prime example of the difficulty in building up a new chapter when campus fraternity men were not supportive. Established in 1945 as UNC's fifth national sorority, the Gamma Epsilon chapter struggled for years, appearing to suffer a poor reputation among a majority of the student body.[46] In fall 1963 members of UNC's Advisory Committee on Special Sorority Problems discussed ΑΓΔ and its small pledge class. The sorority "expressed a deep concern over the number of rushees dropping out of their rush parties . . . for no apparent reason other than derogatory rumors and stories being spread among the student population." The sorority wanted to ensure that all other members of UNC's College Panhellenic were dedicated to the flourishing of every sorority chapter on campus. A letter written by Alpha Gamma Delta grand president Mary McDuffie to the president of the UNC Panhellenic "acknowledged knowing of alleged rumors, i.e., that the ΑΓΔ house would close because of its diminishing size, etc. and the need for the Panhellenic to support their house as a part of the Carolina fraternity system."[47] While it is unknown what the grand president meant to imply with her use of "etcetera," it is likely that she referred to the diminishing "quality" or physical attractiveness of the sorority's members. Derogatory comments about the appearance or the heterosexual dateability of a sorority's members could be highly damaging for a group's reputation on campus. The committee endorsed the letter from AΓΔ and "[urged] Panhellenic and all sorority women to maintain the viability of all campus chapters."[48] For the Advisory Committee to issue such a reminder to the College Panhellenic suggests that relations between some sorority chapters on campus were probably less than friendly. The "honest rivalry" noted by Dean Stacy in 1924 and "healthy competition" observed by Dean Carmichael in 1955 seemed to have been more spiteful than the administrators realized, as some sorority women gossiped about members of other groups.[49] Seemingly, the Alpha Gamma Deltas bore the brunt of this heckling.

If the other sororities were condescending, then AΓΔ needed to bring in the big guns—the fraternity men. Clearly demonstrating that fraternity approval was the key to a sorority chapter's rating on campus, the Advisory Committee "suggested that the support of the IFC [Inter-Fraternity Council] be enlisted" to help bolster the reputation of the Alpha Gamma Delta house.[50] The women of the Advisory Committee were admitting that a sorority's popularity among fraternity men was imperative to its success on campus. To get the IFC to "support" the efforts to strengthen the reputation of the Gamma Epsilon chapter would mean that the fraternities would have to agree to have mixers with the sorority. By showing that they would accept the sorority, UNC fraternities had the power to rebuild the chapter's image among the student body. But with the "Alpha Gams" already branded as undesirable, they would be hard-pressed to get fraternity mixer invitations. Even a lower "rated" fraternity on campus would wish to avoid the stigma of associating with a sorority that had the ignominious distinction of being the butt of campus jokes. Apparently some students referred to the Alpha Gamma Deltas by the nickname "the Gamma ghouls," deriding the group's status with an obvious dig at members' physical appearances.[51] The Advisory Committee failed to discuss the probable difficulty in getting fraternities to lend support to the AΓΔ rehabilitation effort. While it is unclear how, or even if, this plan came to fruition, the fact that Gamma Epsilon withdrew from the UNC campus during the 1965 school year implies that the fraternity men and the other sororities had not been terribly interested in helping save the chapter.[52] Even if the members of other GLOs had stopped their gossiping and made a concerted effort to meet the Alpha Gamma Deltas on an even playing field after the 1963 Advisory Committee meeting, the damage had already been done.

If a chapter was largely excluded from campus heterosocializing because of the physical appearance of its members, it would be very difficult for them to continue to gain new conventionally attractive members who could help build the chapter's reputation. Rush was the most important time of the school year for sororities, when the "look" of the chapter was reinforced by pledging a new group of girls who met the chapter's standards of physical appearance and conservative behavior. But preparations for rush commenced months before the actual event, as alumnae proffered opinions on young women who might appear among the rushees at their sorority in the fall. While the postwar public saw more to dislike about sorority rush and membership selection, the NPC sororities made no attempts to change the overall system or even to address criticisms as valid. Instead, they sought to tighten control over the rush process and produce propaganda that validated their views on the right to privacy in their manner of membership selection.

CHAPTER SIX

•◦•

"To Discriminate Is a Positive Trait"

THE NPC, "FREEDOM OF ASSOCIATION,"
AND THE MODERN CONSERVATIVE MOVEMENT

*I*n May 1946 *LIFE* followed up on its negative account of sorority rush at the University of Colorado with the story of Crystal Malone, the only African American student enrolled at the University of Vermont (UVM) and, for a short time, a member of Upsilon chapter of Alpha Xi Delta (AΞΔ). The magazine described Malone as a light-skinned woman from Washington, D.C., who received "better than average marks" and was "one of the most popular girls on campus." Yet, *LIFE* reported, AΞΔ national leaders were highly offended by Upsilon's actions in pledging Malone. The sorority's nationals placed the chapter on probation after members failed to heed their request that Malone not be pledged to the sorority. Of the situation, AΞΔ's national president, Mrs. Beverly (Winifred) Robinson of Washington, D.C., commented sardonically, "Life is selective, and maybe it's just as well to learn it while we are young." Even so, the Upsilon chapter members stood by Malone, momentously choosing to burn their charter as a show of will.[1]

Even at all-white institutions, sorority rush had always been a discriminatory practice. But with broadening student body demographics and a greater national and international focus on U.S. civil rights issues in the postwar period, sororities faced new questions about their brand of "democracy." National Panhellenic Conference (NPC) sororities reacted to the heightened attention to civil rights in the United States in these years by adopting a conservative platform and outlook that influenced national sororities' subsequent policy decisions and their member education programs. The NPC's hardline

anticommunist and pro-America stance, their insistence on individual freedoms, and their disdain for U.S. federal government intervention in what they
viewed as private matters paralleled the rhetoric of the growing conservative
intellectual movement of the 1950s and 1960s. By the end of World War II,
sororities defended their processes of membership selection with arguments
about "freedom of association," which would become integral to white Americans fighting to maintain racial segregation of public schooling over the following decade. NPC leaders were at the forefront of the burgeoning modern
conservative movement in these years, collaborating with conservative intellectuals and organizations, and sharing these beliefs with sorority members
across the country.

In the 1940s a new wave of antisorority agitators accused the organizations
of antidemocratic practices—a charge that suddenly became more damning
during wartime. Popular media examples, such as Mrs. Glenn Frank's 1945 essay, focused on the hurtful nature of Greek-letter organization (GLO) membership selection, a process that purportedly left those unselected students
feeling worthless and disengaged during college and in their adult lives. With
mass media sources decrying national sororities as antidemocratic, the NPC
determinedly organized a public relations machine among its own members
to present a positive image of the groups and ostensibly defend their position.[2]
Rather than paint a rosy picture of sorority life going into the postwar era,
however, the NPC chose to fashion a "doom and gloom" scenario where sororities, like "the American way of life" so cherished by their members, faced
certain extinction if the country's citizens and national leaders were unable to
understand and refute liberal policies and communist influences. The NPC
ran defense in much of their PR, responding to such "attacks" on their membership practices by invoking their right to "freedom of association," which
they interpreted as a right guaranteed by the U.S. Bill of Rights. In the postwar period, criticisms of rush, which had previously focused on rushees' "hurt
feelings" resulting from social class and religious discrimination, expanded to
include racial discrimination. While the issue came to the fore earlier at nonsouthern colleges where racial segregation had been a social norm rather than
a codified practice, the push for civil rights in the 1950s and 1960s also brought
sorority chapters at southern colleges under scrutiny. Throughout the entire
period, however, the NPC organized a response that was unanimous and un-
yielding among its member groups and presaged the rhetoric of the growing conservative intellectual movement. Like many conservative leaders, the
women of the NPC used their appeals for rights and freedoms to disguise
their interest in maintaining social segregation of the races.[3] Well before Ala-

bama governor George Wallace stood in the schoolhouse door, NPC sorority alumnae figuratively stood in the sorority house doors of the nation to ensure that membership remained white. Both Greek-letter groups and conservatives would find a haven for these beliefs in the South, as massive resistance to federally mandated desegregation propelled many white southerners toward the conservative movement.[4] Leaders of GLOs were concerned that increased social equality of the races in the United States, a change that they saw as the work of communist subversives, would put an end to their private organizations. Portraying their critics as leftists and possible communists or communist sympathizers, the NPC sororities attempted to indoctrinate their members against liberal thought in the guise of anticommunist rhetoric.

The Coming Threat

By the 1910s, many sorority women publicly evinced strong political beliefs, but their sororities would not officially endorse their ideals and platforms on topics such as woman suffrage and social welfare reform. The organizations did not want to alienate portions of their membership by endorsing a certain position, but sororities' quarterly journals generally allowed members a stage from which to voice individual opinions. As with other women's organizations of the period, the veneer of the national organization obscured a membership with varied interests and political leanings.[5] Sorority alumnae of the late nineteenth and early twentieth centuries had often encouraged their sisters to become informed about current events and exercise their privilege as members of the educated, cultured, and "better" class of women in the United States so as to set an example of positive leadership in their communities. Yet the organizations often avoided attaching the label of "politicking" to these activities. Instead, much of their information was cloaked in the rhetoric of maternalism that softened the perceived masculine edge of politics by presenting women's political work as a natural extension of their family caregiving duties.[6]

Sorority journals also provided a way for sorority women to voice support for antiradical causes stemming from fears of the overreach of government into the traditionally understood private space of the home. By the 1920s, many once-devoted progressive women reformers began to turn against the very social welfare programs they had initially supported, out of fears that they were driven by socialist and Bolshevik influences.[7] Many women reformers too had long held a classist and even xenophobic stance. The 1917 Bolshevik revolution in Russia, which alerted Americans to the possibility of communist subversion in the United States and set off a Red Scare across the nation, only exacerbated the fissures among organized women's groups. As Kirsten Delegard notes in her study of the emerging antiradical movement among American women in the 1920s, "the critical factor in determining" affluent women's political direction in this period depended on their response to revolutionary-style unrest in the United States at the end of World War I.[8]

This shift can be traced through the political messages of NPC sororities. In the 1910s and 1920s, some Greek alumni began to suggest that critics of GLOs had ties to Bolshevism and autocratic rule.[9] By positioning their organizations as the vocal opponents of the "isms"—socialism, fascism, and communism—and staunch supporters of democracy and freedom, GLO leaders hit on a trend that they would revisit repeatedly when faced with external criticism. In the leadership's estimation, sorority and fraternity members were the epitome of "true" Americans and the only ones who could keep the nation out of the power grip of those supposedly seeking to overthrow democracy. Among sorority leaders, the turn toward an antiradical ideology reflected the women's fears of losing control of their status-imparting sisterhoods. As women of varying class, ethnic, religious, and racial background might be found attending college in greater numbers, the middle- and upper-class sorority members, who divined themselves sisters or "descendants" of their sororities' supposedly "aristocratic" founders, were distressed at the possible loss of exclusivity of their clubs. While sororities had always been organized around exclusion of certain women based on class, appearance, religion, and race, the exclusivity began to take on specific targets by the 1910s and 1920s. At the fifteenth NPC meeting in 1917, delegates discussed the question of admitting sororities that might be composed primarily of Jewish women to the congress. The harshest words on the matter came from the national president of Chi Omega (XΩ), Mary Love Collins, who stated that "the Jew will never be an American, he has only a technical citizenship." The motion to allow a Jewish organization to join the NPC was lost, and the delegates refused to entertain a motion that it be held over for discussion at another congress.[10]

Publicly active, white, middle- and upper-class female reformers focused their efforts to maintain cultural supremacy through Anglo-American patriotic and heritage organizations.[11] Groups such as the Daughters of the American Revolution (DAR) (1890), the National Society of the Colonial Dames of America (NSCDA) (1891), the Daughters of 1812 (1892), the United Daughters of the Confederacy (UDC) (1894), the American Legion Auxiliary (ALA) (1919), and NPC sororities provided a way for white middle- and upper-class women to define themselves as true "all-American" citizens while othering those who could not meet the organizations' requirements for membership (or were not chosen during sorority rush). Sorority women who felt threatened by individuals who appeared "different" or not "100% American" began to question the background of affiliates and possible members more specifically.

The DAR, a group in which Collins and a significant number of sorority leaders also held membership, actively sought to promote "Americanism" and assimilation of immigrants into American culture as part of their "patriotic" service. Significantly, the DAR was not only concerned with influencing immigrants to assimilate into American culture and share democratic political ideals but also with searching out individuals who might pose a threat to those ideals. Since the Great War, the DAR had been increasing their criticism of pacifists and other female reformers who they believed held connections to socialist and communist plots that posed danger to the United States and its citizens—most importantly, women and their families. Along with the similarly patriotic women's American Legion Auxiliary, the DAR educated its members to be on the alert against suspicious individuals in the name of rooting out radical activity. At the 1925 annual DAR convention, members voted to establish a National Defense Committee, which was integral in the development of women's antiradicalism. The committee actively researched subversive propaganda and reported their findings in a monthly column of the *Daughters of the American Revolution Magazine*.[12] Much of Collins's vitriol likely originated from material circulated by the DAR.

It is highly probable that Collins, as well as other sorority women who were also members of the DAR and similar elite women's organizations of the early twentieth century, gained experience in antiradical organizing through their relationships with the powerful patriotic heritage group. Although the number of sorority women who were also members of the DAR is unknown, the similarity of the DAR's antiradical propaganda techniques to those that would be marshaled by NPC sororities by 1940 is unmistakable. More importantly, a number of high-ranking, powerful women in the national sororities and the NPC *did* share antiradical sentiments and were in the position to disseminate their political ideology within their respective organizations.[13] Collins was already the highly authoritative and respected national president of Chi Omega and an influential NPC delegate, and she would foster reactionary beliefs among members of the men and women's Greek-letter community for decades to come. A number of sorority and fraternity alumni leaders adopted this antiradical-cum-conservative mentality, shaped it to fit their organizational needs, and promoted its value through GLO publications.

In the 1930s Collins focused attacks on European fascism, establishing the conservative line she and other NPC women would use in the postwar years.

FIGURE 11. "Speaking of Monkey Wrenches." A cartoon from the dinner program of the first NIC/NPC joint meeting in 1941 showed how fraternities and sororities viewed their organizations as integral to American democracy during World War II.
Courtesy of the University of Illinois Archives, National Panhellenic Conference Archives, Record Series (41/82/810).

They saw fascist and communist regimes as not only the death knell of American democracy but also, and perhaps more importantly for GLOs, capable of undoing exclusivity in social realms. Sorority and fraternity members, the NPC believed, were the true inheritors of the democratic spirit, and they repeatedly trumpeted the importance of GLOs in guarding American freedom and democracy (see fig. 11). "Greek letter men and women have a unique stake in democracy," Collins wrote, as she noted that the groups were "carriers of certain ideals of our democracy for a satisfying way of life."[14] While the U.S. government was putting pressure on communists and suspected communists in the United States during this period, the NPC also warned of the threat of communistic influence as it positioned GLOs as the antidote to radicalization of American youth.

In the late 1930s and 1940s, a small but growing contingent of Americans concerned with government overreach in New Deal programs, possible communist infiltration in the United States, and perceived loss of U.S. power abroad following World War II began to coalesce around a values system that prized individual freedoms, private property, and disdain for U.S. federal government intervention in what they viewed as private matters. Proponents of the ideology included such individuals as Clarence "Pat" Manion, dean of the Notre Dame Law School; Robert Taft, Ohio senator and presidential hopeful; and, by the 1950s, William F. Buckley Jr., whose magazine, *National Review*, gave shape to the conservative movement as it became popularly understood over the second half of the twentieth century while it helped build momentum for rising conservative star and Arizona senator Barry Goldwater's 1964 presidential campaign. These years also brought cooperation between anti–New Deal Republicans and southern Democrats, who came together to form the new Special House Committee on Un-American Activities, later known as HUAC, with the goal of rooting out supposed communist influence in labor unions and New Deal agencies.[15] Conservatives outside the South shared concerns of federal government overreach with white southern Democrats, who were fighting to maintain white supremacy in their home states by opposing federal antilynching bills and, by the close of World War II, legislation to abolish the poll tax and the establishment of a permanent Fair Employment Practices Committee (FEPC).[16] Suspicious whites viewed African Americans as particularly susceptible to communist organizers who promised them a better life in an equal society and, like Mary Love Collins and other GLO leaders, also interwove the threat of racial mixing with their warnings against communist takeover. These common threads of conservative understanding would tie the largely Republican NPC women to white southerners in the postwar period.[17]

During World War II the NPC sought to assure the American public of sorority women's patriotism and seriousness of purpose while also offering an image of the groups as integral to a democratic society. They saw the volatile war years as a key time to remind individual members of the need to keep tabs on "agitation aimed at the right of social organizing." The NPC's Committee on Information on War and College Women sent a letter to presidents of NPC groups and NPC delegates reminding them of their duty to help preserve the right of social organizing. This right "alone stands between totalitarianism and democracy," wrote the committee. "Because we live in a revolutionary world, Greek-letter groups must be especially alert to their responsibility in maintaining this right." By linking the continuance of sorority exclusivity to displays of wartime patriotism, the committee paved the way to argue for their "right" to discriminate in membership as a basic American freedom in the 1950s and 1960s.[18]

The NPC and their fraternity counterpart, the National Interfraternity Conference (NIC), were ahead of the conservative curve in connecting private associations and "freedoms" in an American democratic context. The group of sorority and fraternity alumni that would become the Interfraternity Research and Advisory Council (IRAC) by 1946 had its beginnings during wartime when alumni sought ways to control information among the national groups and set a new precedent for positive GLO publicity targeted to counter detractors. Collins and Sigma Chi Lloyd G. "Bally" Balfour (Indiana University Law School, 1907), who served as NIC chairman in the early 1940s, were instrumental in planting the idea at the first joint meeting of the NIC and the NPC in 1940. Balfour initiated the conference as a "result of a desire on the part of the fraternities and sororities to present a united front, particularly on the legislative and public relations programs."[19] At an address to the NPC in 1951, he noted that IRAC had no authority but simply "[reported] factually, and sometimes editorially," while "studiously [avoiding] controversial issues."[20] Yet by the time of IRAC's formal inception at a 1946 meeting in Cincinnati, the group, officially named by Collins, already concentrated on combating what the NPC termed "'discrimination' hysteria." IRAC regularly received news of NPC investigations into "agitation" by "antifraternity" groups.[21]

The NPC's Research and Public Relations (RPR) Committee, a beefed-up version of the NPC Publicity Committee, reorganized in 1945 and also spearheaded by Collins, was the source of much information. Noting that Mrs. Glenn Frank had seen to it that her remarks "appeared in print in a way to gain the widest possible circulation" across the nation, the NPC admitted that "is more than we can say for our own efforts along the same line."[22] Instead of simply creating positive public relations for the NPC groups, however, the RPR Committee sought first and foremost to "educate" their own members about the many perceived threats to GLOs and their white, middle- and upper-class American way of life. As early as January 1946, the RPR Committee expressed these ideas to sorority members through printed pamphlets such as "The Reasons Why!" and "The Price of Rights? Responsibility!"[23] The first pamphlet explicitly connected racial and religious exclusivity to freedom of association, noting that opposition to GLOs might be "based upon the theory that all races and religions should associate and intermarry."[24] The second leaflet, released in March 1946, removed race from the equation, instead focusing on the responsibility of GLO members to "enhance the freedoms upon which all human progress depends" by maintaining the social and cultural structure of the nation. They would use "civilized ways" to enhance their own freedoms, pointedly noting that "speaking in a cultivated way does not minimize firmness."[25]

In 1949, amid congressional debate over the FEPC bill proposed by President Harry S. Truman, the RPR Committee reiterated the "facts about so-called discrimination," tracing it to FDR's initial establishment of the FEPC by executive order in 1941 and the resultant "agitation . . . over jobs in industry . . . at the close of the war." This federal power to investigate charges of discrimination, the NPC explained, "broadened to include jobs in govern-ment" and "recognition in public or semi-public groups."[26] For the NPC and for many white southerners, further evidence of "discrimination hysteria" would come from three Supreme Court decisions, handed down on June 5, 1950: *Sweatt v. Painter, McLaurin v. Oklahoma State Regents*, and *Henderson v. United States*, all of which outlawed forms of racial segregation. The rulings in the first two cases concerned professional and graduate education, while the third dealt with railway dining cars. The legal decisions signaled a shift in so-cial norms, as understood by many white southerners as well as the NPC, and helped solidify, in their minds, the "liberal" position of the Supreme Court. Fearing that the court would continue to overturn provisions for "separate but equal" facilities, white southerners and the NPC saw their states' rights and private rights, respectively, at stake.[27] Eschewing any public racial ani-mosity, however, the RPR Committee took pains to frame its arguments in race-neutral rhetoric. They urged all sorority women to accept the meaning of "discrimination" as the NPC understood it: a "fine word . . . brought into dis-repute." "Those who have the capacity to discriminate," the NPC reasoned, "give quality to whatever they do." In 1949 the RPR Committee argued that "the heart of discrimination is not racial but an effort to preserve deeply rooted American freedom." They claimed that GLOs were "private groups of friends as private as a family." They held that the organizations did not "choose [their] friends on the basis of disliking others" and asserted that "the right to choose our friends and associates is the most dynamic private right in our democracy. The forces trying to destroy that right want to destroy democracy."[28] Aware of the delicate nature of the conversation they entered, the conservative-led NPC pioneered a color-blind rhetoric that asserted GLOs' "fundamental free-doms" guaranteed by the U.S. Constitution, including the right to "form vol-untary associations" as an "essential human right" to be exercised "irrespective of the views of any nonmembers," rather than openly state the racial fears be-hind many of their proclamations.

The NPC's Anticommunist Crusade

The NPC painted their critics as communist-influenced civil rights "agitators," as they envisioned their national sororities as crucial participants in a show-down between democracy and communism. By the late 1940s and early 1950s, a series of events, including HUAC's charges of espionage against former State Department official Alger Hiss in 1948, the culmination of China's commu-nist revolution in 1949, and the widely publicized communist witch hunt led by Wisconsin's Republican senator, Joseph McCarthy, from 1950 to 1953, fostered an environment where fearful Americans could perceive evidence of communist subversion in their own country.[29] In this climate NPC leaders generally were able to disseminate their conservative and anticommunist views to a captive audience without reprisals from the membership.

In the 1950s and 1960s, the NPC sought to ally themselves with conservative, patriotic organizations such as the DAR, the American Legion, and Young Americans for Freedom to publicly demonstrate their commitment to anticommunism. In the early 1950s the NPC perceived so great a need for anticommunist education that the RPR Committee branched out to create the "All-American Committee to Combat Communism."[30] Spurred on by the American Legion's All-American Conference (AAC), the NPC formed their committee to streamline their efforts to "inform those with whom we come in contact, of the national danger of communism." The committee sent NPC delegates a newsletter containing lists of books, magazines, and pamphlets that might aid the sororities in presenting the lessons of anticommunism to their members and urged their assistance in the "nation wide crusade." The newsletter recommended as useful tools in the crusade *The Coming Defeat of Communism* (1950) by James Burnham, who would soon become a regular contributor to *National Review*, anticommunist literature written by former members of the Communist Party, and a pamphlet titled "New List of Subversive Organizations," prepared and released by HUAC (May 14, 1951). The committee warned sororities to "*caution*" their membership against joining any organization unless they were well informed of the group's real sponsors and advised NPC delegates to "*warn everyone* to be on alert for any signs of communist propaganda," suggesting that they would be wise to closely examine candidates for school or public offices to ensure that they were free of "questionable affiliation." To enlist speakers on the topic of Americanism, or anticommunism, the committee recommended that sorority women "check names with the local American Legion chapter of the Americanism committee of the DAR."[31]

The RPR and the AAC Committees, as well as IRAC, were vigilant in their searches for communist subversives on campus. When Balfour spoke about IRAC's activities at the 1951 NPC meeting, he boasted "in confidence" to his audience that "a number of college professors have been fired from the information we have received in reports from their classes."[32] During the same meeting, former Pi Beta Phi (ΠΒΦ) grand president Amy Burnham Onken, a Northwestern graduate who served as her sorority's NPC delegate for twenty-five years, urged attendees to read *God and Man at Yale: The Superstitions of "Academic Freedom"* (1951), William F. Buckley Jr.'s "exposé" accusing Yale's faculty of fostering an antidemocratic, anti-Christian ethos. The situation at Yale, Onken asserted, was "not an isolated [incident]."[33] Sorority women would begin to launch a campaign of distrust against what they believed was a glut of liberal university faculty and, increasingly, student affairs administrators, whom they saw as unfriendly to their organizations.

In addition to monitoring faculty, the NPC and IRAC also concerned themselves with student organizations that they believed to be too liberal, including the National Student Association (NSA) and student Young Women/ Young Men's Christian Associations (YW/YMCAs). The NSA had been formed by a group of American college students returning from the first World Student Congress in Prague, Czechoslovakia, in 1946. National Student Association literature from 1951 described the group as filling the "long-existing need for a representative intercollegiate organization designed to serve the American student community, and to promote student interests and welfare." During the 1950s the group supported such issues as aid to education and a ban on nuclear testing and also established a "very liberal position on civil rights and civil liberties" before those causes gained popularity.[34] The NSA's platform of civil rights for all students deterred many southern campuses from affiliating with the organization and was liberal enough for Collins to proclaim them the "prime movers in this discrimination issue."[35] The NSA had "taken a stand against discrimination in fraternities and [urged] the student governments to take action according to the Michigan Plan," which became the standard for addressing GLO discrimination and was adopted at many universities by the 1960s. In 1950 the University of Michigan's student legislature had proposed the plan wherein the universities' fraternities and sororities remove discriminatory clauses from their constitutions by a certain date (usually within five years) or face removal from campus.[36] Even in espousing racial cooperation, the student YW/YMCAs also presented a problem for NPC women. The groups had long been integral parts of campus life and, particularly in the early years of women's enrollment on campuses, had included many sorority women among their members. However, with newly elevated fears of communist influence and racial integration, the student YW/YMCAs' reminders that they had "wide experience in pioneering on the racial frontier" were certainly not overlooked by the unforgiving eyes of the RPR Committee, as the NPC branded them as likely subversives and enemies to GLOs.[37]

On at least one occasion the NPC recruited a college sorority member to report on the NSA's annual conference. In September 1950 a Kappa Alpha Theta from Syracuse University sent a "confidential" report to former Theta national president Margaret Banta detailing the events and attendants at the NSA conference that August.[38] While she had "expected to find the minority groups [Jewish and African American students] in the majority," she was "surprised" that "in general, the students there were 'typically' college men and women." For the purposes of white sorority women's discussion, the "typical college student" was white, Christian, middle class, and relatively apolitical. She observed "quite a few Jewish students . . . representing various schools, and also a number of Negro students" but said they were definitely not in the majority. The reporting Theta stated that her "own personal feeling" was that the NSA was "very liberal." She described the NSA as "ripe" for communist takeover, but she felt that there were "enough highly intelligent, and truly American students" in the group "to prevent it completely."[39] Yet she also noted that she was "disappointed to find that the fraternity members attending the meeting did not wear their pins." When she asked some of the other girls why they chose not to display their pins at the meeting, their response was that "they didn't think they should" because "they felt NSA'ers looked down on the Greeks." While the Theta claimed she was not aware of much antifraternity feeling at the conference, she also noted that, on the other hand, "there was nothing said for them" either.

Edgewater Fights Racial Desegregation

Even as the RPR Committee tried to pursue a race-neutral approach in their commentary on "freedom of association," the committee members sought a space where they might speak freely about their fears of racial integration in American society and GLOs in particular. The Edgewater Conference, a group that first met in 1952 at the Edgewater Beach Hotel in Chicago, became that place for reactionary alumnae and their fraternity counterparts (see fig. 12). Mary Love Collins, again showing herself as one of the masterminds of the conservative, xenophobic, and white supremacist bent of the NPC in the mid-twentieth century, was instrumental in Edgewater's formation. At the first meeting, the group passed a resolution stating that the organization held "the common interest of the belief in the inherent values of collegiate fraternal organizations and the right of self-determination in the selection of members thereof."[40] The secretive conference would monitor challenges to "freedom of association" and seek to devise legal means to challenge those critics who wanted GLOs to do away with discriminatory practices.

Host To 51 Fraternities And Sororities!

THE EDGEWATER BEACH HOTEL, on Chicago's North-Shore Lake front, has been selected as the meeting-place for fifty-one Conventions of America's Leading Greek-letter Societies. Most of these meetings have set all-time attendance records. Chicago's matchless location and the matchless facilities of the Edgewater Beach will assure complete success for your next national convention. Group meeting rates are surprisingly low. Write for information today!

Under Same Management is the Beautiful Edgewater Gulf Hotel at Edgewater Park, Mississippi, meeting place of 1935 N.P.C. Ideal for Winter Conventions!

WRITE TO W. M. DEWEY, Managing Director, Edgewater Beach Hotel, CHICAGO, ILL.

FIGURE 12. A 1936 advertisement in *Banta's Greek Exchange* for the Edgewater Beach Hotel in Chicago was typical of the resorts frequented by sorority and fraternity national conventions. The hotel was also the founding site of the Edgewater Conference, which started in 1952.

Courtesy of the University of Illinois Archives, Stewart S. Howe Collection, Record Series (26/21/8).

While Edgewater would become the main force behind sororities' pro-segregation measures in the 1950s and 1960s, the group's formation resulted from several high-profile challenges to GLOs' time-honored discriminatory membership policies in the late 1940s. The UVM incident with Crystal Malone, which so riled Winifred Robinson, was a primary cause. A caption in *LIFE*'s coverage of the discrimination by Alpha Xi Delta's national office noted that seven of the sorority's fifty-six chapters were in the South, hinting at an issue that NPC and NIC members would use in their continuing rebuttals against critics of their membership policies. While most NPC sororities had a greater number of chapters at schools outside the South, leaders would refer to the sentiments of their southern sisters when considering the issue of desegregation. Nonsouthern sorority women could cast off the southern aesthetic when they wished to disassociate themselves from supposed "southern" traits such as racist behavior. They hoped to distance themselves from women who advocated racial segregation and blatant racism, all the while continuing their work to keep African American women out of their chapters across the nation. Readers of *LIFE* could hardly ignore the caption that mentioned Malone's dates with white students at UVM.[41] The reminder of possible miscegenation would undoubtedly rile some readers and many GLO alumni leaders. Following the situation at UVM, a number of publicized accounts of fraternity chapters at northeastern schools pledging or attempting to pledge Jewish or African American students also rankled fraternity leadership. With these direct affronts from their own members, both NPC and NIC alumni "could see the handwriting on the wall" and decided to take action.[42]

Collins, along with Sigma Nu's Borden Burr (University of Alabama, 1896) and Theta Chi's Col. Joseph A. McCusker (University of Maine, 1917), helped assemble a specially selected group of individuals sympathetic to the cause of "freedom of association" to meet annually to strategize ways of strengthening their arguments for exclusivity.[43] The original meeting included "twelve or fourteen groups," most of which were still members two years later. At least one representative from nineteen different sororities and fraternities attended in 1954. In addition to Collins, the group included such highly respected NPC women as Chi Omega's Elizabeth Dyer (University of Cincinnati), KΔ's Julia Fuqua Ober (Hollins College), Tri-Delta's Ernestine Grigsby (University of Colorado–Boulder, 1919), Pi Beta Phi's Marianne Reid Wild (University of Kansas), and Delta Gamma's Helen Million Preston (University of Michigan, 1924). Winifred Robinson was also front and center at Edgewater but acted as an individual sponsor of the group, not as a representative of Alpha Xi Delta.[44]

Edgewater remained a secretive group, operating behind the scenes. In a discussion of what to say if asked about Edgewater, Collins guided attendees of the 1953 conference to keep the emphasis on "voluntary associations ... [assuming] responsibility in combating communism," as it did not "raise the question of discrimination."[45]

Sorority and fraternity chapters that faced pressure from university administrators to disclose the details of their membership clauses elicited frequent discussion by Edgewater participants. The conference kept up with situations of concern, giving regular reports on those schools. For example, in 1953 President William S. Carlson of the State University of New York (SUNY) began investigating the discriminatory practices of Greek-letter groups in an effort to remove all racial and religious discrimination in membership selection. While local fraternities (not affiliated with national societies) generally complied with the desired changes to admissions policies, the chapters of national groups met SUNY's requests with what sociologist and leader of the National Committee on Fraternities in Education (NCFE) Alfred McClung Lee termed "stubborn resistance, evasion, and subterfuge." While the university considered fraternities a part of their educational operation and under their supervision, the results of the administration's self-study revealed that SUNY had "actually permitted the development of a double standard of admission to its facilities—a fair one for its classrooms and an unfair one for many of its social fraternities." The university gave the nationally affiliated chapters until October 1958 to sever ties with their national organization or be shut down. On November 8, 1954, six months after the *Brown v. Board of Education* decision, the U.S. Supreme Court upheld a lower court ruling on the right of SUNY to ban GLOs, ruling for "the right of public institutions to define the policies that govern fraternal groups on their campus."[46] Speaking specifically of the investigation at SUNY's Buffalo State College, alumnae at Edgewater stated that administrators had repeatedly asked sorority members if there was anything in their rituals that stated they could not "initiate colored people." They had reportedly asked if any girl could be initiated "even though she [was] Jewish." One of the groups was reported to have responded to the former question by saying that they did not have any "such clauses," but that they would not "initiate a Negro student to prove the fact."[47] Ruth Neidig, an alumna of Pi Kappa Sigma sorority, said that her sorority tried to get around this type of questioning by answering "generally" that they "had nothing in [their] constitution."[48] Clearly having engaged in subterfuge to evade the SUNY investigators, Neidig confided to the conference members, "We have an unwritten law, but we [did not] tell them that."[49]

Sororities' Lessons of Conservative Citizenship

NPC women saw the need to train their membership to understand and approach outsiders' questions about discriminatory clauses as did Neidig and others on Edgewater. Amid prevailing beliefs that communism posed an immediate threat to American society, sororities' national officers created programs of citizenship training within sorority chapters to teach their members to champion the "all-American" values of individual freedom, private property rights, free enterprise, and adherence to the Christian faith. These programs linked conservatism in appearance and thought to sorority ideals for good citizenship. In 1951 Sigma Sigma Sigma (ΣΣΣ or Tri-Sigma) developed a yearlong national education program around citizenship. Mary Hastings Holloway Page, Tri-Sigma's national president, shared the program's details with eager NPC delegates at a special meeting in November 1951 where the group discussed the supposed threats to American democracy and voted to join the American Legion's All-American Conference. Page explained that the idea for the program had grown out of talks on "Sororities in a Democracy" at Tri-Sigma's national convention that summer, which included frank discussions of the "many problems on discrimination" that had arisen for sororities. The ΣΣΣ alumnae wanted to "encourage . . . members on ways and means to become better citizens." The leaders imparted these lessons by sending out materials for what they called "Harmony Hour" programs in each chapter. The first program of the school year dealt with American "heritage" (a popular starting point for contemporary essays by conservative thinkers), the second with issues, the third with the candidates, and the final in the series with the topic of "the articulate citizen." While Page did not detail the topics within each program, the NPC leaders wanted all sorority members to understand and be able to speak about the "issues" facing sororities, meaning antidiscrimination rhetoric and possible communist infiltration, suggesting that the articulate citizen–sorority woman would be well versed in the conservative NPC ideology. The sorority interspersed "Charm School" programs, which dealt with posture, conversation, public speaking, and presiding, with the Harmony Hours. Tri-Sigma's combination of training in political thought and bodily comportment was specially engineered to "develop citizenship through personal characteristics and attributes."[50] Sorority leaders hoped to signify upright citizenry, conservative values, and white middle- to upper-class status through display of "appropriate" grooming, physical beauty, and nonthreatening femininity.

The NPC and its member groups, such as ΣΣΣ, designed their policies to be implemented on a national scale, meaning that college sorority members and alumnae in chapters across the country would learn the same lessons of conservatism. The NPC drew on materials produced by the conservative movement's increasingly powerful network of intellectuals and organizations devoted to the popularization of conservative thought in post–World War II American politics and society. By presenting conservative magazines such as *Human Events* and *National Review*, along with radio broadcasts such as Clarence "Pat" Manion's *Manion Forum of Opinion*, as important informational sources, the NPC leaders simultaneously trained their college and alumnae membership to adopt conservative frameworks for engaging the questions of "freedom of association" and "anticommunism."[51] NPC leaders recited conservative movement ideology nearly verbatim as they reiterated the dangers of communist infiltration and reminded sorority members and alumnae of the conservative view, which held that "liberal" organizations and individuals were soft on communism.

In winter of 1957, on the heels of the Civil Rights Act of 1957 and the formation of the Civil Rights Commission, and three years after *Brown*, the NPC linked their concerns about communism and "agitators" critical of sororities in the *NPC Declaration of Freedom*, a pamphlet commenting on individual rights granted by the Constitution. Like many conservatives and southern segregationists, the NPC believed that these federal legislative and judicial actions unlawfully gave greater power to the federal government to limit activities that the NPC felt were guaranteed by the Bill of Rights. Collins originally drafted and presented the declaration to the 35th Biennial Conference, where she advised her audience that "this is a time for knowledge, courage, and wisdom." The delegates unanimously adopted the declaration. As a result, the NPC women conducted their conservative proselytizing on a more visible level, publishing the pamphlet for members and supporters that asserted the NPC's "responsibility to contribute to accurate and thorough knowledge about the Constitution of the United States and the Bill of Rights and to know the ideologies destructive of our Country." First and foremost, the NPC sought to demonstrate that the First Amendment "right of people peaceably to assemble" guaranteed sororities' rights as "voluntary associations" to choose their members. Although left unsaid, the NPC also interpreted this as the right to *deny* membership to those with whom they did *not* wish to associate. The connections made by the NPC among civil rights "agitators," restrictions on freedom for "rightful" citizens, and the role of communism in this realignment of society were unmistakable.[52]

If the sorority women reading the NPC's *Declaration of Freedom* somehow failed to see that the RPR Committee was drawing a connection between civil rights, desegregation, and communism, a three-page segment of recommended reading and a listing of "creditable organizations fighting to preserve various American fundamentals in accord with the Constitution" directed the women to an extensive listing of books by conservative intellectuals, conservative magazines, and conservative American patriotic organizations. The pamphlet suggested a number of "special articles and editorials," including several of David Lawrence's "Opinion of the Editor" segments in *U.S. News and World Report* from 1957, titled "'Civil Rights' That Breed 'Civil Wrongs,'" "There Is No 'Fourteenth Amendment'!," and "Illegality Breeds Illegality." In these pieces, Lawrence argued against the overreach of federal power into individual states and posited that instances of military enforcement of school desegregation, which he characterized as federal despotism, were based on illegal precedent and blatant disregard for the Constitution as originally written. Lawrence and other conservative movement leaders also held that the Fourteenth Amendment to the Constitution, which guaranteed rights of citizenship and equal protection under the law, should be "considered null and void" because of their belief that it was ratified by illegal measure during Reconstruction. Thus, they contended that the Supreme Court's decision in *Brown*, which found that segregated public schools were in violation of the Fourteenth Amendment's equal protection clause, was also invalid, as they believed the Fourteenth Amendment did not and should not exist.[53]

Significantly, the push by NPC leadership and conservative intellectuals in the mid- to late 1950s to uphold individual rights and protect private property allowed for some whites' engagement in racial discrimination to meet those goals. Many conservatives in this period saw the fight by white southern segregationists to maintain their states' segregation laws as a prime example of individual rights endangered by the overreach of federal government. Some conservative movement leaders, such as William F. Buckley Jr., used blatant white supremacist appeals in support of what they believed was the right of localities to uphold public school segregation in the wake of the *Brown* decision. Others, such as Buckley's colleague at *National Review*, L. Brent Bozell, sought to couch the explosive issue of race in color-blind language, just as the NPC did, which was a tactic that made the conservative agenda palatable to a larger portion of the American population.[54] By moving conservative rhetoric toward the preservation of (white) American rights and freedoms and away from the denial of African American civil liberties, the NPC and conservative intellectuals obscured the critical role of race in their ideology.

The NPC proclaimed their devotion to the cause of the southern prosegregationists, identifying similarities in their respective situations. In 1957 the NPC included as suggested reading material for their constituents a *National Review* book review and essay by University of Chicago professor and southern agrarian Richard M. Weaver titled "Integration Is Communization." Weaver argued that the "racial collectivism" fueled by communism was "being used as a crowbar to pry loose rights over private property." In a *National Review* article from 1960, Nashville agrarian Donald Davidson explained that the Supreme Court would "not stop with school desegregation" and that "every section, North or South" was "under a threat that would not lift" until conservatives came together to "take action."[55] The NPC, having concluded that the next step in the attack would be the prohibition of sororities' and fraternities' abilities to privately choose their own members, would stand with conservatives against that threat.

Likewise, writers and organizations associated with the conservative movement took up the cause of sororities' and fraternities' "freedom of association," presenting the groups as prime examples of private entities whose rights of private property were under attack by "liberal" critics and the federal government. In 1957 conservative commentator Russell Kirk, already well known for his book *The Conservative Mind* (1953), had written a two-part essay in *National Review* titled "In Defense of Fraternities." Although not a fraternity alumnus, Kirk stood up for the groups' rights to private membership. "Regardless of your feelings and my feelings toward Negroes, Jews, and Catholics, it is not you and I who have a right to say what qualities a fraternity should establish for membership." In addition, Kirk argued, "If a fraternity should admit *only* Negroes, Jews, and Catholics, you and I—taking us as members of the general public—would have no right to object . . . for a fraternity is not public property." Following this logic, Kirk contended that, like the general public, a college administration also did not "ordinarily have a right to regulate the conditions of membership in fraternities."[56]

In this same period, individual sororities continued to feed memos to their membership that instructed in conservative philosophies. Elizabeth Dyer sent a copy of a four-page document, "The Record We Must Face," to Chi Omegas to show "what fraternities are up against." The piece, which very much reflected Edgewater Conference discussions, included updates on universities where alumnae understood "freedom of association" to be under attack, listed groups such as the YW/YMCA, NSA, and National Association for Women Deans and Counselors (NAWDAC) as friends of racial integration, and stressed the supposed nationwide assault on Christianity by American Jews.[57] Early in the fall of 1959, Julia Fuqua Ober sent all KΔ chapters a letter supplying information on the NSA, supposedly desired by many delegates at the KΔ National Convention over the summer. The attached five-page report, purportedly written by a student member of another NPC sorority, drew on the usual arguments to portray the NSA as a communist front organization. The writer also used her disdain for many of the NSA's positions as a way to criticize federal monetary aid for public welfare, the "path to the left" supposedly taken by the United Nations Educational, Scientific, and Cultural Organization and the National Education Association, and her feelings on racial integration. "Whether or not one approves of integration," she stated, "the effects of rushing headlong into something which is violently opposed by a large proportion of the population are very obviously damaging to the unity of the United States." The sophisticated writing style bore an uncanny resemblance to that evinced in RPR Committee reports.

The NPC leaders strove to ensure that national and regional sorority officers, other alumnae members, and young leaders at the college chapter level were reading the materials that they, as conservative women, deemed vital to their cause. NPC Citizenship Committee chairman and Alpha Gamma Delta alumna Marguerite Sammis Jansky (University of Wisconsin, 1919) outlined the NPC's "Primer of Citizenship" in early 1960 in an article that read like a conservative campaign pamphlet, supporting HUAC, disparaging labor unions, and planting suspicions about the UN. As educated women whose communities would look to them for leadership, Janksy believed, sorority women should be well versed in conservative ideals *and* prepared to "exert an active influence." Again invoking reminders of the connections between social status and preservation of institutional structures of white power in the United States, she demanded of readers, "Can you measure the worth of your personal citizenship as an influential factor in preserving the heritage which has given you a good life?"[58]

The 1960 Kappa Kappa Gamma (KKΓ) national convention program included a "Leadership School" for alumnae officers organized by Kappa's national president and NPC representative Mary Turner Whitney (University of Cincinnati, 1924) and Edith Reese Crabtree (University of Wooster, Ohio, 1907), secretary of IRAC and chair of Kappa's Fraternity Research Committee. A young woman leaving "the protection of home and college today," Crabtree noted, "will enter a world full of problems. There will be choices to be made, and her wisdom in making these choices will depend upon her ability to think for herself after she has the facts in hand." The "facts," presented by Whitney and Crabtree, detailed the conservative/NPC position, which saw Greek-letter groups under attack by "pressure groups trying to drown out the voice of reason," with the "ultimate goal" of destroying the fraternity system and eroding American freedom. The women closed their session with "one more word from Senator [Barry] Goldwater's *Conscience of a Conservative* [1960]," which suggested that Goldwater's book, an influential tract for grassroots conservatives, had been a key text at the Kappa convention. "If they were made aware of the facts," Whitney and Crabtree quoted Goldwater, a Sigma Chi alumnus, "all thinking Americans would recognize the extreme seriousness of the impending danger to the survival of American Freedom."[59]

By the 1960s, the newly formed Young Americans for Freedom (YAF) spoke directly to Greek-letter groups about the importance of standing up for their "rights" as private organizations. A supposedly nonpartisan, conservative youth organization formed under the auspices of William F. Buckley Jr. in 1960, YAF shared the NPC's and NIC's critique of the NSA as a liberal agitator. Edgewater member and Delta Gamma (ΔΓ) national president Helen Million Preston (University of Michigan, 1924) was a representative at the so-called Sharon Conference, a meeting of young conservatives held at Buckley's home in Sharon, Connecticut, when YAF formed. Yet even before YAF officially organized, the group's soon-to-be leaders Douglas Caddy and David Franke spoke at the EC regarding their work to enforce the requirement of the loyalty oath as a part of the National Defense Education Act (1958). The two returned to the conference in 1961 to share the news of YAF's growth and to reiterate its connection to Buckley's *National Review*. Preston provided her take on "Campus Conservatism" in the *Anchora* of Delta Gamma, where she spoke glowingly of the newly formed YAF and Buckley's *National Review*. The journal printed the first pamphlet of YAF in the pages following Preston's notice, and she urged young ΔΓs to write to YAF for more information if interested.[60]

Young Americans for Freedom and *National Review* appealed to college sorority and fraternity members. In January 1964 Buckley wrote a piece in *National Review* about his university speaking tour. He noted a recent trip to the University of Texas (his father's alma mater) where his "typical day" of meeting with a political science class, debating at the law school, and having coffee at a professor's home also included lunch at a sorority, as well as an evening meeting at a fraternity—where he also lodged during his visit.[61] His apparent welcome by sororities and fraternities during the speaking tour suggests that the groups were likely integral in booking his speaking engagements and that members may have learned from their organizations that they should be supportive of Buckley's views, as well as those of other conservatives who spoke out about the rights of individuals to maintain private property and to associate only with those whom they chose. A blurb in YAF's publication, the *New Guard*, in Sep-

FIGURE 13. Two Sigma Chi brothers from the University of North
Carolina at Chapel Hill wait to greet Arizona senator and Sigma Chi
brother Barry Goldwater at the Raleigh-Durham Airport, ca. 1964.
*Courtesy of the North Carolina Collection, Wilson Library, University of
North Carolina at Chapel Hill, University of North Carolina at Chapel Hill,
University of North Carolina at Chapel Hill Image Collection, 1799–1999.*

tember 1964 supports this assertion. The North Carolina YAF, which was tour-
ing communities in the state, was organizing a "special fraternity-sorority social
program . . . devised to channel interest and enthusiasm among their members."
(See fig. 13.) YAF highlighted their role in helping GLOs "fight off liberal attacks calling for their abolition."[62] Momentum among young conservatives,
particularly in southern states in these years, would be essential to the growth of
the Sunbelt's "silent majority" by the 1970s.

On June 23, 1964, barely a week before President Lyndon B. Johnson signed
the Civil Rights Act of 1964 into law, YAF board member Tom Charles Huston delivered an address to the national convention of Alpha Gamma Delta
(ΑΓΔ). A member of Phi Kappa Psi fraternity, Huston spoke passionately
about what he termed "'Operation Greek'—the effort to destroy the fraternity system." He explained that the program was "well financed" and led "by
the same prophets of equalitarianism who are dedicated to the extermination
of all those institutions and traditions which are part of the American way of
life." These alleged enemies of the fraternity system, Huston argued, "clothed"
their criticisms "in the sacred garment of 'civil rights.'"[63] A young fraternity

alumnus from Indiana University, Huston became YAF's national chairman in 1965. He traveled to many fraternity and sorority national conventions and was a featured speaker at the NPC's annual convention that year. In his 1964 speech to ΑΓΔ's national convention, Huston referred to the NSA as the "left-wing confederation of college and university student governments," directing the "anti-Greek drive . . . in the name of civil rights." With the NSA portrayed as the "radical" enemy, YAF joined the NPC and the NIC in their attempts to remove campuses from NSA affiliation.[64]

With the passage and enforcement of the Civil Rights Act of 1964, the federal government demonstrated a commitment to ending discrimination and desegregation in higher education. For conservatives, the 1964 act was yet another federal signpost on the road to a communistic society. Initially, the Meader Amendment to the Civil Rights Act had prohibited interference in the functioning of private organizations, including sororities and fraternities. In 1965, however, Francis Keppel, U.S. commissioner of education, made clear that the Civil Rights Act charged individual universities with the task of eliminating discrimination by their campuses' Greek-letter societies. Citing Title VI of the act, which disallowed federal funding to programs or activities that fostered discrimination on the basis of race, color, or national origin, Keppel announced that he would cut federal funding to universities that allowed fraternities to continue discriminating on the basis of race.[65]

In order to comply with Keppel's enforcement of Title VI, universities would have to ensure that no student organizations allowed discriminatory clauses. In the cases of GLOs, university administrators requested assurances from national sorority and fraternity officers that their respective organizations' constitutions and bylaws were free of clauses that restricted membership on the basis of race. In doing so, the universities also attempted to convince themselves that simply by asking sororities and fraternities to affirm that their membership selection processes were not bound by discriminatory clauses, they could eliminate racial discrimination by the groups. In reality, a national sorority could claim that their organization did not have any discriminatory clauses even while adhering to an unwritten policy of barring African American or Jewish women from membership. By the mid-1960s, for example, XΩ had removed all discriminatory clauses from its constitution and bylaws, but as Guion Griffis Johnson, a traveling adviser for the sorority, explained, "The [Chi Omega] Governing Council still insists upon 'the right to choose its own members' as guaranteed by the Bill of Rights of the Federal Constitution and withdraws chapters rather than give in on this point." This meant that XΩ's unwritten rule on discrimination remained in effect. Johnson thought it was "foolish to lose chapters on this basis" and noted her belief that both Mary Love Collins and Elizabeth Dyer were "reactionary persons who are using 'the right to choose' as a stick with which to fight off integration."[66]

Southern Universities Seek Removal of Sororities' Discriminatory Clauses

After Francis Keppel publicized his plans to enforce Title VI of the Civil Rights Act of 1964, southern universities moved to ensure that their student organizations were in compliance with the ruling so that they would still be eligible for federal funding. Similar to the timetables laid out in the Michigan Plan of 1950, universities in the American South sought to obtain affirmation of nondiscrimination from the Greek-letter chapters on their campuses. On March 5, 1965, the Faculty Council at the University of North Carolina (UNC) "unanimously passed a resolution calling for the end to fraternity and sorority discriminatory clauses." The groups would have until September 1, 1966, to remove all national or local discriminatory clauses. In cases where "administrations disallowed such clauses," the *Daily Tar Heel* noted, some fraternity and sorority nationals had agreed to "waive" national membership requirements for local chapters. The Panhellenic Council and Interfraternity Council leaders at UNC were unsure of the new ruling's effect on each of the campus's chapters. Kappa Delta had been known to refuse compliance with nondiscriminatory statements on other campuses.[67] A 1964 survey of discriminatory clauses held by UNC's GLOs showed that of the eight national sororities with chapters on campus, four suggested some variation of membership restriction aside from the basic rush recommendation form common to all sororities. Alpha Delta Pi (ΑΔΠ) and Tri-Delta reported that members "must accept Christian ritual," while ΧΩ and ΚΔ had "no comment."[68]

At Duke, President Douglas M. Knight corresponded with national sorority officers over the summer of 1965 in an attempt to confirm that the groups were already in compliance with nondiscrimination or that they would change their policies to reflect Keppel's edict. In his initial letter, Knight directly asked national sorority and fraternity officers if they had "any constitutional limitation forbidding a local chapter from accepting a Negro (boy or girl) if the chapter so wishes." He noted that some groups "require sponsorship from a member in the student's home town" and acknowledged that this "might be difficult to get from members of a previously all-white group." The administration worried that if any of the groups followed such a practice, it could trigger accusations of discrimination. His reminder that the university must "comply not only with the letter, but also with the spirit of the law" suggested that the administration understood that sororities tended to say one thing and do another in regard to discriminatory practices.[69]

While most other NPC sororities with chapters at Duke responded to Knight with a simple statement explaining that they did not have restrictive membership clauses, AΔΠ and KΔ, like Kappa, wrote lengthier replies. Their replies display the delicate nature of these conversations. In her carefully worded response, KKΓ national president Frances Fatout Alexander (De-Pauw University, 1928) of Charlotte, North Carolina, stated that Kappa did not have a constitutional limitation "forbidding the pledging of a Negro girl or of any girl." Seemingly attempting to remove race from the equation, she also wrote that there was no "[practice] or mechanism designed to prevent the pledging of anyone" and that Kappa used a "reference system that is informational, not restrictive" supposedly at "the request of our undergraduate members." She pointed out that the reference system had "been in effect for many years now and is helpful in avoiding an incompatible and uncongenial relationship." Just as the reference system had helped sororities avoid the pledging of undesirable white rushees over the years, it could also aid sororities attempting to keep black women out of their chapters. She appeared to seek understanding from Knight on the racial issue, writing obliquely, "I am sure you will agree . . . we can encourage, but not legislate personal opinions and feelings of individuals." She noted that some Kappa chapters *had* received references on African American women from all-white groups, but "limited by small and rigid quotas, the chapter chose to select those girls who it felt were most compatible and had the greatest potential." For national sorority leaders and many college actives in this period, when choosing new members that were "most compatible and had the greatest potential," a white woman would always rank higher in that nebulous category than an African American woman.[70]

Maxine Blake (University of Washington, 1927) affirmed AΔΠ's use of recommendation forms and, like Alexander, managed to sidestep the discussion of race in her response (see fig. 14). She explained to Knight that "the Duke chapter is a very old one on our chapter roll, it receives far more recommendations than it can consider." This was the same logic that the sorority had long used to defend itself against criticism of discrimination or causing "hurt feelings" among white women. It seemed likely that AΔΠ would simply lump any African American rushees in with the "sheer numbers" of women that the chapter had to turn down. Then they would not have to admit that the real reason for the denial was race. Blake reminded Knight that AΔΠ began at the Methodist Georgia Wesleyan Female College, that their ritual was based on

FIGURE 14. Maxine Blake (second from right), Alpha Delta Pi grand president
(1948–77), meets with sorority women from Duke Woman's College, ca. 1950s.
Courtesy of Duke University Archives.

the Bible, and that they "[expected] members to be able to accept such Ritual." She also noted, however, that the sorority had "members of many, many
faiths in the sorority, including some of Jewish origin," suggesting that the sorority would allow non-Protestant members, so long as they participated in
the Christian rituals.[71]

Meanwhile, Kappa Delta president Genevieve Forbes Morse (Louisiana
Tech, 1932) sent a reply to Knight that neither confirmed nor denied the presence of any discriminatory policies. She did enclose a copy of KΔ's statement
of policy regarding membership, which stated that KΔ was a "Christian social
organization" whose purpose was "to foster the art of true friendship. Prospective members must have qualities compatible with this purpose and the prospective life long friendships and associations which are a part of belonging
to Kappa Delta." The compatibility of a candidate would be judged on a list
of qualifications, including "family, economic and social background, educational fitness, moral standards, religion, and, in general, adaptability for group
association and friendship." Again, the vague, subjective nature of member-

ship qualifications made it easy for NPC groups to obscure discriminatory rush practices.[72] Morse also reminded Knight that as part of a national organization, "a chapter does not have local autonomy in membership selection."[73] National sororities and fraternities repeatedly fell back on the ludicrous idea that any new member would have to be acceptable to *all* members of the national organization.

In August 1965 Edgewater Conference members used their influence on fraternity members in Congress to forge a response to Francis Keppel's challenge. Edgewater chairman J. B. Beaird (Acacia fraternity, University of Oklahoma) and vice president Sherwood Blue (Sigma Chi, Indiana University) joined several other national fraternity leaders in Washington, D.C., with hopes of drafting legislation to circumvent federal oversight of GLOs' membership practices. Louisiana congressman Joe D. Waggoner (Kappa Sigma, Louisiana Tech) introduced the amendment to the Higher Education Bill (H.R. 1567), which prohibited federal interference in the "internal affairs" of GLOs. A conservative Democrat, Representative Waggoner had spoken against the Voting Rights Bill the previous month, just before it reached final vote in the House, and also appeared as a guest on the blatantly white supremacist Citizens' Council's weekly *Forum* television and radio broadcast.[74] The Higher Education Bill readily passed the House but met greater debate in the Senate, where, after a momentous lobbying effort on the part of Edgewater, GLO alumni, and the YAF, the resulting proviso enabled the majority of GLOs to continue their practices of racial and religious discrimination in membership selection. The Senate version of the bill allowed for federal oversight of fraternities and sororities that used university property or lived in university housing, meaning that the ruling affected just roughly 15 percent of GLO chapters, effectively ensuring that the organizations could maintain their discriminatory practices.[75]

Sororities and fraternities at Duke lived in university-owned housing, meaning that they were among the 15 percent of GLO chapters continuing to be affected by Title VI. By October 1967, Duke provost Frank De Vyver reported to Knight that they were doing well in getting sororities and fraternities to sign the nondiscrimination compliance forms. Two fraternities and three sororities had not yet signed, and not surprisingly, KΔ was one of the sororities. As a result, the local chapter had chosen to sever ties with the national. De Vyver felt that KΔ's national office was "afraid the local group might select a Negro girl," since the group "had already defied the National by selecting two Jewish girls." The national office had "changed the national constitution and the local President thought all would be well." Afterward, however, she reported to De Vyver that Morse told the chapter that "though the words were changed the policy was not." It appeared that KΔ hoped to deter the administrative officials while adhering to the *unwritten* discriminatory membership clause. Sigma Kappa sorority, De Vyver noted, also was "holding out although they maintain their constitution is quite clear," and another sorority, unnamed by De Vyver, would reportedly sign, "perhaps under protest."[76] Kappa Delta, in a move that seemed like the ones that Guion Johnson described at XΩ, lost the Sigma Delta chapter at Duke over the issue of membership discrimination.

The close of the KΔ chapter brought anger and disappointment from Duke's KΔ alums. One wrote to the Duke Loyalty Fund explaining that she would be withholding her "small contribution" on account of the KΔ chapter going inactive. The KΔ national officers had written to notify Sigma Delta chapter alumnae of the closure but had not given them the real reason. KΔ had blamed the issue on the university, stating that "the campus situation at Duke University could not be resolved, irregardless of continuous efforts since the mid-1950s." The leadership noted that it had "become increasingly difficult for National Sororities to continue to function" at Duke because "they are granted neither status nor respect."[77] She remarked that KΔ had "meant more to [her] in the years since college than any affiliation [she] had on campus" and was very upset that "Duke co-eds" would be "denied this opportunity" that had been "such a pleasure" for her.[78] Duke's administration was quite disturbed at the possibility of losing support of other university donors, particularly those that might give more than just a "small contribution." Attempting to mend any broken fences with alumnae of the Sigma Delta chapter, President Knight wrote a memo addressing the situation. He explained that "as nearly as [the Duke administration] could understand," after debate, KΔ had voted at their national convention to remove the discriminatory clause from their constitution. Duke then planned to have the KΔ local president and national president, Genevieve Morse, sign a statement confirming this change. Morse, however, refused to sign and refused to allow the Sigma Delta chapter president to sign either. This scenario, Knight reported, left the university "no legal alternative but to take action" itself. He explained that it had been a "matter of judgment" for Duke to decide that, as a desegregated university, "it was not proper to have segregated organizations operating on the campus." Knight made clear that it was not only a matter of judgment but also "an opinion from an outside law firm" that the university had to "assure" itself "that sororities and fraternities did not discriminate in their membership policies." He expressed his disappointment that the chapter had to go inactive and suggested that "perhaps in the future your president will be willing to sign the statement, and we can once again have Sigma Delta Chapter operating on campus."[79]

The issue of discriminatory membership clauses brought sororities visibly into the political realm, a space that they had attempted, or pretended, to avoid throughout their existence. The very visible issue of racial discrimination in the United States in the post–World War II period forced sororities, as well as all other membership organizations, to address this explosive topic, opening up questions about long-standing, implicit forms of discrimination by such groups. The NPC countered with a race-neutral approach as they publicly explained their efforts to preserve "freedom of association" as beneficial to *all* citizens, regardless of race, and not intended to deny the rights of any individual or group. By upholding "freedom of association," they reasoned, Americans would ensure the primacy of the Constitution and the continuation of the freedoms it granted to all citizens. The "freedom of association" argument, however, still catered to whites interested in maintaining their freedom to keep from associating with nonwhites and maintaining their privileged position in relation to minority groups in the United States.[80]

The public relations difficulties arising from the discrimination issue drove a redefinition of Greek-letter groups' relationships with university campuses. With university administrations forcing the groups to comply with nondiscriminatory rules common to all student organizations, sororities and fraternities no longer found favored status on campuses. Sorority alumnae became more skeptical of university administrations, which they saw as chock full of communists or, at the very least, misguided liberals. National sororities' new focus on molding conservative "ladies" through targeted propaganda and their social education programs helped form a model of womanhood signified by white, feminine beauty and knowledge of elite social graces. Many alumnae members gladly signed on to the program, while college members, who were beginning to strain against the generational differences with their sororities' national leaders, would have to decide whether to cast their lot with the status quo for their chapter or seek change within their organizations.

CHAPTER SEVEN

⸱•⸱

"Inequality for All and Mint Juleps, Too"

REINFORCING THE SORORITY WOMAN
AS SOUTHERN LADY

*I*n a February 1964 essay for the University of Georgia (UGA) student newspaper, staff writer Neil Aronstam demonstrated the popular view as he lampooned sororities while criticizing their discriminatory nature.[1] In "Southern Sorority Toured," Aronstam described a visit to the fictional "Alpha Alpha" sorority where the chapter president "Ide Belle Mae Montgomery" described her sorority's founding, "just after the War of Northern Aggression on the principles of 'inequality for all and mint juleps, too.'" She explained that the sorority endeavored "through the years to maintain the same standards, and traditions, and outlooks that our forefathers had during the South's most glorious era." Aronstam asked Ida Belle Mae if she was concerned that their standards were "a bit outdated," but she responded by "muttering something about damnyankees." Aronstam noted that when he arrived at the house the Alpha Alphas checked to make sure that he was wearing a fraternity pin before allowing him in. Apparently viewing men as possible dating material only, they explained to him that they were "employing Darwin's theory of natural selection—only letting 'approved' fraternity men date the Alpha Alphas." Aronstam told the sorority women that he was a reporter visiting the house to do a feature on their sorority, not seeking a date. At that point, the sorority housemother, whose character seemed a compilation of all suspicious sorority alumnae, "began frisking [him] for any hidden tape recorders, paper or pens." "We can't be too careful you know," she said. "The way things are, just anyone could slip in here sometimes." Her allusion to "the way things are" likely referred to the recent racial desegregation of campus, suggesting that, in the current climate, the sisters needed to be on guard since *anyone*, including African Americans, might now be able to enter the sorority house either as rushees or, in what was perhaps to her an even more frightening possibility, as male friends or dates of the white sorority women.[2] Aronstam's satire played on stereotypical images of white southern sorority women even as it suggested that the stereotypes were not that far from reality.[3] Through his portrayal of southern sorority women as simplistic southern belles, he also criticized the groups for upholding an elitist and segregationist ideology among their members. By emphasizing the sorority women's obvious adherence to the southern aesthetic and apparent devotion to the Lost Cause mentality, Aronstam indirectly demonstrated the groups' allegiance to a racially discriminatory ideology.

Sorority women were highly visible models of white southern womanhood on their campuses and in their communities. As Aronstam's piece demonstrated, the image of the white southern lady was alive and well on southern campuses in these years, and sorority chapters were primary locations for her support. Sorority women such as the Alpha Gamma Deltas (ΑΓΔ) at the University of Alabama, who posed on the house veranda in "plantation finery" in 1965, presented white sorority women as a tangible reminder of those whom the National Panhellenic Conference (NPC) sorority chapters welcomed and those whose entry they sought to rebuff. Sororities had trained their members to comport themselves in a manner befitting white middle- to upper-class ladies as a means of reinforcing the conservative ethos of the membership. The sorority women projected a highly controlled form of white beauty and sexuality, which, in the case of southern beauty queens, as Blain Roberts has argued, "[enacted] a quiet form of massive resistance."[4] As women who appeared beautiful, sexual (but supposedly chaste), and beyond reproach in their manners, sorority women presented a direct visual response to the ugliness and violence of the segregationists' protests, even as the women themselves worked to maintain the systems that kept their organizations lily white. The southern aesthetic undergirded racial segregation, and the white southern lady was its fiercest weapon against critics.

Aronstam's essay and other southern belle posturings by sorority women occurred simultaneously with and shortly after the 1961–65 Civil War centennial commemorations in the United States. As some southern states chose to stage public celebrations redolent of Old South mythology, Aronstam's essay tied sorority women to a larger battle for southern public memory, waged by white southerners seeking to forestall racial equality.[5] Perhaps more of a celebration of the white southern aesthetic and a remembrance of the Lost Cause than a solemn tribute, the centennial also underscored white southerners' continuing efforts to reinforce their now-crumbling segregated society. As in the 1920s and 1930s, the 1960s celebrations of the southern aesthetic were not limited to southerners, and they served a larger national purpose of demonstrating a patriotic celebration of American heritage as a show of anticommunist strength. The celebrations also provided good fodder for promoters of marketing and tourism, as they pushed the same *Gone with the Wind* imagery that played so well to a national audience three decades prior.

College sorority women were the attractive faces of these national organizations that labored quietly and insidiously to protect spaces of white Protestant power and influence in the United States. Even as many national sorority leaders worked behind the scenes to keep their organizations white, they advised college sorority women to keep mum on issues of school desegregation. In January 1961, as African American students Charlayne Hunter and Hamilton Holmes prepared to enter classes at UGA, alumnae of Zeta Tau Alpha (ZTA) wrote to their local Gamma Pi chapter forbidding member involvement in student protests. Members of the Gamma Pi House Corporation, an alumnae group that managed the chapter house, warned that "any member or pledge . . . who is involved in any way in any demonstration regarding the integration situation will lose her membership in the fraternity automatically."[6] In a copy of the Gamma Pi House Corporation letter sent to UGA's dean of women, Edith L. Stallings, the alumnae noted that "we prefer to keep our girls completely out of any demonstration against the Negroes and this is the most effective control we have."[7] The refusal to allow sorority women to participate could be read in a number of ways. The ZTAs may have wished to spare the national sorority the negative publicity that could come along with having members pictured in the midst of any protest. They also may have worried about offending other alumnae members, either those supporting or, more likely, opposing desegregation. The directive by the alumnae, forbidding the students to participate in public protest, also signaled a continuance of the outdated, patriarchal belief that women should not involve themselves in politics or appear outspoken in public. Protest of any nature by the sorority women was "unladylike" and out of bounds. Although forbidden from actively participating in any public displays regarding segregation at their schools, the sorority women were complicit in the maintenance of white supremacy and the "southern way of life."

Southern college campuses of the 1960s were at once sites of conformity and resistance to the white supremacist tradition. While conformity was the greater tendency, it did not preclude students from considering alternatives to

the systems and conventions that had guided white southern life for generations. For the most part, sorority and fraternity alumni were correct to think
that the strength of the southern aesthetic could keep their southern chapters
largely shielded from the challenges to membership restrictions that more frequently erupted at progressive campuses outside of the South. Like conservative movement leaders who saw mid-twentieth-century white southerners as
an untapped conservative force awaiting mobilization, the Edgewater Conference, and NPC and National Interfraternity Conference (NIC) groups in general, perceived sorority and fraternity chapters at southern universities as the
last line of defense against the federal incursions. Questioned about any problematic developments at the University of Georgia during the 1960 Edgewater
Conference, one member responded, "Down in that general area I don't think
we need to be concerned too much, although that is not an absolute assurance
we can dismiss it."[8] The Edgewater Conference's estimate of the cultural climate
on southern campuses such as UGA was largely correct at the start of the 1960s,
but as the decade wore on, student activism became harder to ignore.

The 1960s represented a moment of possibility for sororities in the South
and across the nation as social changes and campus upheaval led students to rethink the activities of their college years. By the mid- to late 1960s, larger shifts
in American culture began to erode the power held by "the establishment"—
whether students identified that in the form of their parents, the university administration, or their sorority's national leadership. Students attempted to understand their place as mature individuals within a nation altered by the civil
rights movement, the sexual revolution, the war in Vietnam, the rise of Black
Power, and the women's rights movement. Those students who complied with
the established order and followed conservative modes of dress and behavior
could be distrusted by students who were experimenting with challenges to
authority as well as middle-class norms of physical appearance. Even if the average students at southern universities were not the same ones leading campus sit-ins, the "southern belle/sorority girl" was not the role model sought by
most college women in these years. Sorority alumnae, however, continued to
push the image as the national sorority ideal.

The relationship between sorority alumnae and college actives, which had
deteriorated as a result of generational differences in responses to these social
changes, seemed at its worst. Yet, rather than considering how to transform
the college sorority experience to better fit the changing needs of students,
the NPC groups dug in their heels and sought to reinforce the lady ideal. For
alumnae, saving their sororities from decline meant ensuring the organizations' futures as socially and racially exclusive, backward-looking groups. This

lack of adjustment would pay off for sororities by the latter half of the 1970s and the 1980s when many students sought stable, nonactivist environments on their campuses.

The southern belle/sorority girl image also played a crucial role as southern schools desegregated and some African American women entered Panhellenic rush. Constructing white sorority ladies as the ideal of southern and American beauty and womanhood presupposed African American women's inability, in their blackness, to claim ladyhood, thereby marking them similarly unsuitable for sorority membership. The white sorority belle or lady, positioned on the pedestal provided by the NPC sorority, reinforced the racial dichotomy of the southern region for the entire nation. By continuing to rely on the old-fashioned image and conservative values of the southern lady, historically white sororities positioned themselves to appeal to a new group of white, middle-class college women who desired the social marker of sorority ladyhood and saw women's liberation as a risky proposition.

Actives versus Alumnae

During the 1960s, as student activism pitted students against administrators, and each other, over issues of race, gender, and socioeconomic inequity on campuses, some sorority chapters saw an opening to question or outright turn against their national organizations. Some chapters rebelled for the more nebulous reason of "seeking local autonomy," and others to explicitly condemn the racial discrimination practiced by their organizations. College members' quest for local autonomy—meaning the ability to run their sisterhood according to the chapter members' interests rather than answering to the multitudinous layers of regional and national alumnae officers—only increased tension between college and alumnae members.[9] Even if chapters were not ready to challenge the racial bar, some sorority members at southern schools sought to modify the sorority experience as popularly understood by generations of women. With ongoing campus conversations about rush and the purpose of sororities, sorority members began to constructively criticize their national organizations. Over time, sorority women's questioning of alumnae leadership and reassessment of rush and membership selection also prompted some sorority women to consider the racial inequity of NPC sorority sisterhood. Some sorority chapters would welcome African American women as pledges after black students were allowed to enroll at southern colleges, but others did not. Meanwhile, nonsouthern chapters also continued to fight over these same issues, as some members saw their chapters' membership practices as discriminatory, but many others desired to maintain the "racial purity" of the "sisterhood."

At the Woman's College of Duke University in 1961, prior to campus desegregation, a group of women who claimed to be sorority members voiced their concerns with the sorority system from the safety of anonymity. Writing under the name "SOS"—possibly standing for "save our sororities"—the group urged a reassessment of group goals and advocated that Duke's chapters disaffiliate from their national organizations. In so doing, the local chapters would also "detach" themselves from the "growing national sentiment against national sororities." SOS's two main reasons for a desired break with nationals were to gain autonomy in shaping their chapters' programs and to make their own choices in member selection.[10]

While SOS could have directly targeted the alumnae efforts that stemmed from the work of the Edgewater Conference to keep NPC sororities white and Protestant, the students' reasoning did not overtly refer to race at this point. The undergraduate student body at Duke would remain segregated until 1963, but discussions of civil rights issues and desegregation already swirled on campus. By gaining more localized control of the sorority chapters, Duke students hoped to redirect sorority ideals away from a national focus—a move that signaled a considerable disjoin between active member and alumnae goals for the groups. Although the women still valued their sorority membership, they hoped to find a way to change the system to make the groups more equitable to all students and more meaningful to the individual members. As they saw it, sororities were in "danger" of self-destruction. If the chapters and their national organizations "[challenged] themselves . . . to change the policies that [were] objectionable," SOS wrote, then they might be able to "find a real place in the lives of the members."[11] Perceptively, the members recognized that the contemporary cultural climate appeared increasingly hostile toward Greek-letter organizations (GLOs) and that their organizations needed to change tack to remain relevant on campus.

The Duke sorority women's seemingly liberal attitudes likely resulted from the intermingling of sorority and independent women in living space. This uncommon arrangement meant that the two groups had a chance to interact daily and view each other as individuals, rather than "sorority" or "independent." This may have stimulated more conversations about sorority issues on campus than if the two groups had been spatially separated by place of residence. Another factor may have been the regional diversity of students attending Duke. While it was still very much a southern college in the 1960s, the private school attracted a larger number of students from outside the South than the typical southern-state public institution.[12]

The campus upheavals over the value of the sorority system at Duke posed a long-standing problem from the point of view of the NPC. At the 1962 meeting of the Edgewater Conference, delegates noted that they had been "asleep at the switch" in regard to the situation at Duke.[13] NPC area adviser Eileen Rudolph (Tri-Delta) read the second SOS letter to the Edgewater members. At the same time, she criticized the Panhellenic at Duke for inviting the anonymous SOS authors to their meeting to discuss their concerns. Rather than praising the young women for being open-minded, Rudolph had questioned the Panhellenic president's decision to try to work with the agitators, comparing the move to "inviting a robber into your living room to sit down and discuss what he is going to take."[14] Several women at Edgewater believed that Duke's sorority issues resulted from the lack of sorority houses and the presence of administrators unfriendly to sororities. With concern, the conference members recalled the instance of women agitating and de-sistering in the 1940s. "This is the history of Duke, as Duke," stated Julia Fuqua Ober, KΔ's national president and NPC delegate. By failing to present themselves as the preeminent campus activity, sorority chapters, it seemed, were just another club at the Woman's College. In the NPC leadership's view this was not an acceptable status. "This is a bad situation," Ober observed.[15]

Some campus demonstrations in this period sought to undermine long-standing parietals, which tightly controlled students' behavior but were much stricter for women. The move toward more lenient rules, or even the total removal of all regulations, for women on campuses also affected the power of NPC groups to enforce behavioral norms. Although arguing for training in "finer feminine virtues" seemed outdated by the latter half of the 1960s, a campus that had just removed stringent supervision of female students could be just the place for NPC groups to swoop in to remind administrators and anxious parents of sororities' benefit. Yet NPC sororities' unwillingness to quickly adapt to changing campus trends meant that they could easily render themselves unnecessary on campuses instead of filling the latest apparent void of guidance for college women.[16] In this period, national sorority leaders continued to loom as unwanted advisers to, rather than allies of, college actives on a quest for change, and as an extension of the administrative oversight the students hoped to see scaled back. With students looking for alternatives to the traditional social outlets on campus, GLOs faltered as they failed to change along with campus trends. Students appeared to wonder what they might get out of membership in a sorority or fraternity that they could not achieve by joining another interest group on campus or befriending students in their dorms.

During these years, the student-led College Panhellenic councils at Duke and the University of North Carolina (UNC) saw the need for sororities to revamp their image on campus. Awakened to current social issues and more suspicious of organizations that appeared to represent establishment thinking and conventional standards of behavior, students were less likely to unquestioningly join a GLO simply because their parents had done so, or because "it seemed the thing to do." Overshadowed by the impression that they were elitist and perhaps racist clubs, sororities and fraternities seemed less enticing to the average student arriving on campus in this period.

A March 1967 report by UNC's Panhellenic Council (PC) aptly titled "Panhellenic Plans a New Image" acknowledged the problems caused by sororities, such as "pressure to conform, cliquishness, high expenses, unnecessary stressing of social values and snobbishness." They noted that "the social compassion and acceptance of differences so indigenous to student culture [emerged] in many minds as being diametrically opposed" to the sorority membership selection process. In an attempt to change this impression, the Panhellenic report suggested that the rush recommendation system needed "explanation and revisions if it is to be acceptable to the new American generation."[17] Still, the animosity on the part of the actives largely resulted from their perception of the alumnae playing an oversized role in the daily operations of the chapters and the work of choosing new members. The University of North Carolina's PC advised that the sorority alumnae "need to decide what things need control and what do not in American women," explicitly stating that alumnae should reevaluate their desire to control the collegiate sorority members and seek to diminish their involvement in the sorority programs on campus. At the same time, they challenged students on the council to make decisions on which issues they wanted greater control over at the collegiate level. The lead author of the report reserved her most stinging criticism for rush. She demanded that sororities "look carefully at the image they present in rush with their silly little Alice in Wonderland parties and their vague criterion for selection." The authors of the report attempted to downplay the role of race in their discussions of chapter autonomy. She noted that "training" to select new members who would "make sorority life meaningful" was "a much bigger thing than taking a girl because she is or is not a Negro." While the PC was able to sidestep directly addressing their opinion on race in membership selection, they were more straightforward about what they felt was the outmoded guidance from alumnae. Instead of learning "manners and all the social graces that a girl can absorb," the lead author advocated that "a woman in our world must be able to learn the ability to recognize and develop strength personally."[18] Seemingly a novel concept in a group that thrived on conformity, she wanted the sorority to help women learn to think for themselves.

The manner in which sororities' national officers reacted to the college sorority women's unrest exhibited just how wide the generational gap in thinking had become. Whereas the difference in age between the college actives and the alumnae leaders had spanned five to twenty-five years in the earlier decades of the twentieth century, by the 1960s some of the alumnae officers trying to enforce rules were at least fifty years removed from their college experiences. The social changes of the mid-twentieth century meant that many older alumnae viewed college students of the 1960s as completely different from themselves at the same age. New standards of dress and behavior made some white, middle-class college students—including sorority members—nearly unrecognizable to alumnae. While attempting to engage in social issues of their day, college members became, in the eyes of alumnae, crusaders "mixed up in the dissident affairs" of the time. In August 1969 Maxine Blake, Alpha Delta Pi (AΔΠ) area adviser for the NPC's College Panhellenics Committee, issued a report on her visit to UNC. Blake was distressed by the fact that the UNC Panhellenic and the campus in general was, as she put it, "very determined and set in its ways, yet vastly influenced by free thinking and a great desire to promote the welfare of the individual." Blake believed that UNC's PC placed interest in the individual ahead of the chapter and Panhellenic image on campus. To women of Blake's generation, the tendency of some sorority women of the late 1960s and early 1970s to ignore what alumnae saw as the "best interests of their member groups" was a radical shift in thinking. The propensity of individual chapters or members to instigate their own local programs marked a change that, to women such as Blake, seemed destined to damage sorority life as they knew it.

Concomitant with her criticism of the UNC Panhellenic, Blake voiced concern over student activism on the UNC campus. She cautioned the NPC, "Black militants are at work at Chapel Hill, SDS [Students for a Democratic Society] is getting under way, 'anti-recommendation' feeing was expressed, and [Panhellenic members] felt they should express opinions on world affairs."[19] Her comments displayed familiar NPC themes of fear and distrust of liberal-leaning organizations. She also betrayed the link between their fears of liberal groups such as SDS and racial integration. By prefacing her statement with the warning about "black militants," Blake reaffirmed a belief held by conservative sorority alumnae that liberal student activism was somehow a result of interference by African American students. This harked back to the NPC line on "freedom of association" and its implicit connotations of racial separation as a part of the "freedoms" for white individuals and their organizations and institutions.

Like the UNC PC, the Emory University PC also strayed into what Blake felt was a questionable level of autonomy. Up until the 1968 school year, the Emory PC had sent a copy of their minutes to their Panhellenic adviser, Evelyn Wait (Phi Mu). The apparent unwillingness of Emory's new PC president to involve alumnae advisers came off as hostility toward the alumnae even if the group had just wished to decrease their reliance on alumnae. In May 1968 Blake characterized the Emory Panhellenic president as "an idealist and free thinker, if I ever met one." In a report to the NPC that was peppered with sarcasm, Blake stated that the president "informed" her "that 'sorority 1968 needs remodeling.'" When Blake's visit forced a conversation between the college members and the alumnae, it became clear that the two groups of sorority women held different ideas for the future of sororities. Much to Blake's consternation, the Emory Panhellenic had decided among themselves that they wished to provide "upperclasswomen interested in fall rush" with details about the inner workings of rush, including "the Quota-Limitation system" and "the methods of voting on membership in the various chapters." Blake and Wait "protested" the proposed informational session, saying that it "was no business of outsiders" and suggested that the Panhellenic "might better try to sell their prospects on the values of joining a sorority." To that plan, the younger women had replied, "That's lollypop stuff."[20] What the college members saw as an important opportunity to offer a frank explanation of the confusing and intimidating rush system for prospective members, the alumnae saw as a betrayal of private practices. On the other hand, while the alumnae felt sure that their perennial message that sororities taught lessons of ladyhood in a fun, social environment was still the best method to attract new pledges, the college sorority women saw that as a vague and often empty advertisement.

Clearly advocating for change, some sorority women attempted to work within the system to transform what they saw as its faults. Their efforts, however, often appeared to end in disappointment. In September 1967 the president of the PC at Duke, Margaret "Bunny" Small, resigned her post while issuing the "challenge that sorority women [were] not honest with themselves about Greek life." Before deactivating from her sorority, Small delivered a speech to sorority presidents, rush chairmen, and campus leaders in which she derided rush's "dehumanizing" function. She had hoped that her presidency would help build a greater sense of community while overcoming the "attitude of 'parochialism'" that she saw as a part of the Greek system.[21] One of Small's friends acknowledged that they were part of the "radical-political contingent" at Duke and pointedly noted that such radical figures were "hated on [the] campus. Ninety percent of students can't stand them, and therefore, what they represent."[22] It was more likely that many of the students desired change but did not feel confident speaking out or know what steps to take to achieve it.

Three years later, in October 1970, sorority women again stalled further plans to modernize sorority rush. Duke's Panhellenic president, Jan Kennerty, resigned following the defeat of her proposal, which would have required sororities to extend a bid to a rushee who was recommended by 15 percent of the women in the chapter. The new measure would still allow the rushee to choose which sorority she wished to join, but it would effectively end the rush quota system. Only two sororities, Kappa Alpha Theta and Zeta Tau Alpha, supported the change, while the remaining seven voted against it. One of the main reasons given for dissent among the groups was that the sororities feared their nationals would place them on probation for violating accepted rush practices.[23] Kennerty's letter of resignation, printed in the *Duke Chronicle*, stated her belief that she could no longer serve as an effective president because her "views no longer [represented] the views of the majority." She did not want to "rationalize and defend a practice" that she felt was "an obsolete remnant from a bygone time." While Kennerty wrote that "virtually all Greek women are in favor of reform, it seems that we just can't do it now."[24] The power of the alumnae leadership in influencing the behavior of college members remained strong even when students seemed to desire change. It was frequently easier for sorority chapters to continue on the same path than to attempt a tussle with their nationals over changes in rush policies.

Discussions about local autonomy could lead chapters to a breaking point and insurrection against their nationals, but more often they provided sorority women with a sense of defiance, allowing them to feel they were taking part in the student activist movement while not requiring that they sacrifice any of their white, middle- to upper-class privilege. Unless the private talks of a sorority chapter became part of larger Panhellenic or campus debates over changes to the Greek system, many of the discussions remained hidden from public knowledge. Frequently, college actives took the path of least resistance, bending to the will of the alumnae in regard to membership or other policies because, after all, they had joined the sorority for the social privilege of being a sorority lady, and being at odds with the alumnae could jeopardize that privilege. If the national sorority revoked the chapter's charter or the women desistered, it would be tantamount to throwing away their future social connections along with the likelihood of marriage to a suitable fraternity peer.

Even on nonsouthern campuses that had never officially barred, or had long allowed enrollment of, African American students, NPC sorority chapters remained alert to the possibility of African American women participating in rush. Membership in an NPC sorority, which had become a means of denoting a woman's ladyhood and whiteness, and thereby her beauty and essential value, provided a measure by which white, middle- and upper-class "ladies" could define themselves against African American women, who were "encroaching" on their spaces of higher education, their campus activities, and possibly their white male friends and dates. Still, nonsouthern chapters, like white nonsoutherners overall, tried to recuse themselves from any semblance of "racist" thought or behavior. As NPC sorority women had found, the southern aesthetic could be donned as a convenient marker of ladyhood, but it could just as easily be discarded in situations that recalled the unsavory aspects of southern heritage. Nonsouthern sorority chapters continued to reference the feelings of their southern sisters when women of color appeared at rush events. Certainly *they* (as nonsoutherners) were not against the particular woman in question, the response went, but she would not be acceptable to chapter members in the South.

The Beta Lambda chapter of Delta Gamma (ΔΓ) at Gettysburg College in Gettysburg, Pennsylvania, also met with alumnae disapproval when the members expressed interest in pledging an African American woman named Karen "Kip" Augustine in 1966. Gettysburg College was overwhelmingly white at the time; Augustine was one of two African American women enrolled on campus. She had rushed in the fall of 1965, her freshman year, but she had been cut from all six NPC sororities on campus after the first round. She was active on campus and also played field hockey, where she befriended several members of ΔΓ. Although Augustine did not choose to rush again in her sophomore year, her friends from hockey recommended her to the chapter during rush. As ΔΓ member Kathryn Smith Pyle recalled, the sisters generally agreed to extend a bid to Augustine, which meant that she would be welcomed as a Delta Gamma pledge. However, trouble arose when ΔΓ alumnae advisers and national officers heard of the situation. A local alumna who also served as a regional officer of ΔΓ held a meeting with the chapter to explain that the group could not pledge Augustine. She reminded the Beta Lambda members that when deciding whom to invite into chapter membership, they must also consider the feelings of the sorority sisters across the country—and she specifically referenced the sisters in the South. Another sorority chapter at Gettysburg also used this line of reasoning against pledging Augustine. The Gamma Beta chapter of Gamma Phi Beta sorority did not need alumnae advisers to remind them of their national membership policies; they had an active chapter member who delivered the message that any new member would have to be accepted at any of the sororities' chapters around the country. She too mentioned the issue of southern chapters as she blackballed Augustine from membership.[25] By pointing to the southern members of the national organization as the reasoning behind any racially discriminatory decisions, nonsouthern members were able to cast the blame for their widespread unsavory behavior on southerners, who had already rightfully earned much criticism for years of blatant, codified racism and violent efforts to maintain racial segregation. In the minds of sorority women across the country, pledging Augustine or other African American women would compromise the racial integrity of the national organization.

Pyle, who had grown up in a rural area just outside of Gettysburg, acknowledged that she entered college with a provincial understanding of the GLOs on her college's campus. She was unaware of the national structure of the sorority she joined and the power behind it and other NPC sororities. By the end of the meeting with the alumna, the members had abandoned their position so as to comply with the national organization's directive. Pyle felt disgusted by what had occurred. A senior at the time, with other interests on campus, she chose to walk away from ΔΓ and not look back. While some attempts by college sorority women to integrate their chapters' membership became public record, similar battles over discrimination at chapters across the country occurred as privately as did that of the Beta Lambda chapter of Delta Gamma at Gettysburg. If none of the chapter's members felt comfortable going public with the story, it was easy for the sorority to continue its discriminatory practices indefinitely.[26]

Guess Who's Coming to Dinner at the House: When Race Became an Issue at Southern Chapters

Southern universities that had been slow to address desegregation bowed to federal pressure following passage of the Civil Rights Act of 1964 and the Higher Education Act of 1965 and began to allow African American students to enroll as undergraduates.[27] More than any other issue, southern campus desegregation introduced students to political causes of the day. While southern college campuses were generally more conservative than those outside the South, some southern students defied the status quo and increasingly engaged in activism during the 1960s. Student activism in issues of racial segregation, university reforms, and war protests helped broaden students' perspectives and create spaces on southern college campuses where protesters could speak out in ways that they previously could not.[28] The extent to which this occurred on each campus depended on factors such as the geographic origin of the majority of the students at a school and the overall campus culture. Such aspects could render schools such as Duke or UNC very different spaces for GLOs than the University of Alabama or the University of Georgia.

National Panhellenic Conference sororities had helped their chapters across the country avoid pledging African American members. However, the organizations realized that it was only a matter of time before they would be confronted with black women choosing to register for white sorority rush at southern schools. The preparation for a response to that scenario, however, was hardly straightforward as college members held differing opinions on how to proceed. Even if a national sorority, or a particular chapter, had an unwritten rule against pledging nonwhite or non-Protestant women, the likelihood that all members agreed on the issue was decreasing in this period. The southern white students had grown up internalizing the lessons of Jim Crow. Combined with sororities' institutional teachings and chapter peer pressure, the legacy of a legally segregated society helped keep discriminatory policies largely intact, but conflict was inevitable.

At UGA and Duke, African American students tested the permeability of the sorority system in the late 1960s. Following the schools' racial desegregation in 1961 and 1963, respectively, a small but slowly growing number of black students regularly enrolled at both universities.[29] Generally, white students did not welcome the African American students, and social segregation continued on campuses. With GLOs dominating the social scene on many campuses and historically white colleges offering little in the way of organized social activities for the handful of African American students, a challenge to the pervasive whiteness of the Greek system was not out of the question. Growing up in a socially segregated American society, African American students would not necessarily expect to find the campuses' white extracurricular culture open to them. Many focused intently on their studies, but that did not exclude them from a desire for social outlets while at school. African American sororities began at Howard University in 1908, with the formation of Alpha Kappa Alpha, followed by Delta Sigma Theta in 1913. The National Pan-Hellenic Council (NPHC), or "The Divine Nine" group of African American sororities and fraternities, formed on the Howard campus in 1930. However, by the mid-1960s, previously all-white southern university campuses did not enroll enough black students to

FIGURE 15. Duke School of
Nursing student and Pi Beta Phi
member Donna Allen in 1967.
Courtesy of Duke University Archives.

support new NPHC chapters. If African American women were interested in
joining a sorority, their only choice was to attend NPC sorority rush.[30]

By the end of the 1964 school year, of the six black women enrolled at
Duke, at least four had registered for rush. In 1963 the two registered women
had "dropped out voluntarily," and in 1964 the two freshmen participating in rush were cut right before the round of "Formal Parties . . . attendance
at which," explained Dean Mary Grace Wilson, "traditionally . . . guaranteed that the rushee's name [would] appear *somewhere* on the sorority's preferred list of students to whom bids [would] be extended."[31] In fall 1967, with
fewer than twenty-five black students on campus, Donna Allen, the first African American student in the School of Nursing at Duke, also became the
first black woman to join a Duke sorority, pledging Pi Beta Phi (ΠΒΦ) (see
fig. 15).[32] Racial relations at Duke in this period remained tense. The African
American students at Duke in the mid- to late 1960s recognized Duke as a
"white university" and expressed dismay over the lack of administration and
faculty attention to their unique situation as the first generation of black stu-

dents at Duke. That same fall, black students came together to form the Afro-
American Society (AAS), which provided a much needed space for socializing
and political organizing on campus. In November 1967 AAS members staged
a "study-in" at President Knight's office to insist that the university end its use
of segregated facilities. Three days later, the university complied with the black
students' demands. Against this backdrop of campus unrest at Duke, Donna
Allen joined a traditionally white sorority.[33]

Among the other nursing students Allen found a group of women for
whom their studies were a common goal. In a 1969 interview for the *Duke
Alumni Register*, Allen explained that her relationships with her fellow nursing students made her experience at Duke much easier to bear than her three
years at the white high school in Elizabeth City, North Carolina, which she
had helped desegregate in 1964.[34] Allen explained that most of the friends in
her immediate circle "were from the North and the West, but not so much
from the South."[35] Perhaps as a result of the close-knit group of students in
the nursing program, Allen elected to rush an NPC sorority. Along with her
friends, Allen joined an NPC sorority, but she did not remember why she
and her roommate pledged ΠΒΦ. Allen did not recall whether the dean's office may have directed her toward certain sororities and away from others as
a woman of color. She remembered the experience of having a "big sister" in
the sorority, but she was fuzzy on what activities she did with the sorority.[36]
She did specifically recollect a sorority-related costume event at Hanes House
where she dressed as "pepper" and her roommate was "salt." "I look back on it
and think. I don't remember anything degrading. . . . Whatever we did, I don't
know, I just remember that. But I don't remember anything degrading, so I'm
just leaving that alone. I'm not asking about it, nothing. We just did it and that
was it."[37] With an intent focus on schoolwork, Allen may not have been very
involved with the sorority's activities and thus maintained little memory of
them. She may not have felt strongly about maintaining connections with the
people from this period in her life, or perhaps she later reconsidered her decision to join a historically white sorority.

Following fall rush in 1967, the *Duke Chronicle* asked Panhellenic president
Connie MacLeod to comment on the historic event of Donna Allen pledging a white sorority. MacLeod responded cagily, "This is a personal matter between the woman and the sorority, but of course I'm delighted to see Pi Phi
get a girl who wanted them."[38] MacLeod's carefully worded statement seems
to place responsibility of her membership only on Allen, and not the sorority
or Panhellenic. As MacLeod had noted, Allen wanted *them*. Apparently, a fair
number of the ΠΒΦs must have wanted Allen too, but MacLeod did not attri-

bute that sentiment to the entire national sorority or even the entire chapter. Her answer acknowledged that a black woman joining an NPC sorority could be a highly contested issue among sorority members and alumnae, and likely among the Pi Beta Phi NC Beta chapter members themselves.

By the 1968 school year, the Black Power movement was influencing student activism on southern campuses. With larger numbers of black students enrolling at historically nonblack colleges, organized groups such as AAS at Duke, the Black Student Movement (BSM) at UNC, and the Black Student Union (BSU) at UGA began to set goals and make vocal demands of the university administrations, such as calls for black studies programs, recruitment of more black students, hiring of black faculty members, organization of a black cultural center or dorm, and the removal of racist iconography from campus.[39] That fall, Deborah "Debbie" Williams, an African American student at UGA elected to go through NPC sorority rush. Unlike Donna Allen's choice to rush at Duke, Williams's decision to register for rush at UGA was designed to bring attention to the fact that Greek life was an area of campus life that had remained closed to black students and largely separated from the student activities in which black students were involved. An article on Williams's actions, written by Cynthia Baugh, the first black staff member of the *Red and Black*, explained that UGA sororities and fraternities were "completely white," but the reason "'why' [had] not been questioned."[40] In the article, Williams described the white sorority women's and white rushees' reactions to her presence as "priceless." Many of the white women, she explained, expressed "surprise" and "interest" that she appeared at rush events but did not ask her "just why [she] was there." As southern belles trained to react with grace and restraint, the "surprise" and "interest" they showed likely masked the incredulity, and perhaps the fear, that many of the women may have felt and surely discussed at length during their scratch sessions after the rush parties. In the most telling aspect of her exercise, Williams recognized that rush was an activity where, Baugh noted, "prejudice draws a line between friendship and racial differences." Baugh explained that Williams experienced no "outright ostracism" but that she noticed "the little things that characterize the so-often muted undertones of racism prevalent in situations where people are confronted with the idea of integration." Williams saw that "several of her acquaintances were waiting with her for the rushee buses" but that "none of them spoke or seemed to recognize her presence."[41] Apparently, the white women realized that part of their performance as an ideal rushee was to uphold the sanctity of the segregated space of the NPC sorority.

At all sixteen sorority houses, Williams sensed tension and nervousness on the part of the white sorority sisters who came out of their houses to greet the rushees and saw her among the group. While she was "met with the 'standard procedure' of smiles and 'How are you?' and 'Where are you from?'" Baugh wrote, there remained "the problem of who would take [Debbie] into the house and introduce her around." At each sorority, however, the women recovered sufficiently for a sister to come forth to escort her into the house without noticeable difficulties in their highly choreographed rush movements. Williams was surprised that she was asked back to the next round of parties at three of the sororities. Some of the women asked her why she was going through rush, but Williams also learned from these conversations that "some of the sorority girls . . . were glad to see her there." She explained to them that she was rushing to make the point that white sororities had "made no effort to encourage participation by black students." Williams wanted the white sororities to understand that in the wake of desegregation they would have to accept the fact that more black women would be seen going through rush—although, she pointed out, that did not mean "that all black students that come here want to be part of a sorority or fraternity."[42] Baugh noted in the article that "the possibilities of a black sorority [had] been discussed," but nothing had come of it as of the previous school year. In some instances, the women told Williams that they "thought a black sorority would be good on the campus . . . that it would give black students the chance they wanted to identify."[43] White sorority women's interest in having a black sorority on campus could be read two ways. They may have genuinely hoped that the addition of a black sorority would give black women a social space where they would feel comfortable and could enjoy the promise of "sisterhood" that the white women supposedly enjoyed in their NPC chapters. But the presence of a black sorority could also make it easier for white sororities to continue in their segregated ways, as most black women would likely rush an NPHC group instead. If all African American women directed their interest toward NPHC groups instead of joining NPC rush, then white sororities could remain all white without much effort. Thus, having a black sorority on campus could deflect the bad publicity surrounding NPC groups as discriminatory organizations. As she closed the article, Baugh wondered whether Williams's presence at rush had "challenge[d]" the thinking of the rushees and sorority women. Had "her motives [been] taken lightly?" "Did anyone really understand why a black student rushed white sororities?" The situation among sorority women was well summarized by Williams's final comment on the matter, issued "casually" to Baugh: "Some understood, and some didn't . . . some never will."[44]

While NPC sororities welcomed the establishment of NPHC sororities on their campuses—if only as a means to attract African American women away from NPC sorority rush—the NPC did not necessarily wish to engage the African American groups in existing campus Panhellenics. By the early 1970s, the National Association for Women's Deans and Counselors (NAWDAC) was pushing the NPC to address their relationship with NPHCs. NPC chair Myra Foxworthy felt that NAWDAC had moved into "radical territory."[45] Demonstrating the alumnae leaders' penchant for viewing young student personnel administrators as a liberal, enemy force, she voiced her hope that they could "avoid confrontation with hostile young Panhellenic Advisers" at the NAWDAC meeting in the spring of 1972.[46] While unsure of the feelings of the individual member groups on the issue of cooperation with African American sororities, Foxworthy thought the NPC should prepare itself "to face discussion with the leaders of the NPHC groups," although she did not believe that they would want to join the NPC anyway.[47] As Zeta Tau Alpha and NPC delegate Harriet Frische (Baker State University, 1928) noted in a response on the matter, the NPHC groups "would lose their present opportunities of leadership in their own conference and fall into a 2nd class relationship, in spite of good intentions."[48] It would be better for all involved, the NPC believed, if the groups remained separate.

Sororities and Women's Liberation

The image of the white sorority woman as refined southern lady stood in stark contrast to pictures of late 1960s and early 1970s campus protesters, which included the few publicly self-proclaimed "feminists" on southern campuses. To an American public alarmed by a seemingly outspoken, unkempt, and rude generation of youths, the ideal of a disengaged, reserved, demure lady would provide comfort. For students who sought stability in the years after the rise of the counterculture, the lady, and the social and racial "order" for which she stood, would be a welcome icon and ideal to emulate. Dean Katherine Kennedy Carmichael likely applauded sororities' training in ladylike demeanor during these years as she lamented "activist" students' sartorial choices. In 1970 she described participants in UNC's women's liberation movement as "belligerently feministic" and "reminiscent of 1900–1920," while noting their allegiance to the "cult of the ugly, accompanied by the dirty, the meanly dressed, [and] the foul word." They were a far cry from the women of 1960, who, Carmichael reminisced, were "well-dressed and beautiful in body, speech, and clothes."[49]

Women's liberation organizations arose on southern campuses while many students continued to celebrate traditionally gendered interactions between the men and women on campus. The sexual revolution had enabled a reimagining of sexuality outside of marriage, but women's subordination to men in hetero-social and heterosexual relationships persisted, and the structure of GLOs made them primary supporters of that arrangement. At the University of Georgia, Women's Oppression Must End Now (WOMEN) organized in 1971. That same year, UGA sorority women wrote proudly of being selected as "little sisters" of fraternity men. Sororities assigned "big sisters" to act as mentors to the new pledges, also called their "littles." When this dynamic transferred to the fraternity, the relationship between the "big brother" and "little sister" could present a variety of possibilities.[50] The Delta chapter of Sigma Chi at UGA had started a "Little Sigmas" chapter for women who were pinned to Sigma Chis and for the chapter sweetheart (generally chosen for her physical beauty), but the Little Sigmas had quickly expanded to include other sorority women. In their newsletter, the university's Alpha Delta Pi (AΔΠ) chapter proudly announced that seven of the twenty women chosen by the Delta chapter to be Little Sigmas were AΔΠs. The picture accompanying the story shows member Inez Moore ironing clothes. The caption reads, "Inez Moore finds out what it means to be a Little Sigma as she irons her boyfriend's bluejeans."[51] She apparently labored contentedly at what looked like pledge hazing or the daily routine of a homemaker or servant. Inez and the rest of the Little Sigmas strove for this type of "recognition" by the Sigma Chis at UGA. While pockets of women organized around liberal causes, many white women on southern campuses continued to adhere to the conservative line implicitly *and* explicitly propagated by their sorority chapters, by preserving conventionally gendered activities. The fact that the Little Sigmas and similar groups were acceptable to and even revered by sorority women of the early 1970s illustrated the point that the women's liberation movement made directly—that sororities classified women in an unnatural and hurtful way, and in so doing they damaged the ability of these women to work together to overcome gender inequality in U.S. society. Particularly since sororities so effectively perpetuated the idea that acceptance by men was a direct measure of women's value as individuals.

At Duke during the 1971 school year, a group called Duke Women's Liberation, which had formed in the fall of 1969 as Female Liberation No. 11, posed a direct challenge to campus sororities. They argued that instead of creating a kinship network among their members, sororities actually "divide women because they are based on competition and selective sisterhood," which "degrade women as persons." The women's liberation group not only blamed the sororities for choosing rushees that fit a certain image but also chided rushees for choosing to pledge a sorority based on its ability to "satisfy [their] social needs."[52] In their view, both the sorority chapter and the rushees used one another to reach their goal of attracting men. By highlighting the point that "most men still view women in the superficial terms of appearance and physical appeal," Duke Women's Liberation claimed that in catering to male interest, sorority women gained "an excuse to view and to judge other women in these same terms."[53]

Some Duke sorority women stood up for their organizations in response to the claims of the women's liberation group. In letters to the *Duke Chronicle* they argued that Duke Women's Liberation was misguided in its attempt to boil sorority sisterhood down to a superficial group, built around fake friendships. Instead of seeking a certain "type" of member as some sort of attempt to appeal to a target group of men, the letter writers explained, their sorority chapters had helped them form friendships with other women, not all of whom were "beautiful with nice figures."[54] They maintained that sorority membership was "about getting to know the girl for her own individual personality" and that it allowed women to meet other female students outside of their dorms.[55] While sorority women viewed the accusations by Duke Women's Liberation as an unwarranted attack on their sisterhood, they failed to see that the entire sorority system created a culture that derived a woman's value from her appearance and the likelihood that she would be found attractive by a certain group of male students. Even if white female students supported some goals of the women's movement, joining a women's liberation group on a southern college campus was not a widely popular activity. At a 1971 panel discussion held by Duke Women's Liberation as an "alternative for freshman women currently undergoing sorority rush," the Duke *Chronicle* noted that most of the women in attendance were members of Women's Liberation.[56]

Beyond the campus, sorority alumnae also perceived challenges from the women's movement's push to ratify the Equal Rights Amendment (ERA) in 1970. Although many educated, white, middle-class women supported ERA, per usual, NPC sororities did not take an "official" position on the politicized issue. However, the longtime conservative positioning of the NPC leadership suggested that the amendment would not gain support from national sorority officers. The primary provision of ERA stated, "Equality of the rights under the law shall not be denied or abridged by the United States or by any state on account of sex."[57] Conservatives, led by the indomitable Phyllis Schlafly, understood ERA as an attack on "traditional" family values, instigated by women who, they believed, rejected their true, feminine nature and wished to be men. The conservative antiratificationists were unwilling to separate biological sex from social role for either women or men and feared that ratification of the amendment would exacerbate the damage to American families that they believed the women's liberation movement had started. If all women joined the workforce, Schlafly's cohort argued, children would be taken from their mothers and reared by government-run day care centers.[58] The idea easily signaled a communist conspiracy for women who had spent decades obsessing over the threat of communist infiltration.

In March 1975 Barbara Cook, associate dean of students at Purdue University and president-elect of NAWDAC, wrote to NPC chairman Virginia Friese Jacobsen with concerns that some individual members of NPC sororities were circulating letters to alumnae and college chapters "urging the membership to oppose ratification of the Equal Rights Amendment."[59] NAWDAC had reaffirmed their support for ERA in their 1974 Conference Resolutions and encouraged members to work individually, through their state associations, and in other women's groups "to support passage of the ERA in those states which have not yet ratified it," setting the stage for new opposition between their membership and the NPC.[60] Cook explained that the sorority alumnae's letters suggested an erroneous connection between the 1974 U.S. Department of Health, Education, and Welfare Proposed Title IX Requirements and ERA. Title IX of the Education Amendments of 1972 provided that no person, on the basis of sex, should be subjected to discrimination under any education program receiving federal funding. Cook reminded Jacobsen that "it is a fact that Congress has exempted sororities and fraternities and youth organizations from the requirements of Title IX." Cook also noted that a recent Interfraternity Research and Advisory Council (IRAC) Bulletin article by a sorority alumna featured "an anti-ERA stance" and seemed to suggest that the NPC sanctioned that position.[61] For conservative whites who were still angered by the previous two decades' erosion of white supremacy in the name of racial equality, sex equality was the next battlefield.[62] By connecting it to Title IX and other legislation that challenged the private, sorority "family," conservative alumnae were able to raise alarms within their national membership.

Jacobsen replied to Cook's query by stating that she had not seen any such letters against ERA from alumnae and that the NPC "[had] taken no action, nor issued any position statement, relative to ERA." She agreed that Title IX and ERA "must not be confused" but left room for the suggestion that they were related legislation, noting that "to be fully understood, each would require study in depth." Jacobsen neither supported nor opposed ERA in her letter but reiterated the understanding that sororities and fraternities would remain exempt from the proposed Title IX guidelines.[63] In a 1978 interview, Kappa Delta national president Jean Tucker Jackson demonstrated the lingering concern over possible ERA ratification among sorority women. When asked about the future probability of coed GLOs, Jackson replied, "Of course, if the Equal Rights Amendment is ratified it will mean that we can no longer remain a single-sex organization."[64] Her misunderstanding of ERA suggested a continued conflation of the amendment with Title IX and an unwillingness to accede that the typically GLO-friendly Congress would likely make provisions for GLOs in their enforcement of ERA, as they had with Title IX. This reading of ERA also provided a convenient way for NPC sororities to be anti-ERA because of the supposed threat to their organizations. The same year, Delta Gamma national president Mary Ann Lummis Bowyer (Denison University) suggested that the women's liberation movement had not directly affected the function of the sorority because the organization did not "deal in matters regarding to full equality with males." Rather, Boyer felt that the most pressing issue for ΔΓ in the realm of women's rights was keeping up with new regulations put forth by universities.[65] She likely referenced the recent GLO "victory" in gaining an exception to the Title IX ruling from Congress so as to remain single-sex organizations. This gave sororities protection from what they believed was increasing infringement on their organizations by campus administrators.

Conservative sorority alumnae saw the current cultural climate as an affront to white middle-class women's femininity. They constantly felt that sororities were under attack by special interest groups who sought to diminish the cultural authority of white, middle- and upper-class families. By appealing to young women who saw the "value" in maintaining an emphasis on fixed gender identity tied to biological sex, sororities could continue their lessons of ladyhood for a new generation of college members. The image of the southern lady was a natural fit for these groups that required an emblem of traditional womanhood displaying grace and refinement, as well as an affinity for the domestic sphere and family values. Hardly relics from a bygone era, the southern belle and lady persevered as icons that represented a complex mix of physical beauty, hyperfemininity, white southern heritage, and an endurance of reactionary ideals.

"Ladies First":
Selling Sororities to a New Generation of Women

In 1973 Adele Williamson of Louisiana, a former national president of Phi Mu, then serving as an NPC area adviser for Georgia, Louisiana, and Mississippi, sent NPC College Panhellenic chairman and Pi Beta Phi Helen B. Dix a report expressing her belief that "the next few years" would bring "renewed growth to the Fraternity System" in the Deep South if the NPC could continue to build trust with members of College Panhellenics and keep them involved.[66] Not all incoming college women were aware of sororities' recent history of massive resistance to changes in their membership policies. Many young white women, and particularly those in the South, could approach the southern lady as a timeless and appealing model of beauty and desirability worth emulating. Sorority leaders realized that to overcome the student disinterest of the late 1960s, they would have to find a way to make the organizations appear vital to contemporary student life. Just as they had worked to demonstrate their purpose to students and administrators in the early decades of the twentieth century, NPC sororities needed to reaffirm their supposed necessity to campus life.

During the spring of 1974, NPC area adviser and Tri-Delta Kathleen D. Nye (University of Iowa, 1943) issued a report to NPC delegates with chapters at the University of Michigan. In the encouraging report, Nye noted that sororities at Michigan had experienced a 120 percent increase in pledging from 1973 to 1974.[67] Perhaps one of the most heartening signs for the sorority alumnae was a shift from the raucous protests of 1960s. Legal and political action had emboldened social movements that challenged discrimination over race, gender, and sexuality, thereby altering long-standing norms of social interaction in the United States. College students of the 1970s inhabited the new social landscape wrought by their 1960s predecessors, while Americans more broadly continued to face a transformation of society. By the first half of the 1970s, U.S. troop withdrawal from Vietnam, the Watergate scandal and President Richard Nixon's impeachment, and a major economic recession meant that many white middle-class Americans' sense of purpose and security began to falter.[68] The search for direction and identity in an increasingly pessimistic but also newly permissive and experimental culture likely influenced some students to seek the apparent structure imposed by sorority and fraternity life. In 1975, with the number of women pledging sororities at the University of Georgia steadily increasing since the 1970 low of 253, Panhellenic adviser Carol Veatch suggested that the primary reason for sororities' return to popularity at UGA and elsewhere was "a return to a little bit of a conservative trend" on college campuses. GLO advisers noted that students had distanced themselves from structured organizations during the social activism of the mid- to late 1960s, but by the mid-1970s they again sought a "place to belong," particularly on larger, impersonal campuses.[69]

Even as GLOs hoped for a return of the conservative student, sororities considered new methods to appeal to a broader audience. In a move that sig-

naled a departure from NPC sororities' previous strategies, the nationals began to colonize chapters at former junior colleges and other schools that
would not have met their academic or social standards in earlier years. In seeking new areas of expansion for their organizations, sororities expanded their
acceptance of white women from working-class backgrounds and less ex-
alted academic pedigrees. In so doing, sororities were able to offer introduc-
tory training in ladyhood to women from backgrounds that sorority members
of the earlier twentieth century might not have seen as worthy of the title. In
turn, for white women from working-class backgrounds, the picture of the sorority woman as southern lady was an alluring ideal that helped reinforce commonality of race over class. By expanding their definition of ladyhood, NPC
sororities could entice new markets of young women to join their organizations while at the same time inviting a wider swath of white women to partake
in their world of racially based privileges. Bringing these women into the sorority enlarged the group of white women beholden to the powerful national
GLOs and showed sororities' affinities for race over class as legalized segregation fell away.

With longtime sorority leaders retiring from duties or passing away, a
new generation of leadership would take the helm, steering sororities in the
post-activist era. Even as a number of national leaders continued down the
path trod by Mary Love Collins, Maxine Blake, and others of their generation,
some Greek alumnae showed openness to working with college sorority members rather than against them. NPC leaders again turned to their public relations experts to spread the gospel of sisterhood while fine-tuning their messages to reduce the appearance of association with reactionary groups. Even as
they shifted away from proclamations such as those issued by the Research and
Public Relations (RPR) Committee over the previous three decades, the leaders continued to trend conservative.

In a move to retool the profile of GLOs, alumni consultants also reinforced
a conservative image with a "school of manners" approach that mirrored earlier efforts at social education. The GLO resocialization program would seek
a return to what some alumni felt was a more genteel time in sorority and
fraternity life. Instead of directing chapter funds toward beer-soaked parties,
the groups should use the money once again for house "decor and beauty." If
the fraternity members refocused and were not constantly drunk or drugged,
the alumni believed, they would be available as dates for sorority women. Apparently, the lack of social contact—"many sorority leaders had few dates all
year"—had led to girls depledging because they could have a greater social network as "unorganized dorm [residents]."[70] The alumni concerns showed an ef-

fort to reestablish the heterosocial and conventionally gendered order of sorority and fraternity relations.

At the 1973 NPC meeting, leaders unveiled the new Public Relations Committee, noting the important role it could play in crafting a new NPC image. The new plan for PR would focus on the supposed good of sororities in providing camaraderie, social connections, and professional training for young women, while shifting their lessons of citizenship away from the overt connections to anticommunism and "freedom of association" that had branded the groups as holdovers from the 1950s and early 1960s. However, this did not mean that the alumnae were ready to abandon conservative principles. NPC chair Myra Foxworthy (Alpha Gamma Delta, University of Oklahoma, 1960) acknowledged that "among our own membership NPC has attained an image that may not be altogether true or flattering."[71] In 1971, during her first year as chair, Foxworthy and other sorority alumnae began to discuss the damage that could result from the "reactionary" reports long issued by the RPR Committee. In correspondence with other alumnae, Foxworthy expressed her fears that the mailings could "do harm if they fell into the wrong hands." "And coming from a conservative like me," she noted, "that is saying something!" Foxworthy found the content in the reports so inflammatory that she had chosen to withhold them from her sorority's council. When she learned that the committee was sending the reports *directly* to the various sorority headquarters rather than only routing them through the NPC delegates, she worried that the reactionary reports, laden with conspiracy theories, could be distributed beyond the circle of sorority alumnae who knew how to control their contents.[72]

Expansion

As the NPC and individual nationals worked to change popular perceptions of their organizations and mend fences with existing college chapters, they also branched out, building new relationships with recently accredited colleges, which they had formerly shunned for their lack of academic and social credentials. To continue showing evidence of "growth," even as some older chapters might be shutting down from lack of new members (or after losing their charters for defying their nationals), sororities would have to find new campuses to saturate. As the number of women entering sorority rush dropped in the late 1960s and early 1970s, national officers continued to tout the establishment of new chapters as a way of demonstrating the sorority system's "success." For many years, sororities had been very careful about placing new chapters only at universities with a solid reputation and students of high academic, cultural, and financial caliber.[73] In search of new campuses, however, they now steered expansion toward universities that had formerly been normal colleges or had only recently gained full degree-granting accreditation. In spring 1975 Delta Gamma's NPC delegate wrote a column in the *Anchora* that explained how the national sorority had planned its expansion to new campuses in recent years. As "many parents refused to send their sons and daughters to what were called the 'liberal campuses,'" they instead turned to the "'emerging' state schools, many of which were former teachers' colleges and where the atmosphere was more conservative." In the minds of alumnae, a conservative environment made the campuses ripe for Greek life. While the alumnae believed that the "trouble" with activist students was beginning to die down at flagship state universities by the mid-1970s, they also continued to seek out new types of campuses that they would have refused in previous decades for a supposed lack of social exclusivity in students.[74] By considering the establishment of chapters at junior colleges, sororities would be instituting a major change in their approach, which had long relied on social class exclusivity as a means of defining membership.

By 1973 the NPC drew up a list of five hundred possible "junior and community colleges" that might be interested in NPC sororities. Myra Foxworthy explained that while the NPC had originally felt that expansion into junior colleges would "constitute a lowering of standards," changes in higher education over the past seventy years had shown that the schools often became "feeder schools" for "upper division and graduate universities."[75] With the goal of expansion, national sororities seemed ready to replace their previous fears of "lowering standards" with a policy of quantity over supposed quality. A possible expansion to junior colleges, or recently designated four-year institutions, also signaled a possible shift toward a more inclusive understanding of Greek life. While consideration of such a move signaled a broadening of sororities' visions of acceptable members, officers' reports regarding expansion evidenced some of the typical elitism shown by sorority women regarding selection of members. In late 1973, following a trip to Pembroke State University (now UNC-Pembroke) in Pembroke, North Carolina, NPC area adviser Pat Merrill (Kappa Delta, Ohio State) accompanied Martha "Marty" Huggins Pugh (Phi Mu, Howard College) on her visit to the nearby University of North Carolina at Wilmington.[76] NPC sororities would have overlooked these schools for many years. Pembroke State began as the state college for American Indians, remaining nonwhite until 1953, while UNC-Wilmington began as a UNC satellite learning center in 1946, becoming the accredited junior college, Wilmington College, in 1948 and retaining junior status for the next two decades.

After the visit, Merrill sent the NPC a report, directed to delegates of Phi Mu and Zeta Tau Alpha, which had chapters on the Wilmington campus. She was greatly concerned about the strength of the chapters at Wilmington. Phi Mu had sixteen members, while ZTA counted eleven. "The girls appear to be quite apathetic," Merrill noted. "Their rush rules were full of 'don'ts, can'ts, and must nots' until I fear everything appeared so negative and full of 'orders.'" She worried that many of the rushees dropped out because of the regimentation. The college women's interest in creating strict regulations for their chapters may have stemmed from a desire to demonstrate a mastery of middle-class or elite social conventions. Students at flagship public universities and exclusive private colleges with middle-class or elite upbringings who felt more socioeconomically secure may have been comfortable flouting conventional rules of behavior. Their working-class counterparts, on the other hand, may have been eager to attain markers of middle-class acceptability and were thus less inclined to challenge authority. Merrill also opined that "many girls from the nearby town do not have funds for sororities, and many of them are hippie-freaks, not interested in affiliation, and would undoubtedly not be the type of women who would be a good sorority woman." In short, to Merrill these women were not southern lady material. While the NPC decided to limit expansion to four-year institutions and not move into two-year junior colleges, Merrill, likely along with a number of alumnae, continued to express concerns about the "type" of woman who might join an NPC sorority chapter at any less established university.[77]

Rebuilding a Sorority Following

Even though Pat Merrill and other sorority leaders may have held reservations about the caliber of women joining new sorority chapters at recently accredited universities, the alumnae believed that NPC sororities were well positioned to reemerge as fundamental organizations on college campuses in the latter half of the 1970s. A student panel speaking at a 1977 sorority housemother's seminar in Columbia, Missouri, identified contemporary students as "independent, [preferring] a casual lifestyle" with relaxed manners, and "[disliking] discipline," but they also described the students as "establishment oriented." Supposedly, students were more "pessimistic, self-centered, and materialistic," and more concerned with landing a job that would make money. In what was termed the "Me Decade," a time when Americans appeared to nurture self-interests at the expense of larger social and familial pursuits, the private, inward focus of GLOs could provide a refuge for white college students. The students also described their peers as more conservative and less political than those of the 1960s.[78] This characterization suggested that GLOs would stand a better chance at drawing new members from the current crop of students than they would have ten years before. By adopting a less authoritarian approach to their alumnae advising and returning to a program of social training that combined heterosocial skills with professional polish suitable for a variety of activities beyond college, NPC groups found a new generation of women eager to gain the supposed benefits of membership.

Sororities geared their revamped social education toward professionalization and building contacts for adulthood, which suggested an outlook beyond parties and dates in college and the goal of immediate heterosexual marriage after graduation. Greek-letter organization advisers at UGA believed that the organizations were attracting students in "pre-professional curriculums." Panhellenic adviser Carol Veatch was "amazed at the number of women going through fall rush [who were] interested in the academic standing of the sororities."[79] Both the women's liberation movement and the rising cost of living influenced more women to enter the paid workforce.[80] Women began looking at sorority membership as a way to open doors on their career paths rather than just as a social outlet during the four years of college. While some sororities had offered job placement services in the 1910s and 1920s, the professionalization model of the 1970s and 1980s was about networking and sharing privilege. The organizations sought to parallel old boys' networks of white male power in their programs of career and social advancement, as fraternity men had long relied on fraternal connections to establish their careers.

Like the generation of sorority alumnae during the first quarter of the twentieth century, these alumnae also sent mixed messages about "preferred" activities for sorority women. New career services programs sprung up within the organizations, but at the same time, sorority journals shared stories about volunteer work and featured entrepreneurial women who turned their crafts and hobbies into small businesses. While demonstrating drive and ambition, the laudable female entrepreneurs did not seek careers in conventionally male professions or try to work their way up the corporate ladder.[81] In an article carried in multiple sororities' journals, Phi Mu alumna Annadell Craig Lamb wrote of the importance of women who filled volunteer roles. Lamb noted that volunteer work could help sorority alumnae move into paid positions in the same field, but the primary purpose in her writing was to refute the idea that all women wanted a career outside the home. She saw this as a negative effect of the "Women's Lib advocates" who had "bombarded the public with consciousness-raising." Lamb's angle also assumed that most if not all sorority alumnae would have a financial support network, in the form of a bread-winning husband or family money, that would make volunteer work feasible.[82] Like the southern lady, she would exist in the vaunted realm of white privilege, where she would have time available to dabble in her own interests or, if in the Ellen O'Hara vein of ladyhood, minister to those less fortunate. Even as the national sororities expanded to commuter and former junior colleges, sorority alumnae still acted as though the membership came from solid middle- to upper-class backgrounds.

Some student personnel administrators saw students' "fear of failure" as a stimulus in campuses' renewed interest in GLOs. The generation of 1970s college students was the first to graduate into economic uncertainty since those in the Depression years. The postwar economic boom had stalled out with soaring inflation and a slowing economy.[83] For students worried that they would be less well off than their parents' generation, a support network of strong alumnae connections provided an added draw. The renewed focus on refined living in the sorority house, which had gone by the wayside during the anti-establishmentarianism of the late 1960s and early 1970s, meant a return to practicing social graces. Weekly formal dining at the chapter house, for example, followed protocol and offered a veneer of order.[84] Perhaps the complete removal of campus parietals, some college administrators ventured, led students to seek guidance in the form of Greek-letter affiliation.[85] Kappa Kappa Gamma chapter house rules regarding men's visitation and sisters' "key privileges," or the freedom to come and go as they pleased, were more stringent than the regulations found on some campuses in the mid-1970s.[86] The combination of social training and social-class camaraderie provided a sense of tradition and safety.

The increased student interest in GLOs also may have resulted from students' desire to oppose the rebelliousness of the 1960s students. Many had held hopes that continued economic prosperity and progress in race relations would enable the nation to realize the utopian dream of early 1960s activists. By the 1970s, however, some white middle-class Americans wondered whether the resulting changes in U.S. society were of benefit to them or not. For NPC leaders who entered the 1960s seeking ways to hold back the tide of social activism and change, the newly skeptical, self-directed, and self-preservation–driven students of the 1970s and the early 1980s appeared more to their liking.[87] The 1978 film *National Lampoon's Animal House*, which followed the sophomoric exploits of the fictional Delta Tau Chi fraternity at Faber College (drawn from the Dartmouth College undergrad experiences of one of the film's writers), provided a nostalgia trip for white Americans who saw the film's 1962 setting as a "simpler time," before the turbulence of 1960s activism or the defeat and corruption associated with 1970s foreign and domestic affairs. Sure, the "bad guys" in *Animal House*'s "snobbish," WASPy fraternity looked like they were primed to host a Young Americans for Freedom convention, but the "good guys" at the Delta house (who ended up on "double secret probation") were heavy drinkers, objectifiers of women, generally lackluster students and campus contributors, and, really, not convincing in their roles as heroes.[88] In National Lampoon's depiction, there was a suitable GLO experience for every white student who wanted to find the perfect mix of "brotherhood" and hedonism on their respective college's fraternity row. With the "fun" on campus again seeming to center on fraternities by the late 1970s, increased student involvement in sororities was not far behind.

While sororities began the 1970s with their status in question on many campuses, they were able to regain stature among students as the decade progressed. The late-1960s moment of possible change slipped away with little alteration in national sororities' operations. Shifting trends in campus culture aided the sororities as students withdrew from activism and became more introspective and privately focused. A renewed interest in traditional campus activities also boosted GLOs in these years. While the South was indeed a stronghold for the groups, as the Edgewater Conference members opined, sorority chapters continued to flourish at schools in the Midwest, West, and Northeast. But the quintessential public image of the sorority woman remained that of the southern lady. The intense focus on physical appearance, heterosocializing, and a stylized, hyperfeminine performance all aligned with the archetype of the southern lady. "A woman by birth . . . a lady by choice!" was the slogan of a 1973 *Key* article about the importance of maintaining personal values.[89]

Ladyhood might be the choice of the sorority that selected the woman as a sorority lady, or the choice of the individual woman who followed the sorority's behavioral prescriptions to attain "ladyhood," but it simultaneously defined those women who did *not* have a choice and would not be viewed as ladies in popular understandings of the term. The mantle of ladyhood denoted privilege and automatically othered women who were not ladies in the eyes of NPC sororities because of their class, race, religion, or physical appearance. With the southern lady standing in as the preeminent lady figure, the sororities went forth reinforcing a specific, limited vision of power and influence among American women.

CONCLUSION

·•·

An Alpha Phi-asco and
Other Peculiar Institutions

*I*n the summer of 2015, when the women of the Beta Mu chapter of Alpha Phi sorority at the University of Alabama released and then quickly tried to delete a much-criticized publicity video, the episode was just one in a recent spate of negative exposure for NPC sororities in the United States. The video, created to entice new, suitably eligible young women to consider Alpha Phi during sorority recruitment, showed a bevy of thin, white, scantily-yet-designer-clad young women with flowing tresses frolicking around their professionally decorated sorority mansion in Tuscaloosa.[1] The message was clear: If you fit this limited image from the spectrum of womanhood, you too could aspire to become an Alpha Phi at 'Bama. Intertwined with this call to all "southern belle" wannabes was, of course, the pronouncement to local fraternity men that Alpha Phis are beautiful and sexy—in the conventional American understanding of contemporary attractiveness where thin, white women of the privileged class are the standard-bearers.

The display of fun and physically attractive white women to "sell" the popularity of a sorority chapter is nothing new. As I have shown, national sorority chapters across the United States have continually relied on standards of physical beauty as a major factor in choosing new members—to the point where this ingrained practice has led to a public expectation of physical beauty when referring to sorority women. Since sorority membership remains largely white at colleges in the South *and* outside of it, this only reinscribes the idea that whiteness is a prerequisite for beauty among American women. Additionally, the recent focus on NPC sororities' long-standing adherence to a problematic "southern aesthetic" couples the understandings of beauty and "acceptable" womanhood with southern, white women and a southern culture that is greatly influenced by persisting institutions of white supremacy. While today's practice of a southern aesthetic among a certain privileged class of southern white women may include such things as the promotion of what we might call "y'all culture" as a regional identifier, monogramming everything (including your car), coveting Lilly Pulitzer dresses, and aspiring to the lifestyle depicted in magazines such as *Southern Living* and *Garden and Gun*, these superficial markers cloak the underlying desire to self-consciously construct a nationally appealing southern culture that is elite, white, and suburban—or perhaps, if urban, in a safely gentrified form.[2]

However, recent presentations of southernness-as-whiteness have also delved into the Old South themes that captivated sorority women of the early twentieth century. Nostalgic images of the "belle" have manifested on contemporary college campuses in scenarios such as the southern-founded fraternities Kappa Alpha Order's and Sigma Alpha Epsilon's respective Old South Ball and Magnolia Ball—weekends filled with fraternity men in mock uniforms of the Confederate Army and sorority women laced into rented hoop skirts and frilly dresses. The University of Georgia's recent decision to ban the practice of wearing hoop skirts for such events bespeaks the larger yet unaddressed issue at hand—NPC sororities' continued adherence to a southern aesthetic. Premised on a connection to the mythologized Old South, the aesthetic signals yet never explicitly speaks of that time and place where slavery and its attendant characteristics of violence, racism, and classism were practiced norms. Historian Elizabeth Boyd has noted that contemporary, hoop-skirted, white women's "southern belle performances routinely staged on campuses across the South constitute a choreography of exclusion."[3] Buying into the aesthetic, sorority women across the nation claim power through the quietly commanding imagery of the white southern lady—an image that had previously been seen by many white students as an innocuous counterpart to such maligned Old South symbols as Confederate uniforms or the Battle Flag of the Army of Northern Virginia, now popularized as the Confederate flag. In the hoop-skirted incarnation, she is the plantation mistress, publicly perceived as morally above reproach and pedestalized for her virtues, but also a stark reminder of the legacy of black enslavement and brutalities committed against emancipated African Americans.

The Alpha Phi debacle followed on the heels of the University of Alabama's highly publicized 2013 scandal when white women in several NPC sorority chapters on campus came forward with admissions that they had cut an exceptional candidate from their rush lists solely because she was African American.[4] This news confirmed that at least some chapters of NPC sororities were continuing to practice racial discrimination in their membership selection, even after stating otherwise to campus officials in the 1960s. It also definitively connected the practices of racial exclusion with a southern image of sorority women. Of course, Alabama may be an easier target with its well-known history of highly visible racist behavior. These accounts may yield nothing more than a "well, it's *Alabama*" and a knowing look from the national public. Yet even the University of Alabama is becoming a more diverse institution, as nearly 60 percent of students came from out of state by fall 2019.[5] Similarly, many current residents of the South have moved there from other regions of the United States, a demographic shift that continues to change the cultural and sociopolitical makeup of the contemporary South. As I have shown, however, sororities nationwide have a deep history of practicing discriminatory behavior and teaching its "benefits" to members. In recent years, numerous instances of racial, ethnic, and gender insensitivity have occurred at sorority and fraternity chapters across the country.[6] At the same time, NPC leadership and that of national sororities seem loathe to address the skeletons in the closet in regard to their earlier blatant white supremacist ideology. Without knowing the history or assiduously working to overcome these issues, sorority members and alumnae continue to propagate the idea that college students engaging in such behaviors are simply "having fun," "don't know any better," or "made a mistake."

In the spring of 2019, as I was completing edits on this manuscript and waiting to meet a friend for lunch in the overwhelmingly white and (of late) upper-middle-class town of Yarmouth, Maine, I overheard two young women at a nearby table, one of whom was detailing her hopes for college. She gushed about visiting the state of North Carolina with her family, noting that she would like to go to school there and "be a southern belle." Here was a New Englander dreaming of a lifestyle in the southern aesthetic. Were sororities in her mind when she threw out the term "southern belle"? Why did the idea of being a southern belle sound so appealing? Would more college-bound white women think twice about joining sororities or longing for the southern aesthetic if they fully understood the unsavory history tied up in both?

Current NPC history, as presented in polished PR form on the organization's website, makes no clear mention of or apology for sororities' discriminatory positioning during the Cold War and the civil rights era. Instead, the NPC again falls back onto a familiar line, suggesting that "anti-fraternity crit-

ics"—described *not* as communists this time, but as "political subversives"—
were the cause of an upsurge of "negative opinion" against sororities that continued into the 1960s. The groups met these offenders, the NPC explains,
with new efforts to establish "the constitutional right of fraternities to exist
by virtue of freedom of assembly" and to "re-educate the public . . . about the
value of women's fraternities."[7] The euphemistic description glosses over some
of the most fraught and ugly years of sorority leadership, while reaffirming a
color-blind version of institutional racism.

As were their predecessors before them, contemporary sorority and fraternity leaders appear more concerned with maintaining GLOs in their traditional fashion than making organizational changes, which could bring them
in closer alignment with present student interests. The Fraternity and Sorority Political Action Committee, or FSPAC, established in 2005, has solic-
ited donations to lobby on behalf of legislation friendly to GLOs. They claim
to be bipartisan and have donated to both Republican and Democratic congressional candidates who support their interests—of which the protection
of "freedom of association" is still a top contender. However, a 2013 FSPAC
newsletter showed that in the 2011–12 election cycle, the group offered monetary support to nearly twice as many Republican candidates (66) as Democrats (34), suggesting that a conservative Republican ideology is still more in
line with GLO interests. Many of the current (2018–19 cycle) top contributors to FSPAC hosted a 2012 benefit for Romney Victory, Inc., headlined by
none other than University of Mississippi fraternity alum and racial regressive
Trent Lott.[8] Lott was also hired by FSPAC to lobby for the 2015 Safe Campus Act, which would help protect students (often fraternity men) accused
of sexual assault from campus punishment. Rep. Pete Sessions (R) of Texas,
a staunch supporter of FSPAC, was one of the three Republican representatives who introduced the act in the House. Fraternity *and* sorority alumni of
FSPAC backed this legislative measure, but criticism eventually led the NPC
and the NIC to pull back support.[9] Among the NPC's recent legislative prior-
ities was the 2018 attempt to reauthorize the Higher Education Act of 1965. In
a legislative overhaul led by House Republicans, the bill supported a conservative agenda, which included the right of universities and campus student organizations to discriminate. Sororities and fraternities strongly support protec-
tions for single-sex social clubs. Coming in response to Harvard University's
2016 decision to penalize students who choose to join single-sex social clubs
on campus by keeping them from other campus leadership positions or withholding the college's endorsement for prestigious fellowships, the Higher Education Act revamp included a provision to keep schools from punishing so-

rorities and fraternities that remain single-sex organizations.[10] The House did not vote on the higher education bill in 2018, and as of December 2019, Democrats and Republicans in Congress have not come to any agreement on the bill's final form. In the meantime, several national sororities and fraternities filed lawsuits against Harvard, arguing that the policy against single-sex clubs was a form of sexual discrimination.[11] Since that time, Harvard has rescinded the policy against students joining single-sex clubs, as they realized their policy could be viewed as discriminatory and likely would not stand in a court of law. Again, the perceived need to fight for "freedom of association" is alive and well.

At the same time, GLOs have continued to foster heterosocial spaces that contribute to the exploitation of and violence against women. With this being the case, why do women seek to join an NPC sorority (or charter a chapter of an NPC sorority on their campuses if none exist) if all that is needed is a women-only space, as the sorority women at Harvard argue? Would not another women's organization, or localized women-only club on campus, provide a better option—specifically, one without the long history of connection to men's fraternities, drunken partying, traditional gender roles, and sexual violence against women? Certainly, sororities provide future social connections, but in the case of the women at Harvard College we might say—they're already Harvard students, so what more do they need in the way of connections? The connection to campus fraternities and their parties is likely also enticing, but more importantly, sorority membership also confers ladyhood. As sorority women, members are not just drunken college women at a fraternity late-night; they are "ladies." They are not just the unaffiliated women on campus who might be conventionally unattractive or come from working-class or non-Protestant backgrounds; they are "ladies" who also might fall under some or all of those categories but who elevate themselves by claiming distance through the veneer of sorority-defined ladyhood. The Harvard women's desire to join NPC sororities shows that the sorority brand of ladyhood holds its own value in American culture and that in some spaces, I would argue, it holds as much cachet as (if not more than) the Harvard degree.

Similarly, we might wonder why women at Swarthmore College in Pennsylvania recently sought to restart sororities at a college that is known for its Quaker values and commitment to financial accessibility. In May 2019 Swarthmore banned fraternities and sororities (again) after the release of documents by one of the two fraternities on campus, which contained derogatory comments about women and the LGBTQ community and made jokes about sexual assault. The one NPC sorority on campus had only been reestablished on campus in 2013, eighty years after the school abolished sororities on the basis of the groups' discrimination against Jewish women.[12] Again, why would the women need an NPC sorority sisterhood to make their women-only social club "legitimate," particularly on a campus that only had two fraternities, one of which was no longer affiliated with its national organization? The lure of exclusivity—even if the members need specialized payment plans in order to afford the sorority's dues—privilege, and ladyhood conferred by membership in an NPC sorority appear worth the undeniable negative aspects of the Greek-letter community. Ladyhood remains the requirement for white women's power vis-à-vis white men and the institutional power structure in the United States.

Even the ignoble Edgewater Conference continues to meet in some form or fashion. While the archival remains of Edgewater from the late 1980s and early 1990s afforded little information about the group's activities or intentions, the group still feels the need to keep their meetings underground. A tweet from January 2012 by University of Virginia dean of students Allen Groves provided evidence that the EC still meets and still likes to fly under the radar. "Headed to Tampa for the Edgewater Conference a mtg of national fraternity and sorority leaders. I'm speaking on Saturday afternoon."[13] A fraternity man himself, Groves apparently saw no problem publicizing this information. However, the tweet no longer exists on his Twitter feed, suggesting that someone thought better of publicizing the conference's continuation and let him know that. So long as GLOs perceive outside threats to the existence of their organizations, members will see a need for a space such as the Edgewater Conference.

Harvard and Swarthmore are two very different campuses, and their students are certainly not the same as those you typically find at the University of Alabama or the University of Mississippi, but all of these college women want their shot at ladyhood as built on the foundations of the southern ladyhood imaginarwy, despite the antifeminist and misogynistic culture that is upheld by the GLO system. By bringing new young women into the white privilege of the sisterhood, sororities continue to normalize discriminatory behavior for succeeding generations of Americans. Armed with an understanding of these organizations' ideology and how little they have changed their positioning over the past century, we can more forcefully ask members, alumnae, and college administrators why they still wish sororities to occupy such a significant position on many campuses across the United States and to consider the ramifications if their power remains unchecked.

NOTES

⁘

Introduction. Where Y'all Does Not Mean All

1. *Corolla*, 1965, 307, UA.

2. The NPC formed in 1902 as a way for the national sororities to deal with issues arising from rush season. It became a conference where sorority alumnae from the various national groups could discuss issues of mutual concern. Each national sorority that held a membership in the NPC had an alumnae delegate to the organization. The chairmanship of the NPC rotated among the member sororities. "Adventure in Friendship: A History of the National Panhellenic Conference," 2017, https://npcwomen.dynamic.omegafi.com/wp-content/uploads/sites/2037/2017/10/Adventure-in-Friendship-2017-Web.pdf.

3. For the purpose of this work, I am including the following as "southern" states: Alabama, Georgia, Kentucky, Louisiana, Maryland, Mississippi, Missouri, North Carolina, South Carolina, Tennessee, Texas, Virginia, and the District of Columbia.

4. Sixteen Pledged to Active Group as School Opens," *Iota Lyre* 1, no. 1 (November 1934): 1–2, box 2 (26/21/4), HC, UI.

5. Silber, *Romance of Reunion*, 86–87; Blain Roberts, *Pageants, Parlors, and Pretty Women*, 17.

6. Lassiter and Crespino, *Myth of Southern Exceptionalism*; Kruse, *White Flight*; MacLean, "Neo-Confederacy versus the New Deal"; McRae, *Mothers of Massive Resistance*; Ward, *Defending White Democracy*. Historians who have investigated conservative women's grassroots organizing outside of the South include McGirr, *Suburban Warriors*; Delegard, *Battling Miss Bolsheviki*; Kempker, *Big Sister*; and Nickerson, *Mothers of Conservativism*.

7. Robbins, *Pledged*.

8. The southern belle is described as the younger counterpart of the southern lady. See Farnham, *Education of the Southern Belle*, 4–5, 127; Cahn, *Sexual Reckonings*, 307; McPherson, *Reconstructing Dixie*, 149–54.

9. I use the terms "belle" and "lady" interchangeably throughout the text. The southern belle is understood as the young, unmarried southern lady. I tend toward the use of "lady" for both married and single sorority women, as that has become the more frequently deployed term in modern descriptions of the archetype.

10. On the Lost Cause, see Blight, *Race and Reunion*; Cox, *Dixie's Daughters*; Foster, *Ghosts of the Confederacy*; Hale, *Making Whiteness*; Janney, *Burying the Dead*; Osterweis, *Myth of the Lost Cause*; Wilson, *Baptized in Blood*. Wilson explains the Lost Cause as the "civil religion" of the South, 10–14.

11. White southern men, figuratively emasculated by their fall from economic and political power in the wake of the war, sought to reclaim their virility by protecting white southern women from the concocted image of black men as oversexed, serial rapists. See Hale, *Making Whiteness*; Williamson, *Rage for Order*.

12. Jones, *Tomorrow Is Another Day*, 15–19; Ruoff, "Southern Womanhood," 107–11; Hall, *Revolt against Chivalry*, 151. On the process of disfranchisement and dates of adoption in southern states, see Woodward, *Strange Career of Jim Crow*, 84–85, 97–109. On the erasure of sexual violence against black women in scholarly analysis of the relationship between race, sex, and violence during segregation, see LaKisha Simmons, *Crescent City Girls*, 2–3.

13. Scott, *Southern Lady*, 17, 21; McPherson, *Reconstructing Dixie*, 19–20, quotation on 19. McPherson bases her understanding of elite white women's return to the pedestal on the work of Drew Gilpin Faust. See Faust, *Mothers of Invention*, 253–54.

14. Lydia Mattice Brandt, "Re-Creating Mount Vernon," 95–96; Lindgren, *Preserving the Old Dominion*, 4–7; Kammen, *Mystic Chords of Memory*, 218–20. While holding their first Inter-Sorority Conference (predecessor to the NPC) in April 1891, sorority women began to coordinate "a practical Pan-Hellenic plan for the World's Fair." In discussing plans for a concurrent meeting, members at the 1891 conference noted that they "could but feel 1893 represented an opportunity not to be lightly set aside." Although the efforts of the ISC appear lost to larger histories of the Columbian Exposition, the NPC's brief account of the Chicago meeting described a successful "Congress of college fraternities" on July 19 and 20, 1893. However, even the scant notes from the 1891 conference demonstrated the importance of the exposition in the minds of the sorority women. As educated white women from Greek-letter organizations, they likely envisioned their participation in the exposition as a duty and a privilege. See Fran Becque quoting the Kappa Kappa Gamma invitation to the first Panhellenic Conference in "April 16, 1891—The Meeting Before the First NPC Meeting in 1902," April 16, 2014, https://www.franbecque.com/april-16-1891-the-meeting-before-the-first-npc-meeting-in-1902/; "National Panhellenic Conference: An Historical Record of Achievement," 1957, 3–5, box 1, Publications (41/82/800), NPC, UI; Weimann, *Fair Women*, 51.

15. Turk, *Bound by a Mighty Vow*, 114–17; Walter B. Palmer, "Antagonism to Fraternities, a Review," *Banta's* 8, no. 1 (December 1919): 7–10.

16. Chi Omega national president Mary Love Collins noted the importance of maintaining Panhellenic as an "American institution"—an extension of the "American college"—by keeping some "barriers" against sectarian groups (here referring to Jewish and Catholic sororities) until they "knew more about them." 18th NPC, 1923, NPC Proceedings (41/82/10), NPC, UI.

17. Schulman, *Seventies*, 36–37; Lassiter, *Silent Majority*, 4, 227–32.

18. Kevin Kruse, Matthew Lassiter, and Nancy MacLean have argued that the modern

conservative movement transitioned from a blatantly racist defense of social segregation to one built on a "color-blind" rhetoric, which appealed to a broader base from the 1950s through the 1970s, and which remains a key component of Republican Party ideology to this day. Kruse, *White Flight*; Lassiter, *Silent Majority*; MacLean, "Neo-Confederacy versus the New Deal."

19. Email correspondence with Ellen Swain, archivist at the Student Life and Culture Archives, University of Illinois, August 29, 2017. Unfortunately, ATΩ has since removed the Edgewater Conference File, 1953–1993, from the ATΩ National Officers File, and it is no longer available to the public.

20. There is no shortage of national news coverage of college sorority and fraternity members caught in public displays of racist behavior in the twenty-first century. See Adam Harris, "Yearbooks Aren't the Only Place to Find Blackface on Campus," *Atlantic*, February 9, 2019, https://www.theatlantic.com/education/archive/2019/02/ralph-northam-college -campus-blackface/582373/; Gabrielle Noel, "Greek Life Needs to Take Racism as Seriously as It Takes Hazing," *Huffington Post*, April 27, 2018, https://www.huffpost.com/entry /opinion-noel-racism-greek-life_n_5ae2b1a2e4b055fd7fca4141; Terrance F. Ross, "A Brief and Recent History of Bigotry at Fraternities," *Atlantic*, March 10, 2015, https://www .theatlantic.com/education/archive/2015/03/a-brief-and-recent-history-of-bigotry-at-fra-ternities/387319/. I further discuss the current use of the southern aesthetic in sororities in my conclusion.

Chapter One. "A Very Wholesome Discipline"

1. "Annual Report, 1922–1923," folder 1, box 1, series 1, Office of the Dean of Women Records (#40125), University Archives, UNC.

2. Shepardson, *Baird's Manual*, 13th ed., 739–95.

3. Turk, *Bound by a Mighty Vow*, 96–97.

4. At the 1933 NPC meeting, Mrs. Frances W. Baker of Sigma Kappa sorority noted, "For most of us, the last few years have been occupied largely with expansion activities and the establishing ourselves firmly on campuses where sororities exist." 23rd NPC Meeting, 1933, 67, NPC Proceedings (41/82/10), NPC, UI.

5. Ladd-Taylor, *Mother-Work*; Gordon, *Pitied but not Entitled*; Mink, *Wages of Motherhood*; Muncy, *Creating a Female Dominion*.

6. "Some Distinguished Members of Kappa Alpha Theta," *Handbook of Kappa Alpha Theta*, 1911, 16–18, Fraternity Publications (26/21/5), HC, UI.

7. The NPC formed in 1902 as a way for the national sororities to handle issues arising from rushing season. Each member sorority sent an alumna delegate to the organization, with a rotating chairmanship.

8. Martin, *Sorority Handbook*, 8th ed., 53–55, 58.

9. The first sorority chapter to build a house had been the Alpha Chapter of Alpha Phi at Syracuse University in 1886. See "America's First Sorority House," *Alpha Phi Quarterly* (Summer 1961): 165–67, *Alpha Phi Quarterly* Articles, Clippings, 1960–61, 1969, 1970–72, box 7, National Fraternity Reference Files (26/21/4), HC, UI.

10. A number of states, including Georgia, North Carolina, South Carolina, and Virginia, were slow to supply funding for women's dormitories at state universities. Prior to the building of women's dormitories, female students were housed in makeshift residences. In the 1910s the University of Alabama used three houses as women's residences, while a small number of girls lived with families in Tuscaloosa. Similarly, UNC provided two houses for women in 1921. Starting in 1914, the University of South Carolina also rented houses adjacent to campus as a way to accommodate the women. Delpar, "Coeds and the 'Lords of Creation,'" 295; Hollis, *University of South Carolina*, 2:309; Dean, "Women on the Hill," 6; Dyer, *University of Georgia*, 179, Whitney, "Women and the University," 89.

11. In the 1920s the University of Alabama built a coordinate campus for women that included sorority houses in its plan for women's residences. The school actively encouraged sorority house construction through the 1920s and 1930s. In 1925, four years after national sororities first appeared on campus, William and Mary began constructing "Sorority Court," centrally locating all campus sorority houses adjacent to the campus. Pi Beta Phi at UNC procured a house in 1929, and the Chi Omega chapter did the same by 1931. However, the small Chi Omega group was not able to fund the venture during the Depression and had to give up the house in 1933. The first sororities at UGA, Phi Mu and Chi Omega, obtained houses in 1925 and 1924, respectively. Wolf, *University of Alabama*, 155; "Annual Report, 1929," "Annual Report, 1931," "Annual Report, 1933," Annual Reports, 1917–1929, Annual Reports, 1930–1936, box 1, series 1, Office of the Dean of Women (#40125), University Archives, UNC; Godson et al., *College of William and Mary*, 556; Ferguson et al., *History of Chi Omega*, 1:238; Lamb, *History of Phi Mu*, 275.

12. 8th NPC, 1909, NPC Conference Proceedings (41/82/10), NPC, UI.

13. "Epsilon Beta," *Eleusis* 25, no. 3 (September 1923): 351; "Annual Reports, 1962–1963," "Reports to the President, 1959–1963," box 58, Woman's College Records, DU; Martin, *Sorority Handbook*, 8th ed., 33–34; Haller, *History of Delta Delta Delta*, 423; Lamb, *History of Phi Mu*, 177–78; Morse, *History of Kappa Delta*, 462–63.

14. "How Omicron's New Home Will Appear," *Omicron Owl* (March 1937), Chi Omega Illinois Chapter—Omicron Owl, box 15, National Fraternity Reference Files (26/21/4), HC, UI.

15. *Sigmagram* (April 1926), Alpha Delta Pi Illinois Chapter, *Sigmagram*, box 5, National Fraternity Reference Files (26/21/4), HC, UI.

16. At the start of the twentieth century, higher education for white women in the southern United States lagged behind that available for white women in other regions of the country. As southern white progressives began advocating education as the key to the South's economic development and social progress, the region's inadequate educational system slowly began to change form. While elite white women could afford education at private women's colleges in the region, educational reform enabled white women from families of lesser means also to receive a college education. Efforts by progressive educators and legislators secured funding for public white women's colleges designed to train teachers for the region's primary schools. Generally farmer's daughters, the women attending these normal and industrial colleges represented the hopes of the growing southern white middle class. However, without standards for institutions of higher education in the South, women's, coeducational, and men's colleges alike suffered from lack of regulation. As of 1917, just

five southern women's colleges met at least the minimum requirements for accreditation by the Association of Colleges and Preparatory Schools of the Southern States (1895). In order to receive a quality education comparable to that offered at women's colleges in the Northeast, white women in the South had few affordable choices. As a result, families that sought a superior education for their daughters turned to coeducational colleges. Farnham, *Education of the Southern Belle*, 3; McCandless, *The Past in the Present*, 18–22, 28, 32.

17. Alumnae Questionnaires, Class of 1925–1926, Laura Parrish Papers, WM; Parrish, "'When Mary Entered,'" 11–12, 20; Sparks, "Handbook of the Alabama Polytechnic Institute," 228–29; Delpar, "Coeds and the 'Lords of Creation,'" 294, 303. At UNC, women's enrollment increased from 32 in 1917–18 to 169 by 1929–30. The number of female students at the University of South Carolina grew from roughly 11 percent of the student population in 1916 to more than a fourth by 1924. See "Annual Report, 1918," Annual Reports, 1917–1929, box 1, series 1, Office of the Dean of Women Records (#40125), University Archives, UNC; "Annual Report, 1929," Annual Reports, 1917–1929, box 1, series 2, Office of the Dean of Women Records (#40125), University Archives, UNC; Hollis, *University of South Carolina*, 2:309, 311.

18. From the time of its founding in 1898 to 1915, seven of the thirteen southern ZTA chapters deactivated—three, including the Alpha chapter at Virginia State Normal School (where the sorority was founded) in Farmville, because the schools were not of collegiate rank. Kappa Delta, also founded at Virginia Normal in 1897, lost four of its sixteen southern chapters founded prior to 1915 also due to academic ineligibility. Phi Mu, founded at the Georgia Wesleyan Female College in Macon, deactivated four of its chapters in 1910 and 1911 so that Phi Mu could join the NPC, which required that member sororities hold chapters in schools of collegiate rank only. See Strout, *History of Zeta Tau Alpha*, 101, 106, 113; Morse, *History of Kappa Delta*, 530, 536–37, 541; Lamb, *History of Phi Mu*, 273.

19. Women's colleges in the South that banned sororities included Salem College, Winston-Salem, North Carolina (1909); College for Women, Columbia, South Carolina (1910); St. Mary's College, Raleigh, North Carolina (1911); Georgia Wesleyan College, Macon, Georgia (1914); Judson College, Marion, Alabama (1919); Hollins College, Hollins, Virginia (1929); Goucher College, Baltimore, Maryland (1942); and Randolph-Macon Woman's College, Lynchburg, Virginia (1960). When May L. Keller became the first dean of women at Westhampton College in Richmond, Virginia, in 1914, she chose to prohibit sororities on campus. Although a lifelong member of Pi Beta Phi who served as the sorority's national president, Keller observed that "the class structure" at the school "served, in effect, the purpose of a sorority by defining a small group within a larger body." Beta Sigma Omicron, founded in Missouri in 1888, specifically aimed their national expansion at southern women's colleges. However, *Baird's Manual* (1935) stated that "so many chapters were killed by faculty opposition and anti-fraternity legislation" that by 1925 the sorority was left with only seven active chapters from its twenty-four charters. See Lamb, *History of Phi Mu*, 273; Haller, *History of Delta Delta Delta*, 32; Morse, *History of Kappa Delta*, 537, 539, 544, 546; Strout, *History of Zeta Tau Alpha*, 282; Shepardson, *Baird's Manual*, 13th ed., 308–9.

20. McCandless, "Preserving the Pedestal," 45–46. Women's enrollment at UNC was limited to junior and senior transfers. See McCandless, *The Past in the Present*, 83, 90–91, 93.

21. Delpar, "Coeds and the 'Lords of Creation,'" 302–11; Durden, *Launching of Duke*

University, 26, 253; McCandless, *The Past in the Present*, 91; Reed, *History of the University of Georgia*, 3413.

22. McCandless, *The Past in the Present*, 55, 85; Solomon, *In the Company of Educated Women*, 60–61. Whereas arguments against women's higher education in the 1870s and 1880s were based on fears that mental strain would damage women's physical and reproductive health, by the 1900s objections to coeducation centered on psychological consequences of educating women and men together.

23. McCandless, *The Past in the Present*, 87–91.

24. Newcomer, *Century of Higher Education*, 46, 49; see increasing enrollment statistics, page 2–3.

25. Barrow, "Co-Education at the University," 9.

26. The position of the dean of women had only recently become a recognized profession, and the duties of the office varied by school. The professional organization of the National Association of Deans of Women was formed in 1916, and Wisconsin's dean of women, Lois K. Mathews, published the first book on the subject, *The Dean of Women* (1915). See Nidiffer, *Pioneering Deans of Women*, 14. Alabama Polytechnic Institute (API) hired Minnie Fisher in 1921. The University of Georgia appointed Mary Lyndon as dean in 1919. Sparks, "Handbook of the Alabama Polytechnic Institute," 227; Delpar, "Coeds and the 'Lords of Creation,'" 298; "Program from Mary Lyndon Day, 1964," folder 1, box 1, Mary Lyndon Dean of Women Papers (UG97–105:153), UGA; "Annual Report, 1918," Annual Reports, 1917–1929, box 1, series 1, Office of Dean of Women Records (#40125), University Archives, UNC; West, *University of South Carolina*, 43.

27. The Southern Association of College Women merged with the American Association of Collegiate Women in 1921 to form the AAUW. See Bashaw, "*Stalwart Women*," 4.

28. The V.D.W. sorority began in 1910, but no history of its organization remains. It is unknown what words the letters "V.D.W." stand for. See Patrick, "Front Line," 117, 121.

29. Baldwin, "Woman's College," 36.

30. Abland, *Sisters*, 169; Hollis, *University of South Carolina*, 2:316. A charter member of Alpha Delta Pi's Beta Epsilon chapter at the University of South Carolina remembered that AΔΠ was to be the first group installed on campus, but they were beat out by Chi Omega. "Chi Omega officials came down the first day of the week of our installation. They got the Chi Omega girls out of class and installed the chapter. So they were the first." In their chapter report to nationals, AΔΠ women referred to Dean Dillard as "our best friend and advisor." See Mary Fitch Oral History, SC; "Beta Epsilon Chapter of Alpha Delta Pi Chapter Report, 1931–1932," Chapter Reports, Beta Epsilon Chapter—University of South Carolina, AΔΠ.

31. In 1905 deans of women invited members of the Inter-Sorority Conference to their conference to discuss their common goals in working with collegiate sorority women. The NADW regularly held a joint session with women from the NPC at their annual meetings. "Report on the Joint Meeting of the Deans and Advisors of Women in State Universities and Representatives of the Inter-Sorority Conference," 1905, box 1, NPC-NADWAC Historical File, 1905–1941, Committee File (41/82/50), NPC, UI; NPC Proceedings, 1935, 11–15, NPC Proceedings (41/82/10), NPC, UI; Turk, *Bound by a Mighty Vow*, 121–22.

32. Michel Foucault argues that through disciplining, subjects can be trained to exhibit desired behaviors. In time, these behaviors will become habitual or "normalized" in the minds of the subjects. Foucault, *Discipline and Punish*, 170–94, esp. 179–83.

33. Palmer, "Higher Education of Young Women"; Alumnae Questionnaires, Class of 1921–1924, Class of 1925–1926, Class of 1939, Laura Parrish Papers, WM; *Women's Student Government Handbook, 1931–1932*, 27, in Frances C. Cosby Nettles Papers, WM; McCandless, "Preserving the Pedestal," 47. For example, the 1924–25 *Handbook for Women Students at the University of North Carolina* lists just six rules for women, three established by the dean of women and three by the students themselves. In sharp contrast, the 1958–59 *Handbook* includes six pages of rules, including social rules, regulations for coed organizations, house regulations, dismissal from the university, graduate rules, and an entire section of regulations specific to freshmen. See *Handbook for Women Students at the University of North Carolina*, 1924–1925, 7, NCC, UNC; *Women's Handbook*, 1958–1959, 32–37, NCC, UNC; Dean, "Women on the Hill," 11; Bailey, *From Front Porch to Back Seat*, 84–85.

34. "House Rules," *Trident* 19, no. 3 (April 1910): 385–89.

35. Alumnae Questionnaires, Class of 1921–1924, Laura Parrish Papers, WM; *Carolina Handbook*, 1930–1931, 7–10, NCC, UNC.

36. Christina Simmons, "Companionate Marriage."

37. Solomon, *In the Company of Educated Women*, 56–57, 119–22.

38. The journals increasingly tempered their presentation of career women with discussion of the individuals' feminine qualities. While touting the pathbreaking positions held by alumnae, the magazines also portrayed the women as conventionally feminine by highlighting their attractive physical appearances, their winning personalities, or their "private lives" as wives and mothers. By featuring these types of profiles in the sororities' journals, the groups suggested that their alumnae had achieved success and authority in the workplace—even in traditionally male professions—precisely because, as sorority women, they maintained a nonthreatening femininity. Zella Brown Ragsdale, "A Former Dean of Women Looks at Homemaking," *Themis* 31, no. 3 (March 1933): 225–27; Adele Parsons Conselyea, "Houston City Club's Boast, A. D. Pi Is Outstanding Woman Surgeon," *Adelphean* 28, no. 2 (June 1935): 24–25; Worth Tuttle Hedden, "A Brief Course in the Theory of Marriage," *Angelos* 30, no. 2 (January 1934): 138–41; Worth Tuttle, "Autobiography of an Ex-Feminist," *Atlantic Monthly* 152, no. 6 (December 1933): 642–49.

39. For example, Mary Love Collins, the highly respected leader of Chi Omega and a major player in NPC development, appeared to have had a companionate relationship with at least one other Chi Omega over the course of her sorority membership. A contemporary Chi Omega biographical sketch of Collins notes that no one ever saw her husband, "a Mr. H. M. Collins," but that apparently no one ever questioned what had happened to him either. She was listed as "Mrs. H. M. Collins" in early issues of the *Eleusis*.

40. In her study of fictional accounts of women at college, Shirley Marchalonis identifies a number of sorority-themed stories between 1870 and 1930. Marchalonis, *College Girls*, 115–27, quotations on 119.

41. *Pledge Manual or Freshman Training Guide for Kappa Alpha Theta*, 1927, 14, National Fraternity Publications (26/21/5), HC, UI.

42. "Active Chapter Letters and Notes, Sigma Delta—Trinity College," *Angelos* 10, no. 2 (March 1914): 137–38; "Chapter Letters and Notes, Sigma Delta, Trinity College," *Angelos* 20, no. 4 (June 1924): 480.

Chapter Two. *"A Laboratory in How to Get Along with People"*

1. Jenn Coltrane, "The Worth of Sororities," *Banta's Greek Exchange* 1 (December 1912): 277–79.

2. Minnie Allen Hubbard, "What Alpha Delta Pi Offers the College Girl," *Adelphean* 32, no. 2 (1939): 3–4.

3. Mowry, "Fraternities and Sororities," 512–14.

4. Walter B. Palmer, "Fraternities on the Defensive," *Banta's Greek Exchange* 1, no. 1 (December 1912): 43–48. After 1897, when the South Carolina legislature, riding "Pitchfork" Ben Tillman's wave of populist sentiment, prohibited students at state universities from joining fraternities, other states—including Arkansas (1902) and Mississippi (1912)—made similar moves. Laws banning fraternities were also introduced in Wisconsin and Kansas. Palmer referenced "attacks" from presidents or faculties of many universities such as "Cornell, Wisconsin, Minnesota, Missouri, [and] Stanford," which came as a result of studies that suggested the scholarship level of fraternity men fell below the university average.

5. Turk, *Bound by a Mighty Vow*, 113, 122.

6. Section 1–9, NPC Review, 1902–1937, (41/82/813), NPC, UI.

7. When the inspector was a young alumna, she may have served as a positive role model for the college members. In 1914 a number of ZTA chapters excitedly reported on visits from Gladys Ayland, ZTA's second inspector, and by all accounts, a superstar in the eyes of the actives. "She was an inspiration," gushed Nu chapter at the University of Alabama. The women "enjoyed every minute of her stay, even while [they] were being tested on [their] knowledge of ZTA past, present, and future." "Nu—University of Alabama," *Themis* 12, no. 4 (July 1914): 602.

8. Section 1–10, NPC Review, 1902–1937 (41/82/813), NPC, UI.

9. Bailey, *From Front Porch to Back Seat*, 1–7; Fass, *The Damned and the Beautiful*, 368–69. For discussion of the twentieth century's emerging "culture of personality," as compared to the nineteenth century's celebration of an individual's "character" as a measure of his or her worth, see Susman, "'Personality,'" 277–81.

10. Turk, *Bound by a Mighty Vow*, 208n13. By 1941, at the invitation of Sara Blanding, dean of women at the University of Kentucky and president of the NADW, the two groups formed a joint committee where the groups could address topics of concern to both. See "Report of the Conference of a Committee of Deans of Women and National Panhellenic Congress Representatives," NPC-NAWDC Historical File, 1905–1941, box 1, Committee File (41/82/50), NPC, UI; Bashaw, "*Stalwart Women*," 11–12, 37–38.

11. Mary Alice Jones, "The Fraternity Membership: Today and Tomorrow," 24th NPC Meeting, 1935, 205–6, NPC Proceedings (41/82/10), NPC, UI. While many deans of women in this period were supportive of sororities, some found them problematic, particularly as a result of rush. See chapter 5 for further discussion.

12. Audrey Moore Stewart Oral History Interview, May 1, 2001, 6, UI.

13. Solomon, *In the Company of Educated Women*, 81–85.

14. The University of Alabama first offered home economics courses during the 1914 summer session. Regular courses began in the College of Arts and Sciences in 1917–18. Alabama Polytechnic Institute (API) also began teaching home economics classes in the summer of 1914 as a way to prepare the increasing number of home demonstration agents in the state. It introduced a home economics department in 1920. The University of Georgia added a curriculum for the degree in home economics in 1918 and began admitting women for a two-year course. William and Mary added a home economics department to coincide with the admission of female students in the fall of 1918. See Delpar, "'Coeds and the Lords of Creation,'" 302–4; Atkins, *Blossoms amid the Deep Verdure*, 16–17; Reed, *History of the University of Georgia*, 2413–15; Parrish, "'When Mary Entered,'" 26; McCandless, "Pedagogy and the Pedestal," 271–73.

15. Marie Casteen, "A New Field for Women," *Angelos* 26, no. 3 (1930): 335–39.

16. Agnes Ellen Harris, "Administrative Problems of a College in Relation to Fraternities," 24th NPC Meeting, 1935, 14, NPC Proceedings (41/82/10), NPC, UI. Born in Cedartown, Georgia, in 1883, Harris was the daughter of a school superintendent who encouraged her pursuit of higher education. She studied home economics at the Oread Institute of Domestic Science in Worcester, Massachusetts, the Georgia Normal and Industrial College for Women in Milledgeville, and later in summer sessions at Teacher's College, Columbia University, where she received her bachelor's degree in the discipline in 1910. During the 1910s, prior to becoming head of the home economics department and dean of women at Alabama, she worked in various capacities for the U.S. Department of Agriculture home demonstration agency in the state of Florida. At the same time, she served as dean of the School of Home Economics at the Florida State College for Women. Bashaw, "*Stalwart Women*," 26–27. In later years the Alpha Zeta chapter of Phi Mu at the University of Alabama inducted Harris into membership. "Death Claims Two 'Distinguished Alumnae' Citation Winners," *Aglaia* 47, no. 2 (1953): 7–8.

17. November 14, 1935, series 2, Phi Mu, Gamma Epsilon Chapter Records, DU; Report of the Dean of Women, 1931–1932, 3–4, binder 3, box 9, Annual Reports (41/3/2), Office Dean of Student Personnel and Dean of Women, UI. Throughout the book, inflation figures are calculated using Bureau of Labor Statistics, CPI Inflation Calculator, http://www.bls.gov/data/inflation_calculator.htm.

18. 24th NPC Meeting, 1935, 41, NPC Proceedings (41/82/10), NPC, UI.

19. Christine Stansell demonstrated these class tensions in the case of working-class women and middle-class moral reformers as well as in the relationship of domestic servants and their employers in nineteenth-century New York City. See Stansell, *City of Women*, 66–69, 74–75, 156, 163–65.

20. Margaret L. Freeman, "To Seek the Good," 307–19.

21. Audrey Moore Stewart Oral History Interview, May 19, 2001, 7, UI.

22. *Pledge Manual of the Delta Gamma Fraternity*, January 1936, 6–7, National Fraternity Publications (26/21/5), HC, UI.

23. *Handbook for Women Students at the University of North Carolina*, 1924–1925, 6–7,

NCC, UNC; *Handbook for Women Students at the University of North Carolina*, 1930–1931, 8, NCC, UNC.

24. *Kappa Alpha Theta Pledge Training Book*, 1927, 12–13, National Fraternity Publications (26/21/5), HC, UI; Ballard and Ward, *Tri Delta Hostess*, 1937, 6, National Fraternity Publications (26/21/5), HC, UI; *Ladies First*, 1966, 2, 4, National Fraternity Publications (26/21/5), HC, UI.

25. *Kappa Alpha Theta Pledge Training Book*, 1.

26. *Pledge Manual of the Delta Gamma Fraternity*, 66, 71, 75, 79.

27. *Kappa Alpha Theta Pledge Training Book*, 12–15.

28. Ibid., 1.

29. Peril, *College Girls*, 207–16.

30. *Kappa Alpha Theta Pledge Training Book*, 1, 14.

31. *Pledge Manual of the Delta Gamma Fraternity*, 7.

32. November 14, 1935, series 2, Phi Mu, Gamma Epsilon Chapter Records, DU. At the November 1940 chapter meeting, a motion was made and passed to raise the initiation fee from fifty to sixty dollars. There had been no mention of changing initiation fees at any other point in the recorded minutes from the collection, beginning in 1934. See November 11, 1940, series 2, Phi Mu, Gamma Epsilon Chapter Records, DU.

33. *Tyee*, 1932, 62, https://digitalcollections.lib.washington.edu/digital/collection/uw-docs/id/29186; *Cactus*, 1936, 230, https://repositories.lib.utexas.edu/handle/2152/61604.

34. See chapter 4, p. 16.

35. Ballard and Ward, *Tri Delta Hostess*, 5.

36. Bailey, *From Front Porch to Back Seat*, 26–27; Waller, "Rating and Dating Complex," 730.

37. Wilson, *Judgment and Grace in Dixie*, 144–47.

38. Ballard and Ward, *Tri Delta Hostess*, 6.

39. Ibid., 15–31.

40. Ordell Griffith, a business administration student at Louisiana State University in the early 1930s, recalled that most female students majored in either education or home economics. Ordell Griffith Interview, 28, LSU.

41. Hartmann, *Home Front and Beyond*, 86, 90.

42. Ballard and Ward, *Tri Delta Hostess*, 30.

43. The student personnel movement had grown up as a product of military training in World War I and began to be implemented in higher education in the 1920s and 1930s. Robert A. Schwartz, "Reconceptualizing the Leadership Roles of Women," 512–17; Schwartz, "Rise and Demise," 227–28.

44. *Instructions for Pledge Training for Kappa Kappa Gamma*, 1944, 15, 17, Fraternity Publications (26/21/5), HC, UI.

45. Ibid., 15–18.

46. February 13, 1947, series 2, KKG, Delta Beta Chapter Records, DU.

47. February 5, 1940, March 6, 1946, series 2, KKG, Delta Beta Chapter Records, DU.

48. November 18, 1946, September 29, 1947, series 2, KKG, Delta Beta Chapter Records, DU.

49. Since the 1921 NPC meeting, the groups' national officers had officially promoted socializing between their members and women on campus who were unaffiliated with sororities.

50. "Entertaining Outside Girls," *Adelphean* 13, no. 2 (1922): 445.

51. For example, during the 1951–52 school year, students at the University of Georgia held 310 authorized social activities. More than half (175) of these events were held by social fraternities and sororities. See Annual Report, 1951–1952, folder 6, box 1, Dean of Women Records: Edith L. Stallings and Louise McBee UG97–119, UGA.

52. February 17, 1938, series 2, Phi Mu, Gamma Epsilon Chapter Records, DU. At Duke in the fall of 1937, the administration asked each sorority to "give a tea for non-sorority girls." See November 22, 1937, series 2, Minutes, KKG, Delta Beta Chapter Records, DU.

53. January 26, 1935, November 14, 1935, series 2, Phi Mu, Gamma Epsilon Chapter Records, DU.

54. April 17, April 24, 1939, series 2, Minutes, KKG, Delta Beta Chapter Records, DU.

55. Elaine Tyler May, *Homeward Bound*, 14, 68, 150. Woman veterans also took advantage of the G.I. Bill funding. See Meyer, *Creating G.I. Jane*, 182. While it is unclear how well the program served African American veterans, the educational benefits also helped them enroll at black colleges or complete vocational training courses that they could not have afforded without government aid. See Mettler, *Soldiers to Citizens*, 54–57, 72–76.

56. Eisenmann, *Higher Education for Women*, 49–51.

57. Ibid.

58. Linda Long, "Dean Honored by Alma Mater," *Lyre*, n.d., Clippings Personal, box 6, series 2.3, Office of the Dean of Women Records (#40125), University Archives, UNC; Dalgliesh, *History of Alpha Chi Omega*, 284, 285, caption.

59. Carmichael, "The Sorority Woman Moves into the World of the Future," 17, box 4, series 2.2, Office of the Dean of Women Records (#40125), University Archives, UNC.

60. Carmichael, "Speech at Birmingham-Southern College," 3, box 4, series 2.2, Office of the Dean of Women Records (#40125), University Archives, UNC; Carmichael, "Sorority Woman Moves," 18.

61. Mary Alice Jones, "The Fraternity Membership—Today and Tomorrow," 24th NPC Meeting, 1935, 198, Proceedings (41/82/10), NPC, UI.

62. Ibid., 1.

63. Hubbard, "What Alpha Delta Pi Offers," 3–4; Carmichael, "Sorority Woman Moves," 17.

Chapter Three. Southern Belles and Sorority Girls

1. E. M. F. [Erna M. Fergusson], "Our Southern Heritage," *Aglaia* 15, no. 3 (March 1920): 16–19. The article was reprinted from the *Aglaia* of March 1915.

2. Michael Ann Sullivan, "Erna Fergusson: First Lady of American Letters," December 20, 2013, newmexicohistory.org/people/erna-fergusson.

3. E. M. F., "Our Southern Heritage."

4. Gregory, *Southern Diaspora*, 48.

5. Nonsouthern-founded sororities Alpha Phi, Kappa Alpha Theta, Kappa Kappa Gamma, and Pi Beta Phi had placed chapters at the University of Toronto by 1915. Southern-founded Chi Omega had placed a short-lived chapter at Hellmuth Woman's College in London, Ontario, in 1899. Brown, *Baird's Manual*, 408, 414, 434, 443, 454.

6. Delta Gamma, which began in 1873 in Oxford, Mississippi, at the Lewis School for Girls, originally focused on placing new chapters at southern institutions but found its way onto campuses outside of the South by the end of the decade, thanks to the attention of George Banta, a Phi Delta Theta at Franklin College in Franklin, Indiana. Kappa Delta and Zeta Tau Alpha, formed at the State Normal School in Farmville, Virginia (now Longwood University), in 1897 and 1898, respectively, also limited their initial expansion to other southern colleges. ZTA sought membership in the NPC in 1905 and, with it, national establishment of chapters. KΔ approved northern expansion in 1906. Sigma Sigma Sigma and Alpha Sigma Alpha also began at Virginia Normal School in 1898 and 1901, respectively, but they became members of the Association of Educational Sororities (AES), which was limited to normal schools, until the NPC voted to admit those organizations in 1947. Alpha Delta Theta formed at Transylvania College in Lexington, Kentucky, in 1919. While national, it remained small and was absorbed by Phi Mu in 1939. "A Record of the Delta Gamma Fraternity," *Anchora* 72, no. 2 (Winter 1955): 7–12; Strout, *History of Zeta Tau Alpha*, 87, 97; Morse, *History of Kappa Delta*, 126–27; Hubbard, "What Alpha Delta Pi Offers the College Girl," *Adelphean* 34, no. 1 (November 1939): 3–5.

7. Fran Becque, "NPC Organizations That No Longer Exist; A Reflection on National Badge Day," March 3, 2013, https://www.franbecque.com/npc-organizations-that-no-longer-exist-a-reflection-on-international-badge-day/.

8. Shepardson, *Baird's*, 10th ed., with data compiled by author.

9. On the Lost Cause, see Blight, *Race and Reunion*; Cox, *Dixie's Daughters*; Foster, *Ghosts of the Confederacy*; Hale, *Making Whiteness*; Janney, *Burying the Dead*; Osterweis, *Myth of the Lost Cause*; Silber, *Romance of Reunion*; Wilson, *Baptized in Blood*. On southern ladyhood, see Cox, *Dixie's Daughters*; Gilmore, *Gender and Jim Crow*; Janney, *Burying the Dead*; Joan M. Johnson, *Southern Ladies, New Women*; Scott, *Southern Lady*; Wheeler, *New Women of the New South*.

10. Blain Roberts has shown how this image of southern beauty in the twentieth century was "deeply racialized." See *Pageants, Parlors, and Pretty Women*, 7.

11. On racial discord in the North, see Gregory, *Southern Diaspora*; Wilkerson, *Warmth of Other Suns*, 271–75; Wiltse, *Contested Waters*, chapters 5 and 6.

12. Silber, *Romance of Reunion*, 41–54.

13. Lindgren, *Preserving the Old Dominion*, 4–5.

14. Starting shortly after Reconstruction, nonsoutherners learned about the South and its people through journalistic accounts, novels, and travelers' reports. This "education" continued in the early twentieth century with popular music and motion pictures. Nonsoutherners valued what they perceived as the character of the South—a pastoral refuge from the dirty, crass, and impersonal modern American city of the industrialized era, with inhabitants descended from Anglo-Saxon aristocracy. Southerners were always polite and genteel, and above all the southern lady represented the pinnacle of southern perfection. See Silber, *Romance of Reunion*; Cox, *Dreaming of Dixie*.

15. E. M. F., "Our Southern Heritage," 11.

16. "Program of the Forty-Fifth Annual Reunion of the United Confederate Veterans, Fortieth Convention, Sons of Confederate Veterans, Thirty-Sixth Convention, Confederated Southern Memorial Association," Internet Archive, https://archive.org/details/Forty -fifthUnitedConfederateVeteransReunionFourtiethConventionSonsOf, accessed January 16, 2020.

17. Lamb, *History of Phi Mu*, 90, 91, 274. Hayes served as state recording secretary and state registrar of the UDC in Georgia.

18. UDC membership statistics from Cox, *Dixie's Daughters*, 29.

19. United Daughters of the Confederacy, *Minutes of the Fourth Annual Meeting*, 124; Morse, *History of Kappa Delta*, 87, 88.

20. "Paducah Has a Street of Women Presidents," *Evening Independent* (Saint Petersburg, Fla.), July 20, 1921.

21. Lamb, *History of Phi Mu*, 15, 16.

22. "United Confederate Choirs of America," *Eleusis* 11, no. 4 (1909): 405–8; Cox, *Dixie's Daughters*, 134–40.

23. "Kappa Alpha," *Angelos* 10, no. 3 (1914): 230–31; "Richmond Alumnae," *Themis* 13, no. 4 (1915): 647.

24. "Three Southern Colleges," *Trident* 22 (1913): 485.

25. Silber, *Romance of Reunion*, 67; Yuhl, *Golden Haze of Memory*, 171; Lindgren, *Preserving the Old Dominion*, 4–5.

26. "Delta Delta Delta Enters the Old South," "Three Southern Colleges," *Trident* 22 (1913): 475–87.

27. "Bobby and Bette," *Key* 56, no. 3 (December 1938): 272.

28. "Confessions of a Southern Girl," *Hoot* 7, no. 5 (June 25, 1932): 4, Kappa Kappa Gamma—The Hoot (2 of 2), 1928–1994, box 27 (26/21/4), HC, UI.

29. "Sixth Biennial Convention," *Eleusis* 12, no. 1 (February 1910): 11; Mary Gayle, "Traditions of Lexington," *Eleusis* 12, no. 1 (February 1910): 13–16.

30. "Down in Birmingham, August, 27–31, 1917," *Angelos* 14, no. 1 (November 1917): 15, 17–19.

31. Morse, *History of Kappa Delta*, 173–76.

32. "Homestead 'Darky Help' Combines Smiling Service . . . Southern Charm," *Adelphean* 33 (1941): n.p.

33. On the interconnection between the Lost Cause and Colonial Revival movements, see Lindgren, *Preserving the Old Dominion*, 2–7, and Lydia Mattice Brandt, "Re-creating Mount Vernon," 81–82, 95–96.

34. Bishir, "Landmarks of Power," 156–61.

35. Jane Armstrong, "The Glory That Is Georgian at Syracuse," *Key* 49, no. 2 (April 1932): 172.

36. Mills von Frühthaler, "Welcome Kappas! To the First Alumnae Chapter House!" *Key* 55, no. 4 (December 1938): 371–73. Kappa hoped to build other Hearthstone alumnae homes, but it was not a financially feasible model. See Kylie Towers Smith, "We Should Live Together When We're Old! Kappa's Boyd Hearthstone," December 10, 2012, https:// www.franbecque.com/we-should-live-together-when-were-old-kappas-boyd-hearthstone/.

37. "Kappa Houses across the Country," *Key* 54, no. 1 (February 1937): frontispiece.

38. "How Omicron's New Home Will Appear," *Omicron Owl* 13, no. 2 (March 1937): 1–4; Chi Omega Illinois Chapter Omicron Owl, 1930–1936, 1965, box 15 (26/21/4), HC, UI.

39. Margaret W. Read, "Have You Seen Our New House?" *Key* 54, no. 1 (February 1937): 5–9.

40. Yuhl, *Golden Haze of Memory*, 208n27; Lydia Mattice Brandt, *First in the Homes*, 79.

41. La Verne Bryson, "In the Georgian Manner," *Themis* 38, no. 4 (May 1938): 136–40; "From English Stucco to Georgian Colonial," *Themis* 38, no. 4 (May 1938): 148–49.

42. Bryson, "In the Georgian Manner," 137.

43. Helen Knox, "Lee Memorial Is Restored Mansion, Plantation Serves Liberty's Cause," *Key* 57, no. 3 (October 1940): 313–16.

44. "The Key Visits the Deep South," *Key* 64, no. 2 (April 1947): 77–91.

45. Ibid., 90–91.

46. By 1947, KKG had fifty-seven active chapters at nonsouthern universities and only thirteen at southern universities. More than half of the southern chapters had been established in the previous twenty years, meaning Kappa's presence was much less pronounced in the South than in other regions. See Kappapedia, "Chapters," http://wiki.kappakappagamma.org/pages/Chapters, last modified August 28, 2017, accessed January 16, 2020.

47. On the plantation school writers and historians, see Hale, *Making Whiteness*, chapters 2 and 3.

48. Ferguson was born in Homer, Louisiana, in 1895. She was a 1917 graduate of the University of Arkansas, where she was a member of the originating Psi chapter of Chi Omega. She was longtime editor of the *Eleusis. Razorback*, 1917, https://digitalcollections.uark.edu/digital/collection/Razorbacks, accessed February 13, 2020; Ferguson et al., *History of Chi Omega*, 44, 45, 48.

49. Strout, *History of Zeta Tau Alpha*; Kreig, *History of Zeta Tau Alpha*; "Shirley KreaSan Krieg," *Themis* 22, no. 1 (1923): 15, 16; "Shirley KreaSan Weds C. P. Kreig," *Daily Illini*, November 7, 1920, 2, Student Life and Culture Archives, UI.

50. Stinson, *Years Remembered*, 2.

51. Page, "Social Life in Old Virginia," 192.

52. Ibid., 220.

53. Patterson, *Brown v. Board of Education*, xiii.

54. Stinson, *Years Remembered*, vii.

55. Shirley Kresan Strout, "Journey to Virginia," *Themis* 55, no. 2 (Winter 1957): 94, 96; Strout, *History of Zeta Tau Alpha*, 191. With her somewhat exotic surname of "Kreson" (sometimes spelled Kre'San in earlier publications), Strout may have been hesitant to research her own genealogy, since it likely would not offer her blood ties to a desired colonial heritage in early America.

56. Osterweis, *Myth of the Lost Cause*, 113; Silber, *Romance of Reunion*, 105–21; Blight, *Race and Reunion*, 216–31; Margaret Freeman, "A Sunny Southerner or a Beautiful Alien?" *Magazine of Albemarle County History* 71 (2013): 34–59.

57. Cox notes that most southern states used pro-Confederate textbooks by the 1920s. See *Dixie's Daughters*, 160.

58. "Sixteen Pledged to Active Group as School Opens," *Iota Lyre* 1, no. 1 (November 1934): 1–2, box 2 (26/21/4), HC, UI.

59. "How the Chapters Rush," *Angelos* 13, no. 1 (November 1916): 22.

60. Eagles documented numerous instances of sororities and fraternities practicing blackface minstrelsy at the University of Mississippi in the 1940s and 1950s. See *Price of Defiance*, 59.

61. *Yackety Yack*, 1949, 298, NCC, UNC.

62. Ballard and Ward, *Tri Delta Hostess*, 1937, 57, National Fraternity Publications (26/21/5), HC, UI.

63. Silber discusses the place of black characters in late nineteenth-century conciliation dramas, arguing that in a time of demographic flux throughout the country, it was comforting for whites from both North and South to see African Americans as docile laborers who reinforced the understood "class obligations" of the whites and blacks in the South. See *Romance of Reunion*, 109.

64. "Save Your Confederate Money," *Beta Nu's Letter* 1, no. 1 (June 1961): 4, Beta Nu Chapter History—University of Georgia, AΔΠ.

Chapter Four: Standardizing Sexuality

1. Daphne Cunningham, "Zeta, University of Alabama, April 27, 1914," *Angelos* 10, no. 2 (1914): 227–28; Daphne Cunningham, "Zeta, University of Alabama, July 26, 1914," *Angelos* 10, no. 4 (1914): 309–10.

2. Daphne Cunningham Diary, May 1, 12, 15, 18, 19, 1913, UA; Dorr, "Fifty Percent Moonshine," 46. On 1920s dating culture see Bailey, *From Front Porch to Back Seat*; Fass, *The Damned and the Beautiful*.

3. The KΔ events took place on February 22 and December 10, 1913. The numerous fraternity events are sprinkled throughout Cunningham's two diaries from 1913 and 1914, both at UA.

4. For further discussion of changes in sexual permissiveness in American society by the 1920s, see D'Emilio and Freedman, *Intimate Matters*, chapter 11, esp. 239–42.

5. Cahn, *Sexual Reckonings*, 5–10.

6. Sociologist Lisa Handler noted a similar tendency in her study of 1990s college sorority women, noting that sororities "make decisions for the 'collective good' of the group," and these decisions are "filtered through the goal of attracting male attention." Handler, "In the Fraternal Sisterhood," 249.

7. Syrett, *Company He Keeps*, 183–86, 218–19.

8. Cahn, *Sexual Reckonings*, 38.

9. Alumnae Questionnaires, Post-1945, Laura Parrish Papers, WM; September 23, 1929 minutes, box 1, folder 1, Women Students' Cooperative Government Association Records, WM.

10. On treating, see Peiss, *Cheap Amusements*. Elizabeth Clement explained the self-policing of "treating" culture among young working-class women, where "girls looked to each other to define acceptable and unacceptable modes of exchange" on dates. These girls attempted to push the limits of sexuality and receive "treats"—in the form of entertain-

ment, material goods, or rent payments—without being publicly branded as prostitutes. She notes that "treating provided the model for the economic and sexual exchange that became a hallmark of dating" in the middle class as well. Clement, *Love for Sale*, 56–57, 227.

11. John R. L. Johnson Jr. Oral History, 6, University Archives Oral History Collection, WM.

12. Syrett, *Company He Keeps*, 191.

13. *Kappa Alpha Theta Pledge Training Book*, 1927, 14, National Fraternity Publications (26/21/5), HC, UI.

14. Ibid.

15. Lucy Mercer, "Omega [Chapter]," *Section Two of the Adelphean 19* (1927): 111–13.

16. Fass, *The Damned and the Beautiful*, 310. During Prohibition, the "cocktails" developed to make the most of low-quality bootleg liquors diluted hard liquor's potency and introduced suitable beverages for women drinkers. The Eighteenth Amendment and the Volstead Act, which outlawed transportation and sale of liquors but allowed consumption of homemade wines and beers, repositioned private homes as drinking establishments rather than saloons. The serving and responsible drinking of alcohol thus became "domesticated" among Americans of all social classes, and young women more easily became equal partners in the youth drinking culture. See Rotskoff, *Love on the Rocks*, 39–40.

17. Rotskoff, *Love on the Rocks*, 42–45.

18. October 18, 1934, series 2, Minutes, Delta Beta Chapter Records, DU; Jane Porter Middleton interview, 15, T. Harry Williams Center for Oral History Collections, LSU.

19. Pauline Linebarger McClain Oral History Interview, 12–13; Kay Fishbaugh Carr Oral History Interview, 5; Florence Hood Miner Oral History Interview, 15, all from Oral Histories of the Great Depression, Student Life and Culture Archives, UI.

20. Fass, *The Damned and the Beautiful*, 318–19.

21. D'Emilio and Freedman, *Intimate Matters*, 244–45.

22. Grigsby, "A Direct Social Program," *Banta's Greek Exchange* 23, no. 3 (July 1935): 221–24; Priddy, *Detailed Record of Delta Delta Delta*, 599.

23. Fass, *The Damned and the Beautiful*, 200.

24. "Message of the National President to Convention," *Section Two of the Adelphean* 27 (1934): 13; "Report of the Standards Committee by M. L. Collins," 23rd NPC, 1933, box 1, NPC Proceedings (41/82/10), NPC, UI.

25. While continuing to socialize was the norm for sororities, sometimes financial concerns could keep groups from organizing parties where they would be expected to pitch in for decorations and food. In October 1938 Gamma Epsilon chapter of Phi Mu at Duke had been invited to go in with two other sororities to host a tea dance at the end of the month but decided "due to exorbitant cost, it would not accept." See Minutes, October 17, 1938, series 2, Phi Mu, Gamma Epsilon Chapter Records, DU.

26. In addition to raising monthly membership dues by $1.25 to a total of $4.25 a month for the 1931–32 school year, Duke's Delta Beta chapter of Kappa Kappa Gamma also approved a recommendation that members pay an additional social tax of twenty-five cents a month and that pledges pay $2.50 for a social tax for the months October through January. Minutes, April 8, 1931, April 26, 1932, May 10, 1932, series 2, KKΓ, Delta Beta Chapter Records, DU.

27. *Iota Speaks*, June 1943, Kappa Alpha Theta, Cornell Chapter Newsletter, 1924–26, 1927–36, 1938–44, box 27, Subject Files (26/21/13), HC, UI; *Adelphean* 36, no. 3 (December 1943): 79, AΔΠ. Each Saturday night at Duke, one sorority and two fraternities would take charge of the dance to be held in the Ark. See Minutes, March 15, 1943, series 2, Phi Mu, Gamma Epsilon Chapter Records, DU.

28. Class of 1944 respondent, Laura Parrish Papers, WM; *Colonial Echo*, 1944, 84, 169.

29. Martha Pet Edfeldt, "The Wartime Sorority," *Aglaia* 39, no. 1 (November 1944): 26–27.

30. Winchell, *Good Girls*, 116–34.

31. Mary Grace Wilson to Katherine Warren, January 18, 1951, Drinking Regulations, 1942–1958, box 29, Woman's College Records, DU. While often eclipsed by the 1920s and 1960s "sexual revolutions," some historians have argued that social changes during World War II were part of a continuing escalation of, rather than just an aberrant period of increase in, Americans' sexual behavior and cultural acceptance of sex. See Petigny, *Permissive Society*, chapter 3; Meyerowitz, "Liberal 1950s?"; Littauer, *Bad Girls*, 3–4.

32. Mary Grace Wilson to Katherine Warren, January 18, 1951, Drinking Regulations, 1942–1958, box 29, Woman's College Records, DU.

33. Historians have noted that during both World War I and II, some young women sought to entertain, date, and sometimes consent to sex with servicemen as part of what they—or the servicemen—perceived to be women's patriotic "duty" on the home front. Military doctors and government officials sought to keep servicemen from coming into contact with young women (both working prostitutes and "good girls"), whom they painted as the source of sexually transmitted diseases around military bases. See Allen Brandt, *No Magic Bullet*, chapter 5; Clement, *Love for Sale*, 145–47, 151, 153; Hegarty, *Victory Girls*, 112–14, 50–52, 56–58; Littauer, *Bad Girls*, chapter 1; Meyer, *Creating G.I. Jane*, 101–4; Winchell, *Good Girls*, 76, 86–87.

34. Wilson to Warren, January 18, 1951.

35. Straus and Bacon, *Drinking in College*, 146–55.

36. Rotskoff, *Love on the Rocks*, 51, 59. She notes that changes in the drinking culture by the 1930s and 1940s had enabled heterosocial settings for drinking but had not entirely removed the masculine connotation of hard liquor. Through the work of advertisers, she explains, consumption of alcohol became part of the postwar "American way of life," defined by "bountiful domestic pleasures."

37. Wilson to Warren, January 18, 1951.

38. "Annual Report, 1952–1953," folder 7, box 1, Dean of Women Records: Edith L. Stallings and Louise McBee UA97–119, UGA. A tally of the WSGA court offenses showed that while no one broke the drinking rule during 1952–53 or 1955–56, two women in 1953–54 and seven in 1954–55 were found guilty. See "Annual Report, 1954–1955," folder 11, box 1, Dean of Women Records: Edith L. Stallings and Louise McBee UA97–119, UGA.

39. "Comments from Survey of Lucy Cobb Dorm Residents," February 11 (no year given), folder 6, box 2, Dean of Women Records: Edith L. Stallings and Louise McBee UA97–119, UGA.

40. Rotskoff, *Love on the Rocks*, 198–201.

41. *Instructions for Pledge Training for Kappa Kappa Gamma*, 19, Kappa Kappa Gamma

Pledge Manual, 1944, 1963–63, box 29, National Fraternity Reference Files (26/21/4), HC, UI.

42. Moran, *Teaching Sex*, 113, 127, 144. Contrary to conventional understandings of sex roles, social scientists of the postwar era proposed that masculine and feminine characteristics were not biologically determined at birth but were instead, as Moran notes, "achieved through individual effort and a supportive environment." Postwar family life education (FLE) courses were "intensely interested in the question of sex roles." While sororities did not explicitly link their teachings to sex education or FLE courses, they were in a much better position to monitor and correct heterosocial adjustment of adolescent females on the cusp of adulthood.

43. For discussion of sex education and heteronormative gender roles for girls in this period, see Susan K. Freeman, *Sex Goes to School*, chapter 5.

44. Burgess et al., *Courtship, Engagement, and Marriage*, 26.

45. "Report of the Sorority Evaluation Committee," 1951–1952, Reports and Evaluations, 1949–1959, box 1, Panhellenic Council Records, 1938–1996, DU. In the 1951–52 survey, 311 sorority girls and 89 independents believed that sorority membership increased dating opportunities, while 196 sorority girls and 143 independents did not think membership helped in dating.

46. "Panhellenic Questionnaire," Fall 1961, Reports and Evaluations, 1960–1969, box 1, Panhellenic Council Records, 1938–1996, DU.

47. On the near universal goal of marriage and family for all Americans during the long 1950s, see Coontz, *Marriage, a History*, chapter 14. On perceived importance of marriage and the nuclear family in the Cold War era, see Elaine Tyler May, *Homeward Bound*, 17–20; McEnnany, *Civil Defense Begins at Home*, 4–5, 72–78.

48. November 5, 1951, November 15, 1951, June 7, 1952, series 2, Phi Mu, Gamma Epsilon Chapter Records, DU; "Chapel Administrative Leadership Timeline," *Friends of Duke Chapel Newsletter*, Third Quarter 2008, 4, https://chapel.duke.edu/sites/default/files/08_3Q.pdf.

49. November 10, 1955, series 2, Phi Mu, Gamma Epsilon Chapter Records, DU.

50. "Minutes on the Advisory Committee on Sororities," 1948, Advisory Committee on Special Sorority Problems, 1950–1955, box 1, series 12, Office of the Vice Chancellor for Student Affairs Records (#40124), University Archives, UNC; Carmichael to Tri-Delta member, December 4, 1953, Correspondence, 1937–1957, box 1, series 10.2, Office of the Vice Chancellor for Student Affairs Records (#40124), University Archives, UNC.

51. Carmichael, "The Sorority Woman Moves into the World of the Future," 17, box 4, series 2.2, Office of the Dean of Women Records (#40125), University Archives, UNC.

52. *For She's an Alpha Chi! A Handbook of Collegiate Social Customs*, National Fraternity Publications (26/21/5), HC, UI. The handbook's authors were Peggy Henry Matthews and Phyllis Boynton Conrad of Alpha Lambda chapter at the University of Minnesota. At time of publication Matthews was midwest editor for *Mademoiselle* magazine, and Boynton was the chapter chairman of the sorority's Collegiate Social Development Committee. Both women would have been around forty years old when developing the booklet. Conrad's obituary, August 1, 2010, http://www.legacy.com/funerals/washburnmcreavy

-minneapolis/obituary.aspx?pid=144430417; Matthews's obituary, January 28, 2018, https://www.legacy.com/obituaries/sandiegouniontribune/obituary.aspx?n=peggy-henry -matthews&pid=187997033.

53. *Design for a Duchess*, 1962, 8, 10, Reference "Design for a Duchess" 1962, series 7, Order of the White Duchy Records, 1925–1968, DU.

54. *For She's an Alpha Chi!* 3.

55. Ibid.

56. On going steady see Bailey, *From Front Porch to Back Seat*, 49–55; Breines, *Young, White, and Miserable*, 115–24; Littauer, *Bad Girls*, 117–19, 127–29.

57. Syrett, *Company He Keeps*, 274–83.

58. Greene, *Sex and the College Girl*; Douglas, *Where the Girls Are*; Steinem, "Moral Disarmament."

59. Portia Allyn Smith Oral History Interview, 17, Oral Histories of the Great Depression at the University of Illinois, UI.

60. Littauer, *Bad Girls*, 127–28.

61. Christina Simmons discussed the public belief in "male sexual necessity" during the pre–World War II period and a tendency for marriage manuals of this era to rely on the convention of "male initiative" in sexual activity. The normalization of a dominant male sexuality could teach young women to expect or resign themselves to boorish male behavior, which today would be recognized as sexual harassment or assault. See *Making Marriage Modern*, 205–9.

62. In Peggy Goodin's 1950 novel *Take Care of My Little Girl*, freshman sorority pledge Liz is pressured to date Chad, a "Big Man on Campus" from a popular fraternity. Her "sisters" see Chad as "good advertising" for their sorority. Unfortunately, he also happens to be a dull, closed-minded drunkard who dates around and whom her sisters consider "beyond reach and dangerous." Still, this knowledge did not deter the sorority women from endorsing him as a significant catch. See Goodin, *Take Care of My Little Girl*, 57–60, 109–11.

63. In 1944 the UNC Women's Honor Council documented four cases of women's drinking-related misconduct. In two instances coeds "were found in a fraternity house in which alcoholic beverages were being consumed in their presence." One of the women drank with the men while the others abstained. All were served with nearly identical social probations. In the other cases women received social probation for storing and drinking beer or liquor in their dorm rooms. It is unclear whether the women were sorority members. See "Honor Council Report for 1944" and "Rules and Regulations for Women Students of the University of North Carolina, 1944–1945," Woman's Association, 1935–1945, box 1, series 1, Office of the Dean of Women Records (#40125), University Archives, UNC.

64. Duke Woman's College Judicial Board to Mary Grace Wilson and attached survey, March 20, 1958, Drinking Regulations, 1942–1958, box 29, Woman's College Records, DU.

65. *Handbook for Women Students at the University of North Carolina*, 1924–1925, NCC, UNC; *College of William and Mary Women's Student Government Handbook*, 1931–1932, Frances C. Cosby Nettles Papers, 1931–1935, WM. By 1948 UNC mentioned the prohibition of drinking in the dormitories. Women who needed to keep liquor in their rooms "for medicinal purposes," however, could do so, but they had to report it to the house presi-

dent. See *Handbook for Women Students at the University of North Carolina*, 1948–1949, 20, NCC, UNC.

66. Fass, *The Damned and the Beautiful*, 318–19; NADW-NPC Joint Committee Meeting Minutes, March 1950, 14–15, NPC-NAWDAC Liaison Committee, 1947–1957, Committee File (41/82/50), NPC, UI.

67. Grand Council of Kappa Alpha Theta to Thetas and friends of Theta, December 11, 1957, Vice President of Student Affairs Records AU RG-793, folder 4, box 2, AU. Rotskoff argues that the medicalization of the "problem drinker" by the mid-twentieth century fueled Americans' concern with alcoholism, and primarily the alcoholic male. See *Love on the Rocks*, 85–86.

68. Grand Council of Kappa Alpha Theta to Thetas and friends of Theta, December 11, 1957, Vice President of Student Affairs Records AU RG-793, folder 4, box 2, AU.

69. Carmichael to Dr. Loren C. McKinney, February 11, 1955, Advisory Committee on Special Sorority Problems, 1950–1955, box 41, series 12, Office of the Vice Chancellor for Student Affairs Records (#40124), University Archives, UNC; Minutes of the Advisory Committee on Special Sorority Problems, March 8, 1962, Advisory Committee on Special Sorority Problems, 1956–1964, box 41, series 12, Office of the Vice Chancellor for Student Affairs Records (#40124), University Archives, UNC.

70. Annual Report, 1964, 5, Office of the Dean of Women Records, 1928–1974, WM.

71. Sharon Sullivan Mujica interview, 16, 50, SOHP, UNC.

72. Carmichael, "Why Educate Your Daughter?" n.d., 5, 8, box 5, series 2.2, Office of the Dean of Women Records (#40125), University Archives, UNC.

73. *Chapter Keystones*, no. 7 (September 1961): 5, *Chapter Keystones*, 1961–1962, series 4, box 1, ΚΚΓ, Delta Beta Chapter Records, DU.

74. Syrett, *Company He Keeps*, 241.

75. Carmichael to Bill Redding, February 27, 1958, General: Parties, 1955–1962, box 32, series 10.2, Office of the Vice Chancellor for Student Affairs Records (#40124), University Archives, UNC; Fred Weaver to Committee Members, January 2, 1940, Fraternities: Interfraternity Council (IFC): IFC Visitation Agreement, 1936–1950, box 32, series 10.2, Office of the Vice Chancellor for Student Affairs Records (#40124), University Archives, UNC.

76. Fred H. Weaver to Chancellor R. B. House, January 21, 1952, Fraternities: Interfraternity Council (IFC): IFC Visitation Agreement, 1951–1953, box 32, series 10.2, Office of the Vice Chancellor for Student Affairs Records (#40124), University Archives, UNC.

77. University of North Carolina Interfraternity Council Visiting Agreement, 1940, Fraternities: Interfraternity Council (IFC): IFC Visitation Agreement, 1936–1950, box 32, series 10.2, Office of the Vice Chancellor for Student Affairs Records (#40124), University Archives, UNC.

78. Carmichael to Redding, February 27, 1958, General: Parties, 1955–1962, box 32, series 10.2, Office of the Vice Chancellor for Student Affairs Records (#40124), University Archives, UNC. This group was called the House Privileges Board in 1940s UNC yearbooks. See *Yackety Yack*, 1947, 188, NCC, UNC.

79. Carmichael to Redding, February 27, 1958.

80. Ibid. Much to the chagrin of Carmichael *and* the women who attended the frat par-

ties, weeknight events could run from 5:00 p.m. to 11:00 p.m. The Panhellenic Council had repeatedly asked the IFC to cooperate to limit these parties, but the IFC "annually refused to take action." While such a social schedule could easily derail a woman's academic requirements if study took a back seat to the parties, a woman's sorority chapter, as well as the host fraternity, expected their presence at mixers.

81. In Anne Rivers Siddons's novel *Heartbreak Hotel* (1976), set in 1956, the housemother at the "Kappa" sorority is the widow of a judge, described as "a gentlewoman in suddenly reduced circumstances and left with no close, encumbering family." Finding herself out of touch with the lives of mid-century college women, she spends most of her time alone in her apartment drinking whiskey-laced tea or coffee. See *Heartbreak Hotel*, 31–33.

82. Carmichael to Redding, February 27, 1958.

83. Ibid.; Ruth Duncan to President Frank P. Graham, March 15, 1946, Fraternities: Interfraternity Council (IFC): IFC Visitation Agreement, 1936–1950, box 32, series 10.2, Office of the Vice Chancellor for Student Affairs Records (#40124), University Archives, UNC.

84. Carmichael to Redding, February 27, 1958.

85. Ibid.

86. Historian Leisa Meyer described a similar situation for women in the Women's Army Corps during World War II. She explains that the "norms of 'appropriate sexual behavior'" for women in this period "[allowed] for the presence of active sexual desire in women" but "continued to rest on the idea that men had a greater sex drive than women and characterized women as having a special responsibility to 'curb male lust.'" See Meyer, *Creating G.I. Jane*, 125.

87. Panhellenic Court Judicial Board Minutes, November 9, 1961, Sororities: Panhellenic Court, 1961–1965, box 33, series 10.2, Office of the Vice Chancellor for Student Affairs Records (#40124), University Archives, UNC.

88. Ibid.

89. Dean Charles Henderson Jr. to Mel Underdahl, General Secretary, Zeta Psi Fraternity, December 14, 1961, Fraternities and Sororities Correspondence, 1961, box 32, series 10.2, Office of the Vice Chancellor for Student Affairs Records (#40124), University Archives, UNC.

90. *Ladies First*, 46, box 77, National Fraternity Reference File (26/21/4), HC, UI; "Manning Woman Writes Book Titled 'Ladies First,'" *Sumter Daily Item*, July 5, 1966, https://news.google.com/newspapers?nid=1979&dat=19660705&id=YJciAAAAIBA-J&sjid=X6oFAAAAIBAJ&pg=5647,218990.

91. Bailey, *Sex in the Heartland*, 7–11.

92. Loren Tipton Cornette Oral History Interview, 15, University Archives Oral History Collection, WM.

93. Borstelmann, *1970s*, 93; Douglas, *Where the Girls Are*, 64–65.

94. Butterworth, *Ideally Speaking*, 31–34, National Fraternity Publications (26/21/5), HC, UI; Barbara Burns Hiscock, "Ideally Speaking . . . in This Changing World," *Crescent* 68, no. 1 (March 1968): 3–5; Stein, *Stranger Inside You*.

95. D'Emilio and Freedman, *Intimate Matters*, 312–14; Borstelmann, *1970s*, 93–95.

96. Syrett, *Company He Keeps*, 297n19, 369–70; Program of NPC 49th Session, 1985, NPC Proceedings (41/82/10), NPC, UI.

97. Syrett, *Company He Keeps*, 297.

Chapter Five. "The Chosen Are Happy, the Rest Are Crushed"

1. Betty White, *I Lived This Story*, 32–33. White was a 1929 graduate of Northwestern University. *I Lived This Story* won the first annual contest organized by *College Humor* magazine and Doubleday, Doran and Company publishers for the best story about college life in 1929. How much of the story White actually "lived" is unclear, but details suggest the book was autobiographical. She included ritual songs of Kappa Kappa Gamma in the prose, suggesting an insider's knowledge of the sorority, and newspapers implied that she had been a sorority member but was forced to resign after publishing the novel. The critical novel left little room to argue that sororities were beneficial to campuses. Following the book's success, White went to Hollywood as a scriptwriter for Paramount Pictures. The studio produced *Confessions of a Co-Ed* (1931), a film loosely based on White's novel. See "Current Magazines," *New York Times*, May 25, 1930, 70; R. Grantham, "Pipe and Pen," *Ubyssey* [student newspaper of the University of British Columbia], January 5, 1932, 2.

2. Turk, *Bound by a Mighty Vow*, 62–67.

3. "National Panhellenic Conference: An Historical Record of Achievement," ca. 1957, 7, box 1, NPC Publications (41/82/800), NPC, UI.

4. "Fifty Years of Rushing—Evolution to Modern System," NPC Proceedings, 1951, 40, box 2, NPC Proceedings (41/82/10), NPC, UI.

5. 32nd NPC Meeting, 1951, 40, NPC Proceedings (41/82/10), NPC, UI.

6. 22nd NPC Meeting, 1931, 233–34, NPC Proceedings (41/82/10), NPC, UI.

7. NPC Meeting, 1951, 40–42, box 2, NPC Proceedings (41/82/10), NPC, UI; 26th NPC Meeting, 1939, 62–65, NPC Proceedings (41/82/10), NPC, UI.

8. Carmichael to Ferne Hughes, October 20, 1948, Sororities, Rushing, 1945–1956, box 3, series 10.2, Office of the Vice Chancellor of Student Affairs Records (#40124), University Archives, UNC.

9. Turk, *Bound by a Mighty Vow*, 125.

10. "Report of Committee for Study of Rushing," 26th NPC Session, 1939, 64, NPC Proceedings (41/82/10), NPC, UI. The entire range of expenses reported was from $7 to $1,000.

11. "What to Wear during Rush," in "Eta Etchings," 1961, Eta Chapter, Alpha Delta Pi, University of Alabama, AΔΠ.

12. Jean Martin, "Are You Worth While?" *Aglaia* 39, no. 1 (1944): 27.

13. September 22, 1944, series 2, Phi Mu, Gamma Epsilon Chapter Records, DU.

14. November 16, 18, 19, 22, 1942, Diary, July 1, 1942–December 31, 1942, Margetta Doris Hirsch Doyle Papers, WM.

15. Mrs. Glenn Frank, "Heartache on Campus," *Woman's Home Companion*, April 1945, 20–21, 41. The article was reprinted in other outlets, including the *Milwaukee Journal* and *Reader's Digest*. See George Starr Lasher, "Fraternities Will Continue to Serve American Youth," *Rattle of Theta Chi* 33, no. 4 (1945): 13–16.

16. "College Sororities: They Pose a Social Problem," *LIFE*, December 17, 1945, 97–105.

17. Betty Jones, "Report on Duke University Agitation," October 23, 1945, 3, Alpha Delta Pi Chapter Histories—Omicron, Duke University, AΔΠ.

18. "Open Discussion on Sororities at Duke University," October 4, [1945], 1, Reports and Evaluations (Rush and Otherwise), 1945–1959, box 1, Panhellenic Council Records, 1938–1996, DU.

19. Ibid., 2.

20. Stanard to Members of Grand Council, October 9, 1945, Alpha Delta Pi Chapter Histories–Omicron, Duke University, AΔΠ.

21. Minutes, October 18, 1951, Order of the White Duchy Records, 1925–1968, DU.

22. "Report of the Sorority Evaluation Committee," 1951–1952, Reports and Evaluations (Rush & Otherwise), 1945–1959, box 1, Panhellenic Council Records, DU.

23. Arney R. Childs, Biographical File, Records, Dean of Women, 1926–1945, SC.

24. Childs to Edwin G. Seibels, August 4, 1941, Fraternities/Sororities, 1931–1945, Records, Dean of Women, 1926–1945, SC.

25. Childs to Helen Barbour, n.d., Sororities, Records, Dean of Women, 1926–1945, SC.

26. Ibid.

27. Advisory Committee on Sororities Minutes, 1948, Fraternities and Sororities, box 2, series 12.1, Office of the Vice Chancellor of Student Affairs Records (#40124), University Archives, UNC.

28. Annual Report, 1949–1950, 22, box 2, series 2.1, Records of the Office of the Dean of Women (#40125), University Archives, UNC; Nancy Iler Burkholder, telephone interview by author, May 11, 2010.

29. Minutes of the Advisory Committee on Special Sorority Problems, October 17, 1963, Fraternities and Sororities: Advisory Committee on Special Sorority Problems, 1950–1964, box 41, series 12, Office of the Vice Chancellor for Student Affairs Records (#40124), University Archives, UNC.

30. "An Analysis of Sorority Rushing (Deferred)," [1948?], 1, 3–5, Panhellenic Council Records, 1938–1996, box 2, Deferred Rush, 1947–1968, DU.

31. Ibid.

32. Chi Omega Rush Policies, 1952, folder 1113: UNC Panhellenic, 1948–1963, series 10.1, Guion Griffis Johnson Papers (#04546), SHC, UNC.

33. "Confidential Recommendation of Prospective Member," ca. 1939, Delta Delta Delta Ohio State Chapter—The Nus News, box 18, National Fraternity Reference Files (26/21/4), HC, UI.

34. Minutes of the Advisory Committee on Sororities, December 7, 1948, Fraternities and Sororities: Advisory Committee on Special Sorority Problems, 1950–1964, box 41, series 12, Office of the Vice Chancellor for Student Affairs Records (#40124), University Archives, UNC.

35. Ibid.

36. These exchanges are found in subseries 3.1: General Chi Omega Materials, folders 250–275, Guion Griffis Johnson Papers (#04546), SHC, UNC.

37. Sarah Theusen's article on Guion and Guy Johnson is the best source for biographical information on the couple. See Theusen, "Taking the Vows of White Southern Liberalism:

Guion and Guy Johnson and the Evolution of an Intellectual Partnership," *North Carolina Historical Review* 74, no. 3 (1997): 284–324.

38. Ibid., 313–14. Theusen suggests that Guion jumped into club work with great gusto during this period as a direct result of threats from university trustees and administrators against her husband's job.

39. I have used pseudonyms for the names of prospective rushees and their families discussed in the Chi Omega correspondence of the Guion Griffis Johnson Papers.

40. Johnson to Collins, May 11, 1951, folder 250: Correspondence, 1951, series 3.1, Guion Griffis Johnson Papers (#04546), SHC, UNC.

41. Collins to Johnson, May 14, 1951, folder 250: Correspondence, 1951, series 3.1, Guion Griffis Johnson Papers (#04546), SHC, UNC.

42. Collins to Johnson, August 16, 1951, folder 250: Correspondence, 1951, series 3.1, Guion Griffis Johnson Papers (#04546), SHC, UNC.

43. Johnson to Collins, August 24, 1951, folder 250: Correspondence, 1951, series 3.1, Guion Griffis Johnson Papers (#04546), SHC, UNC.

44. Syrett discusses how men's fraternities' reputations relied largely on the status of the university where the chapter was located and the chapter members' prosperity. It was less the individual members' moral reputations, in contrast to sorority women influencing the reputation of their chapters. *Company He Keeps*, 82–94.

45. Sorority members use the term "hot" rushee to describe the women going through rush whom the sororities on campus view as the most desirable future pledges. In this case, "hot" is not used to describe appearance, as in popular modern terminology, but is meant to include all of the desirable characteristics in a prospective pledge, such as scholarship, activities, background, personality, appearance, and recommendations.

46. Memorandum from Mary S. McDuffie to Faculty Committee on Sororities, February 13, 1946, Fraternities and Sororities: Faculty Committee on Sororities, box 41, series 12, Office of the Vice Chancellor for Student Affairs Records (#40124), University Archives, UNC; Minutes of the Faculty Committee on Fraternities and Sororities, February 12, 1963, Fraternities and Sororities: Faculty Committee on Sororities, box 41, series 12, Office of the Vice Chancellor for Student Affairs Records (#40124), University Archives, UNC.

47. Minutes of the Advisory Committee on Special Sorority Problems, October 17, 1963, Fraternities and Sororities: Advisory Committee on Special Sorority Problems, box 41, series 12, Office for the Vice Chancellor for Student Affairs Records (#40124), University Archives, UNC.

48. Ibid.

49. Annual Report, 1923–1924, box 1, series 1, Office of Dean of Women Records (#40125), University Archives, UNC; Carmichael to Dr. Loren C. McKinney, February 11, 1955, Fraternities and Sororities: General, 1941–1971, box 41, series 12, Office of the Vice Chancellor for Student Affairs Records (#40124), University Archives, UNC.

50. Minutes of the Advisory Committee on Special Sorority Problems, October 17, 1963, Fraternities and Sororities: Advisory Committee on Special Sorority Problems, box 41, series 12, Office of the Vice Chancellor for Student Affairs Records (#40124), University Archives, UNC.

51. Off-the-record source to author.

52. "Report of the Faculty Committee on Fraternities and Sororities, 1964–1965," 6–7, Fraternities and Sororities: Annual Reports, 1929; 1949; 1957–1971, box 41, series 12, Office of the Vice Chancellor for Student Affairs Records (#40124), University Archives, UNC.

Chapter Six. "To Discriminate Is a Positive Trait"

1. "Sorority Fight," *LIFE*, May 20, 1946; "Dissent on Campus," *Vermont Quarterly*, n.d., http://www.uvm.edu/vtquarterly/vqfall/dessent.html, accessed January 20, 2020.

2. "Publicity and Public Relations Panel," 29th NPC Meeting, 1945, 165–69, NPC Proceedings (41/82/10), NPC, UI.

3. Joseph Lowndes discusses this practice by writers at *National Review* and within the 1964 Barry Goldwater presidential campaign in *From the New Deal*, 44, 51–57.

4. Recent studies such as Kruse, *White Flight*, Lassiter, *Silent Majority*, and Crespino, *In Search of Another Country* illuminate the importance of race in the mobilization of grassroots conservatism in the South. For a party-level analysis of race as it influenced the southern political shift toward the conservative movement and the GOP, see Lowndes, *From the New Deal*. Lewis shows how southern white supremacists used anticommunist rhetoric to remove race from debates over segregation policies in *White South*.

5. Cott, *Grounding of Modern Feminism*, 95–96.

6. Ladd-Taylor, *Mother-Work*; Gordon, *Pitied but not Entitled*; Mink, *Wages of Motherhood*; Muncy, *Creating a Female Dominion*.

7. Cott, *Grounding of Modern Feminism*, 258–63; Delegard, *Battling Miss Bolsheviki*, 182.

8. Delegard, *Battling Miss Bolsheviki*, 15–16.

9. George Banta, "The Sorority Situation at Wisconsin," *Banta's Greek Exchange* 6 (July 1918): 294–97; Mary C. Love Collins, "As Our Sisters See It," *Banta's Greek Exchange* 8 (March 1920): 191; Turk, *Bound by a Mighty Vow*, 208n45.

10. 15th NPC Meeting, 1917, NPC Proceedings (41/82/10), NPC, UI.

11. Cott, *Grounding of Modern Feminism*; Morgan, *Women and Patriotism*; Delegard, *Battling Miss Bolsheviki*; Nickerson, *Mothers of Conservatism*.

12. Delegard, *Battling Miss Bolsheviki*, 95.

13. Other antiradical/conservative sorority women emerging in the post–World War II period include Collins's assistant, companion, and successor at XΩ, Elizabeth Dyer; Julia Fuqua Ober and Genevieve Forbes Morse of KΔ; Ernestine Grigsby of Tri-Delta; Eleanor Bowers Hofstead of KAΘ; Mrs. Beverly Johnson of AΞΔ; and Edith Crabtree of KKΓ.

14. Mary Love Collins, "Democracy—The Issue," *Banta's Greek Exchange* 23, no. 3 (1935): 221–24.

15. Schrecker, *Many Are the Crimes*, 91.

16. Ward, *Defending White Democracy*, 21, 38–40, 78–79; Perlstein, *Before the Storm*, chapter 1.

17. A larger number of sorority alumnae hailed from outside the South in these years and were likely members of the Republican Party. Several early 1930s notices in the *Key* of Kappa Kappa Gamma refer to the overwhelmingly Republican support in the sorority. See *Key* 49, no. 4 (1932): 375; *Key* 50, no. 1 (1933): 3–4.

18. Minutes of Committee on Information on War and College Women, November

15, 1942, box 1, Committee on Information on War and College Women Report, 1942, Committee File (41/82/50), NPC, UI; Committee on Information on War and College Women to Presidents of NPC Fraternities and NPC Delegates, March 15, 1943, box 1, NPC Minutes and Committee on Information on the War and College Women Report, Committee File (41/82/50), NPC, UI.

19. 32nd NPC Meeting, 1951, 131, NPC Proceedings (41/82/10), NPC, UI. For Balfour's background, see Fran Becque, "About L. G. Balfour on Sigma Chi's Founders' Day," June 28, 2012, https://www.franbecque.com/1018/.

20. 32nd NPC Meeting, 1951, 132, NPC Proceedings (41/82/10), NPC, UI.

21. 36th NPC Meeting, 1959, 26, NPC Proceedings (41/82/10), NPC, UI; 31st NPC Meeting, 1949, 116; NPC Proceedings (41/82/10), NPC, UI.

22. 29th NPC Meeting, 1945, 165–66, NPC Proceedings (41/82/10), NPC, UI.

23. 30th NPC Meeting, 1947, 165–66, NPC Proceedings (41/82/10), NPC, UI; 35th NPC Meeting, 1957, 34, NPC Proceedings (41/82/10), NPC, UI.

24. "The Reasons Why!" January 20, 1946, box 1, Publications (41/82/800), NPC, UI.

25. "The Price of Rights? Responsibilities!" March 20, 1946, RPR Committee, 1946–1971, box 1, Committee File (41/82/50), NPC, UI.

26. 31st NPC Meeting, 1949, 116–17, NPC Proceedings (41/82/10), NPC, UI.

27. Bartley, *Rise of Massive Resistance*, 37–38.

28. 31st NPC Meeting, 1949, 116–17, NPC Proceedings (41/82/10), NPC, UI.

29. Schrecker, *Many Are the Crimes*, 157, 175, 242–43.

30. Meeting, 1951, 177–88, NPC Proceedings (41/81/10), NPC, UI.

31. "News Letter," [1951?], Fraternity Affairs File (41/82/9), NPC, UI.

32. 32nd NPC 1951, 135, NPC Proceedings (41/82/10), NPC, UI.

33. Fran Becque, "Happy Birthday Amy Burnham Onken, NPC Chairman, 1945–1947," September 24, 2012, https://www.franbecque.com/happy-birthday-amy-burnham-onken-npc-chairman-1945-47-2/; 32nd NPC, 1951, 231, NPC Proceedings (41/82/10), NPC, UI; Buckley, *God and Man at Yale*.

34. "NSA Contemplates Its Shattered Image," *Washington Post*, February 20, 1967; Eugene G. Schwartz, *American Students Organize*, 219; Johnston, "United States National Student Association," 226.

35. Johnston, "United States National Student Association," 152; Minutes, 1953, 46, Edgewater Conference File, box 1, ATΩ National Officers (41/93/31), ATΩ, UI.

36. Syracuse KAΘ to Mrs. George Banta Jr., September 21, 1951, National Student Association, 1950–1951, box 1, Fraternity Affairs File (41/82/9), NPC, UI; Lee, *Fraternities without Brotherhood*, 62–68, 72–73.

37. 35th NPC, 1957, 53–55, NPC Proceedings (41/82/10), NPC, UI.

38. Margaret Banta was married to George Banta Jr., the national president of Phi Delta Theta fraternity. He ran George Banta Publishing Company, the primary publisher of materials for Greek-letter groups, founded by his family and based in Menasha, Wisconsin. See McComb, *Great Depression and the Middle Class*, 167n158.

39. Syracuse KAΘ to Mrs. George Banta Jr., September 21, 1951, National Student Association, 1950–1951, box 1, Fraternity Affairs File (41/82/9), NPC, UI.

40. Minutes, 1953, 123, Edgewater Conference File, box 1, ATΩ National Officers (41/93/31), ATΩ, UI.

41. "Sorority Fight," *LIFE*, May 20, 1946.

42. James, "Defenders of Tradition," esp. 21–35, which covers situations that arose at men's fraternity chapters at Middlebury, Bowdoin, Amherst, and Dartmouth Colleges between 1946 and 1949. Minutes, 1954, 28, Edgewater Conference File, box 1, ATΩ National Officers (41/93/31), ATΩ, UI.

43. Minutes, 1954, 28–30, Edgewater Conference File, box 1, ATΩ National Officers (41/93/31), ATΩ, UI. Neither Burr nor McCusker were able to fully participate in Edgewater, as Burr died in 1952 and illness led McCusker to step down as conference chairman after 1953. Chairmanship was then passed to Dr. Houston T. Karnes, a Lambda Chi Alpha and a mathematics professor at LSU.

44. NPC sororities with representatives present included XΩ, KΔ, ΠBΦ, ΔΔΔ, and ΔΓ. AES sororities included Pi Kappa Sigma (absorbed by Sigma Kappa, 1959), Delta Sigma Epsilon (absorbed by Delta Zeta, 1956), Theta Sigma Upsilon (absorbed by AΓΔ, 1959), and Alpha Sigma Tau. NIC fraternities included Sigma Chi, Theta Chi, Phi Delta Theta, Alpha Tau Omega, Pi Kappa Alpha, Phi Sigma Kappa, Alpha Sigma Phi, Lambda Chi Alpha, and Kappa Sigma. Sigma Tau Gamma sent a letter of regret. Minutes, 1954, 1–3, Edgewater Conference File, ATΩ National Officers (41/93/31), ATΩ, UI.

45. Minutes, 1953, 73, Edgewater Conference File, box 1, ATΩ National Officers (41/93/31), ATΩ, UI.

46. Lee, *Fraternities without Brotherhood*, 6–7, 54.

47. Minutes, May 29–30, 1953, 42, Edgewater Conference File, box 1, ATΩ National Officers (41/93/31), ATΩ, UI.

48. Pi Kappa Sigma (1894–1959) began at Michigan State Normal College in Ypsilanti, Michigan. It was an original member of the Association of Educational Sororities. In 1959 Sigma Kappa sorority absorbed Pi Kappa Sigma. See Robson, *Baird's Manual*, 792.

49. Minutes, May 29–30, 1953, 42–43, Edgewater Conference File, box 1, ATΩ National Officers (41/93/31), ATΩ, UI.

50. NPC Called Meeting, March 29, 1951, 23–24, NPC Proceedings (41/82/10), NPC, UI.

51. "The NPC Declaration for Freedom," 1957; on the Manion Forum, see Perlstein, *Before the Storm*, 3–16.

52. "The NPC Declaration for Freedom," December 1957, box 1, Fraternity Affairs File (41/82/9), NPC, UI. Lowndes argues that white supremacists gravitated toward conservatism as a means to combat what southern white supremacist Charles Wallace Collins described as "the dual dangers of 'Negro equality and State capitalism.'" See Lowndes, *From the New Deal*, 1–10, quotation on 2.

53. David Lawrence, "'Civil Rights' That Breed 'Civil Wrongs,'" *U.S. News and World Report*, July 19, 1957; David Lawrence, "There Is No 'Fourteenth Amendment'!" *U.S. News and World Report*, September 27, 1957, quotation on 139; David Lawrence, "Illegality Breeds Illegality," *U.S. News and World Report*, October 4, 1957; MacLean, "Neo-Confederacy versus the New Deal," 318–19.

54. MacLean, "Neo-Confederacy versus the New Deal," 312–13; William F. Buckley, "Why the South Must Prevail," *National Review*, August 24, 1957; Donald Davidson, "The New South and the Conservative Tradition," *National Review*, September 10, 1960; Richard M. Weaver, "The Regime of the South," *National Review*, March 14, 1959; L. Brent Bozell, "The Open Question: Mr. Bozell Dissents from the Views Expressed in the Editorial, 'Why the South Must Prevail,'" *National Review*, September 7, 1957.

55. "The NPC Declaration for Freedom," December 1957, box 1, Fraternity Affairs File (41/82/9), NPC, UI; Richard M. Weaver, "Integration Is Communization," *National Review*, July 13, 1957; Lassiter, "De Jure/De Facto Segregation," 29; Donald Davidson, "The New South and the Conservative Tradition," *National Review*, September 10, 1960.

56. Russell Kirk, "In Defense of Fraternities: Part II," *National Review*, May 18, 1957.

57. Dyer to Chi Omega Counsellors, January 1957, Chi Omega Correspondence, 1957, subseries 3.1, Guion Griffis Johnson Papers (#04546), SHC, UNC.

58. Marguerite Sammis Jansky, "A Primer of Citizenship," *Banta's Greek Exchange* 48, no. 1 (January 1960): 34–37.

59. "Dedicated to What?" *Key* 77, no. 3 (1960).

60. Minutes, 1961, 133, Edgewater Conference File, box 1, ATΩ National Officers (41/91/31), ATΩ, UI; Perlstein, *Before the Storm*, 70; Preston, "The Forward Look: Campus Conservatism," Delta Gamma *Anchora* Articles, 1959–1961, 1966, box 18, National Fraternity Reference Files (26/21/4), HC, UI. At the time of YAF's formation, Caddy was a staff writer at *Human Events* and chair of the D.C. College Republicans while attending the Georgetown School of Foreign Service. Franke edited the magazines of the Intercollegiate Society of Individualists (ISI) and College Young Republicans.

61. William F. Buckley Jr., "What Johnny Doesn't Know," *National Review*, January 14, 1964.

62. "Carolina YAF," *New Guard*, September 1964, 24, *The New Guard*, box 1, Subject Files (26/21/13), HC, UI.

63. Tom Charles Huston, "Operation Greek: The Attempt to Destroy the American Fraternity System," 7–8, in Tom Charles Huston, "Fraternities and Freedom," 1965, Young Americans for Freedom, 1965, 1967–1968, box 19, HP (41/2/52), UI.

64. Schneider, *Cadres for Conservatism*, 32–33; Huston, "Operation Greek," 8; "NSA Contemplates Its Shattered Image," *Washington Post*, February 20, 1967.

65. James, "Defenders of Tradition," 102–4; Syrett, *Company He Keeps*, 256; Wallace Turner, "Colleges Face U.S. Aid Cutoff If They Permit Fraternity Bias," *New York Times*, June 18, 1965, 1, 24.

66. Guion Johnson to Mrs. Judson D. [Alice] Willis Mease, March 3, 1964, Chi Omega Correspondence, 1964, subseries 3.1, Guion Griffis Johnson Papers (#04546), SHC, UNC.

67. Pete Wales, "Discriminatory Clauses, Compliance Dates Set Sept. 1, 1966," *Daily Tar Heel*, March 6, 1965, Fraternities, 1963–1969, box 14, Douglas M. Knight Records, DU.

68. Memorandum to the Faculty Committee on Fraternities and Sororities from William G. Long, Dean of Men, Re: Restrictive Clauses, October 22, 1964, Fraternities and Sororities, Discriminatory Policies, 1959–1971, box 32, series 10.2, Office of the Vice Chancellor for Student Affairs Records (#40124), University Archives, UNC.

69. Knight to [Fraternity/Sorority officer], June 28, 1965, Fraternities—Title VI, 1965–1968, box 14, Douglas M. Knight Records, DU.

70. Mrs. Frank H. [Frances] Alexander to Knight, July 13, 1965, Fraternities—Title VI, 1965–1968, box 14, Douglas M. Knight Records, DU.

71. Maxine Blake to Knight, July 19, 1965, Fraternities—Title VI, 1965–1968, box 14, Douglas M. Knight Records, DU.

72. Genevieve Forbes Morse to Knight, "Kappa Delta Statement of Policy," July 20, 1965, Fraternities—Title VI, 1965–1968, box 14, Douglas M. Knight Records, DU.

73. Genevieve Forbes Morse to Knight, September 28, 1965, Fraternities—Title VI, 1965–1968, box 14, Douglas M. Knight Records, DU.

74. Gary May, *Bending toward Justice*, 165; Rolph, "Courting Conservatism," 25–26, 33.

75. James discusses these events in further detail in his dissertation "Defenders of Tradition," 108–10; Marjorie Hunter, "College Aid Bill Passed by the House, 367 to 22," *New York Times*, August 27, 1965, 1, 30; "Senate Approves College Aid Bill," *New York Times*, September 3, 1965, 1, 14.

76. Frank T. De Vyver to Knight, October 23, 1967, Fraternities—Title VI, 1965–1968, box 14, Douglas M. Knight Records, DU.

77. KΔ National President to Alumnae of Sigma Delta Chapter, November 1967, Kappa Delta, 1960s, Dorothy Newsom Rankin Papers, DU.

78. Mrs. William M. Ramey to Duke Loyalty Fund, January 19, 1968, Fraternities—Title VI, 1965–1968, box 14, Douglas M. Knight Records, DU; also cited in Syrett, *Company He Keeps*, 257.

79. Knight to Alumnae of Sigma Delta Chapter of Kappa Delta Sorority, n.d., Fraternities—Title VI, 1965–1968, box 14, Douglas M. Knight Records, DU. After severing ties with the national sorority, the chapter became a local sorority on the Duke campus and conducted rush under the name Kappa Delta Tau. The notice in the *Duke Chronicle* stated that by the end of rush, the group would have formulated plans for the name, program, and other organizational details of the chapter going forward. The chapter was "pleased with its independence and with the accompanying freedom to [choose] whomever they wish as members." Local KΔ president Lucy Brady noted that "the chapter [had] always had a very strong stand against discriminatory policy" and "was more liberal than the national desired, and we decided it was worth it to us to keep our position rather than knuckle under." See Dave Shaffer, "Kappa Delta Goes Local," *Duke Chronicle* 64, no. 8 [n.d.], box 3, Panhellenic Council Records, DU.

80. MacLean, "Neo-Confederacy versus the New Deal," 320; McGirr, *Suburban Warriors*; Lowndes, *From the New Deal*, 55–70; Kruse, *White Flight*; Lassiter, *Silent Majority*; Crespino, *In Search of Another Country*.

Chapter Seven. "Inequality for All and Mint Juleps, Too"

1. Neil Aronstam, "Southern Sorority Toured," *Red and Black*, February 11, 1964, UGA.
2. Pratt, "Long Journey," 110.
3. Aronstam, "Southern Sorority Toured."

4. Blain Roberts, *Pageants, Parlors, and Pretty Women*, 216.

5. Teters, "Albert Burton Moore," 122–25; "Montgomery Holiday—Costume Show Continues Civil War Centennial," *New York Times*, February 16, 1961, 21.

6. Gamma Pi Chapter of Zeta Tau Alpha House Corporation to Suzanne Stewart, January 9, 1961, box 2, folder 1 (Integration), Dean of Women Records: Edith L. Stallings and Louise McBee UA97–119, UGA. On the other hand, UGA fraternities seemed to have no such directives from their alumni advisers. Historian Robert Pratt has described white fraternity men who very visibly protested the university's desegregation at this time by "serenad[ing]" the hanged blackface effigy of Holmes "with choruses of Dixie, singing 'There'll never be a nigger in the _____ [fraternity] house,' whose various names they inserted." See Pratt, "Rhetoric of Hate," 245.

7. Gamma Pi Chapter to Stewart, January 9, 1961.

8. Minutes 1960, 52, Edgewater Conference File, ATΩ National Officers (41/91/31), ATΩ, UI.

9. In July 1965 the Tri-Delta chapter at Colby College in Waterville, Maine, had its charter revoked by nationals because "the college demanded local autonomy and banned required participation in anything of a religious nature," but some sororities still maintained an emphasis on Christian tradition in their rituals. See "Discussions of Local Autonomy," *Banta's Greek Exchange* 53, no. 3 (July 1965): 210–11. Likewise, as discussed in chapter 6, the Sigma Delta chapter of Kappa Delta at Duke lost their charter in 1967 after signing an affirmation that the chapter was nondiscriminatory, against the wishes of KΔ's national president, and the Alpha Xi Delta chapter at UVM gave up their charter rather than give in to their nationals' discriminatory membership policy.

10. S.O.S. "On Sororities," [1961], Newspaper Clippings, 1963–1971, box 3, Panhellenic Council Records, DU.

11. Ibid.

12. Box 31–32, Statistics, 1925–1999, Office of the University Registrar Records, DU.

13. Minutes, 1962, 96, Edgewater Conference File, box 1, ATΩ National Officers (41/93/31), ATΩ, UI.

14. Ibid.

15. Ibid., 97.

16. Some deans of women, such as Katherine Carmichael at UNC, were hesitant to abandon rules of *in loco parentis*. They believed that closing rules, which required women to be back in their dorms or sorority houses by a certain time each night, provided women some protection from male dates who may have been pressing them for sexual activity. Other deans of women, however, such as Emily Taylor at the University of Kansas and Mary Grace Wilson at Duke, saw parietals less as protection for and more as a hindrance to women's learning to make their own decisions. Sartorius, *Deans of Women*, 89; Lucy Gruy, "New Responsibility for Students," *Duke Alumni Register* 55 (March–May 1969): 53.

17. "Panhellenic Plans a New Image," March 1967, 2, Sororities, Panhellenic Council, 1940–1977, box 33, series 10.2, Office of the Vice Chancellor for Student Affairs Records (#40124), University Archives, UNC.

18. Ibid., 4.

19. Maxine Blake, "Report on Requested Visit to University of North Carolina Panhellenic," August 21, 1969, College Panhellenic Area Advisor Reports of Workshops, 1964–1969, box 1, College Panhellenic Committee File (41/82/40), NPC, UI.

20. Maxine Blake, "Memo Concerning: Sororities and Emory University, Atlanta, Georgia," May 22, 1968, College Panhellenic Area Advisor Reports of Workshops, 1964–1969, box 1, College Panhellenic Committee File (41/82/40), NPC, UI.

21. Janis Johnson, "Panhel President Quits Sororities," *Duke Chronicle*, September 20, 1967, Newspaper Clippings, 1963–1971, box 3, Panhellenic Council Records, DU.

22. "Interviews: Steve Johnston, Leo Hart, Anne Oliver," *Duke Alumni Register* 55 (March–May 1969): 12; Thomas B. Rainey and Bunny Small, "The Duke Crisis: 'It Ain't Over,'" *North American Review* 253, no. 2 (1969): 30–33, 46.

23. "Kennerty Quits Panhel as Her Reforms Beaten," *Duke Chronicle*, October 23, 1970.

24. "Text of Kennerty's Letter," *Duke Chronicle*, October 23, 1970.

25. Peggy Eutemark Smith, telephone conversation with author, March 25, 2018.

26. Kathryn Smith Pyle, telephone conversation with author, March 11, 2018.

27. Wallenstein, *Higher Education*, 12, 34–35, 241. Wallenstein notes that by 1955, African American students, including some undergraduates, had enrolled at what he terms "historically nonblack schools" in former Confederate states, including the University of Virginia, Virginia Polytechnic Institute, UNC, the University of Arkansas, and the University of Texas. He argues that "resistance to integrated higher education 'stiffened as a consequence' of the *Brown* decision" (35).

28. Turner, *Sitting In and Speaking Out*, 22, 264–65.

29. Pratt, "Long Journey," 107; Turner, *Sitting In and Speaking Out*, chapter 7, esp. 205.

30. Ross, *Divine Nine*, 424.

31. Mary Grace Wilson to Frank De Vyver, Re: Duke sorority membership, July 6, 1965, Sororities, 1957–1966, box 39, Woman's College Records, DU.

32. "239 Women Get Sorority Bids," *Duke Chronicle*, October 18, 1967, Newspaper Clippings, 1963–1971, box 3, Panhellenic Council Records, DU. Prior to desegregating the Duke Nursing School and the North Carolina Beta chapter of Pi Beta Phi, Allen had been among a small number of black students chosen to desegregate the white high school in her hometown of Elizabeth City, North Carolina, in 1964. See Donna Allen Harris Interview, December 4, 2008, 2, Oral History Program, DMCA.

33. The author contacted Donna Allen Harris about this project, but Ms. Harris did not wish to add any further details of her sorority experience beyond what she had previously stated in her oral history interview for the DMCA.

34. "Interviews: Merrill Ware, Bob Creamer, Donna Allen," *Duke Alumni Register* 55 (March–May 1969): 32.

35. Harris Interview, 14.

36. Ibid., 15, 25.

37. Ibid.

38. "239 Women Get Sorority Bids."

39. Turner, *Sitting In and Speaking Out*, 203–4.

40. David Kross, "A Step Forward for Women's Rights: UGA in the 1960s," *Red and*

Black, March 28, 2002, UGA; Cynthia Baugh, "Black Rushee Relates Exence; Describes Reaction as 'Priceless,'" *Red and Black*, October 1, 1968, UGA.

41. Baugh, "Black Rushee Relates Experience."

42. Ibid.

43. Ibid. By the late 1960s the slow growth in the number of African American students on historically white university campuses in the South led to requests for chapters of historically black fraternities and sororities. At UGA, African American students founded the Zeta Pi chapter of the Alpha Phi Alpha fraternity on May 10, 1969, and the Zeta Psi chapter of Delta Sigma Theta sorority on November 11, 1969. At UNC several African American students founded the Psi Delta chapter of Omega Psi Phi fraternity on February 17, 1973, followed shortly thereafter by the establishment of the Kappa Omicron chapter of Delta Sigma Theta sorority on July 21, 1973. At Duke, NPHC fraternity and sorority chapters arrived in 1974 and 1975. See Alpha Phi Alpha, https://greeklife.uga.edu/content_page /alpha-phi-alpha-content-page, accessed January 23, 2020; Delta Sigma Theta, https:// greeklife.uga.edu/content_page/delta-sigma-theta-content-page, accessed January 23, 2020; UNC NPHC Chapters, https://www.uncnphc.com/chapters, accessed February 16, 2020; Frederick W. Schroeder Jr. to Omega Psi Phi Fraternity, Inc., September 27, 1972, Fraternities and Sororities Correspondence, 1969–1978, box 32, series 10.2, Office of the Vice Chancellor for Student Affairs Records (#40124), University Archives, UNC.

44. Baugh, "Black Rushee Relates Experience."

45. Foxworthy to Page, February 17, 1972, NPC-NAWDAC Liaison Committee, 1972–1977, box 1, Committee File (41/82/50), NPC, UI.

46. Foxworthy to Mary Burt Nash, February 15, 1972, NPC-NAWDAC Liaison Committee, 1972–1977, box 1, Committee File (41/82/50), NPC, UI.

47. Foxworthy to Page, February 17, 1972.

48. Frische to Foxworthy, February 22, 1972, NPC-NAWDAC Liaison Committee, 1972–1977, box 1, Committee File (41/82/50), NPC, UI; Harriet R. Frische obituary, August 15, 2004, https://www.legacy.com/obituaries/azcentral/obituary.aspx?n=harriet-r -frische&pid=2517694.

49. Carmichael, "Notes Concerning the Activist Student Life at the University of North Carolina," July 8, 1970, folder 85, box 3, series 2.1, Office of the Dean of Women Records (#40125), University Archives, UNC. A women's liberation group organized at UNC in 1969.

50. Stombler, "'Buddies' or 'Slutties,'" 297–98. Stombler notes that the little sisters are chosen for their "beauty and sociability." The little sister organizations were viewed critically and that many disbanded by the 1980s and 1990s when the groups became associated with gang and acquaintance rape.

51. "Little Sigma's," *Beta Nu's Letter* 9 (1971–1972): 4, Alpha Delta Pi–Beta Nu, University of Georgia, Chapter Histories, AΔΠ.

52. Duke Women's Liberation, Program and Discussion, February 18, 1971, Newspaper Clippings, 1963–1971, box 3, Panhellenic Council Records, DU. At UGA, Women's Oppression Must End Now (WOMEN) organized in 1971.

53. Ibid.

54. Debby Godfrey, "Letter to the Edit Council, Sororities," *Duke Chronicle*, February 19, 1971.

55. bid.; Mary Hook, "Letter to the Edit Council, Sororities," *Duke Chronicle*, February 21, 1971.

56. "Women's Lib Views Rush," *Duke Chronicle*, February 21, 1971.

57. Mathews and De Hart, *Sex, Gender*, vii.

58. Ibid., 154–57.

59. Cook to Jacobsen, March 12, 1975, Chairman's Correspondence, 1974–1975, box 1 (41/82/20), NPC, UI.

60. NAWDAC Resolutions, 1974 Conference, NPC-NAWDAC Liaison Committee, 1973–1975, Committee File (41/82/50), NPC, UI.

61. Cook to Jacobsen, March 12, 1975.

62. Mathews and De Hart, *Sex, Gender*, 152–56.

63. Jacobsen to Cook, March 28, 1975, Chairman's Correspondence, 1974–1975, box 1, Chairman's File (41/82/20), NPC, UI.

64. "The State of the Sorority: Q&A with the National President," *Angelos* 72, no. 6 (Winter 1978): 271.

65. "An Interview with the President," *Anchora* 92, no. 1 (Spring 1976): 3.

66. Williamson to Dix, 1973, College Panhellenic Area Workshops, 1972–1973, NPC College Panhellenic Committee File, 1955–1980, 1991, box 1, Committee File (41/82/50), NPC, UI.

67. Nye to NPC delegates, Re: Visit to Michigan, February 27–28, 1974, College Panhellenic Committee, 1973–1974, box 1 (41/82/50), NPC, UI; "Obituary for Kathleen Davis Nye," http://www.bryanbraker.com/obituaries/Kathleen-Nye/#!/Obituary, accessed January 23, 2020.

68. Bailey and Farber, *America in the Seventies*, 4–6.

69. "Greeks Having Growth Trend," February 20, 1975, *Red and Black*, 6, UGA; Hoge et al., "Trends in College Students' Values," 263–64.

70. Dr. Frederic D. Kershner Jr., "The Colorado Study, Its Meaning for Women's Fraternities," 1969, Operation Greek, 1969–1971, box 1, Fraternity Affairs File (41/82/9), NPC, UI.

71. NPC Meeting, 1973, 159, NPC Proceedings (41/82/10), NPC, UI; Myra Foxworthy obituary, https://www.dignitymemorial.com/obituaries/oklahoma-city-ok/myra-foxworthy-6657311#, accessed January 23, 2020.

72. Myra Foxworthy to Gwen M. McKeeman and Virginia F. Jacobsen, February 5, 1972, box 1, Research and Public Relations Committee, 1967–1972, Committee File (41/82/50), NPC, UI.

73. Turk, *Bound by a Mighty Vow*, 96–99.

74. Eleanor Smith Slaughter, "Expansion: Healthy, Orderly Growth," *Anchora* 91, no. 1 (Spring 1975): 2–3. Prior to 1951, when members of the Association of Educational Sororities became full members of the NPC, the two umbrella organizations had an agreement

that member sororities would not colonize on each other's campuses. Afterward, NPC groups were free to colonize on campuses that began as teachers' colleges.

75. Foxworthy to Connie Wallace, March 5, 1973, Junior and Community Colleges, 1971–1973, box 1, Fraternity Affairs File (41/82/9), NPC, UI.

76. History of UNC Pembroke, http://www.uncp.edu/about-uncp/history; "About UNCW: UNC Wilmington History and Traditions," http://uncw.edu/aboutuncw /aboutHistory.html; J. Patricia "Pat" Merrill obituary, https://www.tributearchive.com /obituaries/7159464/J-Patricia-Pat-Merrill. All websites accessed January 23, 2020.

77. Pat Merrill to NPC Fraternities with Chapters at UNC-Wilmington, December 8, 1973, College Panhellenic Committee, 1971–1973, box 1, College Panhellenic Committee File (41/82/40), NPC, UI. By the late 1970s, the NPC had decided not to colonize at junior colleges. See "The State of the Sorority: Q&A with the National President," *Angelos* 72, no. 6 (Winter 1978): 271.

78. Audrey Shafer to Gwen McKeeman and Lynn Peterson, Re: Housemothers' Seminar at Columbia, Missouri, June 25, 1977, box 1, College Panhellenic Committee, 1976–1977, College Panhellenic Committee File (41/82/40), NPC, UI; Bailey and Farber, *America in the Seventies*, 7.

79. "Greeks Having Growth Trend," *Red and Black*, February 20, 1975, 6, UGA.

80. Borstelmann, *1970s*, 80–84.

81. The *Key* featured an ad for the new career program of Kappa Kappa Gamma, called Choices. See *Key* 95, no. 2 (Summer 1978): 13. See also "Three Designing Delta Gammas," *Anchora* 93, no. 4 (Winter 1977): 17–19.

82. Lamb, "The Volunteer Professional," *Angelos* 71, no. 5 (Spring 1976): 195–96.

83. Schulman, *Seventies*, 4–8.

84. Andree Brooks, "Greek Row Glows Golden Again," *New York Times*, November 9, 1986, EDUC67.

85. Edward B. Fiske, "Students Don't Go for Anything Goes Anymore," *New York Times*, March 18, 1984, E8.

86. "What's New on Campus," *Key* 90, no. 2 (Fall 1973): 21.

87. Schulman, *Seventies*, 3–7.

88. "Another Round for the Bad Boys," *New York Times*, July 31, 2011, AR10; "Toga! One of the Forces behind *Animal House* Reveals That the Movie Was Truer to Life than You Might Have Guessed," *New York Times*, November 5, 2006, I18.

89. "Are Values Out of Style?" *Key* 90, no. 1 (Spring 1973): 3.

Conclusion. An Alpha Phi-asco and Other Peculiar Institutions

1. In the midst of the Alpha Phi controversy, the Beta Mu chapter's extravagant foyer with winding staircase, faux Georgian paneling, and giant sparkling chandelier was featured in a *Southern Living* website gallery showcasing the South's most outrageously appointed sorority houses, which noted that having a professional decorator is "the new norm." "The South's Most Beautiful Sorority Houses," *Southern Living*, http://www.southernliving.com

/home-garden/decorating/sorority-houses/alpha-phi-university-of-alabama-image, accessed January 22, 2020.

2. "Y'all culture" is my term for the increasing use of "y'all" as a national signifier of "southernness," which includes the recent tendency of attaching "y'all" to other words to denote a southern incarnation of a particularly nonsouthern or neutral term.

3. Elizabeth B. Boyd, "Remove the Southern Belle from Her Inglorious Perch," *Washington Post*, August 14, 2015.

4. Abbey Crain and Matt Ford, "The Final Barrier: 50 Years Later, Segregations Still Exists," *Crimson-White*, September 18, 2013.

5. https://www.ua.edu/about/quickfacts, accessed January 22, 2020.

6. Terrence F. Ross, "A Brief and Recent History of Bigotry at Fraternities," *Atlantic*, March 10, 2015, https://www.theatlantic.com/education/archive/2015/03/a-brief-and-recent-history-of-bigotry-at-fraternities/387319/.

7. "Adventure in Friendship," https://npcwomen.dynamic.omegafi.com/wp-content/uploads/sites/2037/2017/10/Adventure-in-Friendship-2017-Web.pdf, accessed January 22, 2020.

8. "2011–12 Election Cycle Most Successful for FSPAC," FSPAC newsletter, Spring 2013, 2, http://fspac.org/wp-content/uploads/2018/10/Spring-2013.pdf; "FSPAC Donor Honor Roll," http://fspac.org/wp-content/uploads/2019/10/2019-Donor-List-by-Giving-Level-10-14-9.pdf, accessed February 16, 2020; Greeks for Romney-Ryan Fundraising Memo, September 10, 2012, http://images.politico.com/global/2012/09/greek22.pdf; Deroy Murdock, "Disqualified!" *National Review*, December 18, 2002, http://www.nationalreview.com/article/205362/disqualified-deroy-murdock.

9. Eric Levitz, "Frats Hire Trent Lott to Lobby for Fewer Sexual Assault Investigations on Campuses," *New York Magazine: The Cut*, October 18, 2015, http://nymag.com/thecut/2015/10/frats-hire-trent-lott-to-lobby.html; "H.R. 3403—Safe Campus Act of 2015," https://www.congress.gov/bill/114th-congress/house-bill/3403/cosponsors, accessed January 22, 2020; Tyler Bishop, "Forcing College to Involve Police in Sexual-Assault Investigations?" *Atlantic*, November 19, 2015, https://www.theatlantic.com/education/archive/2015/11/forcing-colleges-to-involve-police-in-sexual-assault-investigations/416736/.

10. "Government Relations," https://www.npcwomen.org/priorities/npc-government-relations/, accessed January 22, 2020; C. Ramsey Fahs, "In Historic Move, Harvard to Penalize Final Clubs, Greek Organizations," *Harvard Crimson*, May 6, 2016, http://www.thecrimson.com/article/2016/5/6/college-sanctions-clubs-greeklife/; Anemona Hartocollis, "Republicans Stuff Education Bill with Conservative Social Agenda," *New York Times*, February 1, 2018, https://www.nytimes.com/2018/02/01/us/first-amendment-education-bill.html.

11. Madeline St. Amour, "Next Steps Uncertain after Bipartisan Agreement," Inside Higher Ed, December 5, 2019, https://www.insidehighered.com/news/2019/12/05/senate-has-bipartisan-proposal-what-comes-next; Andy Tsubasa Field, "Fraternities and Sororities Sue Harvard over Its Policy against Single-Sex Groups," *Chronicle of Higher Education*, December 3, 2018, https://www.chronicle.com/article/FraternitiesSororities/245251; Valerie

Strauss, "Harvard Rescinds Policies against Fraternities, Sororities, and Other Single-Gender Organizations," *Washington Post*, June 30, 2020, https://www.washingtonpost.com/education/2020/06/30/harvard-rescinds-policy-against-fraternities-sororities-other-single-gender-organizations/, accessed July 8, 2020.

12. Amanda Epstein, "Kappa Alpha Theta Chapter Official at Swarthmore," *Swarthmore Phoenix*, February 7, 2013, https://swarthmorephoenix.com/2013/02/07/kappa-alpha-theta-chapter-official-at-swarthmore/; "1933 Sororities Abolished," https://www.swarthmore.edu/a-brief-history/1933-sororities-abolished; Zipporah Osei, "After Protests, Swarthmore Will End All Greek Life on Campus," *Chronicle of Higher Education*, May 10, 2019, https://www.chronicle.com/article/After-Protests-Swarthmore/246279.

13. Screenshot of Google search results for "Edgewater Conference" in author's possession. Accessed March 16, 2019.

BIBLIOGRAPHY

Source Repository Abbreviations

AΔΠ	Alpha Delta Pi Archives
ATΩ	Alpha Tau Omega Archives
AU	Auburn University
BSC	Birmingham-Southern College
DMCA	Duke Medical Center Archives
DU	Duke University
HC	Stewart S. Howe Collection
HP	Wilson Heller Papers
LSU	Louisiana State University
NCC	North Carolina Collection
NPC	National Panhellic Conference Archives
SC	University of South Carolina
SHC	Southern Historical Collection
SOHP	Southern Oral History Program
UA	University of Alabama
UGA	University of Georgia
UI	University of Illinois
UM	University of Maryland
UNC	University of North Carolina
WM	College of William and Mary

Manuscript Sources

Alpha Delta Pi Archives, Alpha Delta Pi Memorial Headquarters, Atlanta, Georgia
    Adelphean
    Chapter Files
    Edgewater Conference File

Auburn University, Auburn, Alabama
Special Collections and Archives, Ralph Brown Draughon Library
    Office of the Vice President of Student Affairs Records
    Glomerata
Birmingham-Southern College
    La Revue
College of William and Mary, Williamsburg, Virginia
Special Collections Research Center, Earl G. Swem Library
    Colonial Echo
    Margetta Doris Hirsch Doyle Papers
    Frances C. Cosby Nettles Papers
    The Flat Hat
    Laura Parrish Papers
    Grace Warren Landrum Papers
    Office of the Dean of Women Records
    University Archives Oral History Collection
        Loren Tipton Cornette Interview
        Mary Edwards Interview
        John R. L. Johnson Interview
        Janet Coleman Kimbrough Interview
        Wilfred J. Lambert Interview
        Helen Campbell Walker Interview
    Women's Student Cooperative Government Association Records
Duke University, Durham, North Carolina
University Archives, David M. Rubenstein Rare Book and Manuscript Library
    Alice Mary Baldwin Papers
    Black History at Duke Reference Collection
    Chanticleer
    Duke Alumni Register
    Duke Chronicle
    Kappa Kappa Gamma, Delta Beta Chapter Records
    Douglas M. Knight Records
        Order of the White Duchy Records
    Office of the University Registrar Records
    Panhellenic Council Records
    Phi Mu, Gamma Epsilon Chapter Records
    Dorothy Newsom Rankin Papers
    University Archives Photographic Negative Collection
    Woman's College Records
    YWCA of Duke University Records
Duke Medical Center Archives, Duke University Medical Center
    Donna Allen Harris Interview
Louisiana State University, Baton Rouge, Louisiana

T. Harry Williams Center for Oral History Collections
    Ordell Griffith Interview
    Jane Porter Middleton Interview
University of Alabama, Tuscaloosa, Alabama
W. S. Hoole Special Collections Library
    Corolla
    Daphne Cunningham Diaries
    Agnes Ellen Harris Collection
    Mahout
University of Georgia, Athens, Georgia
Hargrett Rare Book and Manuscript Library
    University Archives
    Dean of Women Records: Edith L. Stallings and Louise McBee
    Mary Dorothy Lyndon Papers
    Red and Black
University of Illinois, Urbana, Illinois
Student Life and Culture Archives
    Alpha Tau Omega Archives
    Daily Illini
    Wilson B. Heller Papers
    Stewart S. Howe Collection
    National Panhellenic Conference Archives
    Office of Student Personnel and Dean of Women Papers
    Oral Histories of the Great Depression at the University of Illinois
        Kay Fishbaugh Carr Interview
        Pauline Linebarger McClain Interview
        Florence Hood Miner Interview
        Portia Allyn Smith Interview
        Audrey Moore Stewart Interview
University of Maryland, College Park, Maryland
Special Collections and University Archives, Hornbake Library
    Terrapin
University of North Carolina at Chapel Hill, Chapel Hill, North Carolina
Louis Round Wilson Library
    North Carolina Collection
        Carolina Handbook
        Daily Tar Heel
        Handbook for Women Students at the University of North Carolina
        University of North Carolina at Chapel Hill Image Collection
        University of North Carolina at Chapel Hill Photographic Laboratory Collection
        Yackety Yack
    Southern Historical Collection
        Henry T. Clark Papers

Guion Griffis Johnson Papers
Anne Queen Papers
Southern Oral History Program
Guion Griffis Johnson Interview
Sharon Mujica Interview
University Archives
Campus Y of the University of North Carolina at Chapel Hill Records
Office of Fraternity and Sorority Life of the University of North Carolina at Chapel Hill Records
Office of the Vice Chancellor of Student Affairs of the University of North Carolina at Chapel Hill Records
Office of the Dean of Women of the University of North Carolina at Chapel Hill Records
Student Government of the University of North Carolina at Chapel Hill Records
University of South Carolina, Columbia, South Carolina
South Caroliniana Library
Manuscripts
Gamecock
Garnet and Black
University Catalog
University Archives
Dean of Women Records
Mary Fitch Oral History Interview

Newspapers and Journals

Adelphean of Alpha Delta Pi
Aglaia of Phi Mu
Alpha Phi Quarterly
Anchora of Delta Gamma
Angelos of Kappa Delta
Atlantic Monthly
Banta's Greek Exchange
Crescent of Gamma Phi Beta
Eleusis of Chi Omega
Greensboro Daily News
LIFE
Lyre of Alpha Chi Omega
Key of Kappa Kappa Gamma

National Review
New York Times
North American Review
Rattle of Theta Chi
Section Two of the Adelphean
Themis of Zeta Tau Alpha
Trident of Delta Delta Delta
Urn of Beta Sigma Omicron
Woman's Home Companion
Ubyssey
U.S. News and World Report
Vermont Quarterly
Washington Post

Published and Unpublished Secondary Sources

Abland, Linda Welch. *Sisters: Celebrating Alpha Delta Pi Sisterhood*. Atlanta: Alpha Delta Pi Sorority, 2001.

Andrew, John A., III. *The Other Side of the Sixties: Young Americans for Freedom and the Rise of Conservative Politics*. New Brunswick, N.J.: Rutgers University Press, 1997.

Atkins, Leah Rawls. *Blossoms amid the Deep Verdure, 1892–1992: A Century of Women at Auburn*. Auburn, Ala.: Auburn University, 1993.

Bailey, Beth. *From Front Porch to Back Seat: Courtship in Twentieth-Century America*. Baltimore: Johns Hopkins University Press, 1988.

———. *Sex in the Heartland*. Cambridge, Mass.: Harvard University Press, 1999.

Bailey, Beth, and David Farber, eds. *America in the Seventies*. Lawrence: University Press of Kansas, 2004.

Baldwin, Alice Mary. "The Woman's College as I Remember It." Unpublished manuscript, 1959.

Barrow, David C. "Co-Education at the University; An Address before the Georgia Federation of Women's Clubs, at the Twenty-Sixth Annual Convention." Athens, University of Georgia, 1922.

Bartley, Numan. *The Rise of Massive Resistance: Race and Politics in the South during the 1950s*. Baton Rouge: Louisiana State University Press, 1967.

Bashaw, Carolyn Terry. *"Stalwart Women": A Historical Analysis of Deans of Women in the South*. New York: Teachers College Press, 1999.

Becque, Fran. "Coeducation and the History of Women's Fraternities, 1867–1902." PhD diss., Southern Illinois University, 2002.

Bederman, Gail. *Manliness and Civilization: A Cultural History of Gender and Race in the United States, 1880–1917*. Chicago: University of Chicago Press, 1995.

Bishir, Catherine W. "Landmarks of Power: Building a Southern Past in Raleigh and Wilmington, North Carolina, 1885–1915." In *Where These Memories Grow: History, Memory, and Southern Identity*, edited by W. Fitzhugh Brundage, 139–68. Chapel Hill: University of North Carolina Press, 2000.

Blight, David. *Race and Reunion: The Civil War in American Memory*. Cambridge, Mass.: Harvard University Press, 2001.

Borstelmann, Thomas. *The 1970s: A New Global History from Civil Rights to Economic Inequality*. Princeton, N.J.: Princeton University Press, 2011.

Brandt, Allen. *No Magic Bullet: A Social History of Venereal Disease in the United States since 1880*. New York: Oxford University Press, 1986.

Brandt, Lydia Mattice. "Re-Creating Mount Vernon: The Virginia Building at the 1893 Chicago World's Columbian Exposition." *Winterthur Portfolio* 43, no. 1 (Spring 2009): 70–114.

———. *First in the Homes of His Countrymen: George Washington's Mount Vernon in the American Imagination*. Charlottesville: University Press of Virginia, 2016.

Breines, Wini. *Young, White, and Miserable: Growing Up Female in the Fifties*. Boston: Beacon, 1992.

Brown, James T. *Baird's Manual of American College Fraternities*. 10th ed. New York: self-published, 1923.

Buckley, William F., Jr. *God and Man at Yale: The Superstitions of Academic Freedom*. Washington, D.C.: Regnery, 1951.

Burgess, Ernest W., Paul Wallin, and Gladys Denny Shultz. *Courtship, Engagement, and Marriage*. Philadelphia: J. B. Lippincott, 1954.

Cahn, Susan K. *Sexual Reckonings: Southern Girls in a Troubling Age*. Cambridge, Mass.: Harvard University Press, 2007.

Cash, Wilbur J. *The Mind of the South*. New York: Alfred A. Knopf, 1941. Reprinted with a new introduction by Bertram Wyatt-Brown. New York: Vintage Books, 1991.

Clement, Alice. *Love for Sale: Courting, Treating, and Prostitution in New York City, 1900–1945*. Chapel Hill: University of North Carolina Press, 2006.

Cohen, Sol. "The Mental Hygiene Movement, the Development of Personality, and the School: The Medicalization of Education." *History of Education Quarterly* 23, no. 2 (1983): 123–49.

Coomes, Michael D., Elizabeth J. Witt, and George D. Kuh. "Kate Hevner Mueller: Woman for a Changing World." *Journal of Counseling and Development* 65, no. 8 (1987): 407–15.

Coontz, Stephanie. *The Way We Never Were: American Families and the Nostalgia Trap*. New York: Basic Books, 2000.

———. *Marriage, a History: How Love Conquered Marriage*. New York: Penguin, 2005.

Cott, Nancy. *The Grounding of Modern Feminism*. New Haven, Conn.: Yale University Press, 1987.

———. *Bonds of Womanhood: "Woman's Sphere" in New England, 1780–1835*. 2nd edition, with a new preface. New Haven, Conn.: Yale University Press, 1997.

Cox, Karen. *Dixie's Daughters: The United Daughters of the Confederacy and the Preservation of Confederate Culture*. Gainesville: University Press of Florida, 2003.

———. *Dreaming of Dixie: How the South Was Created in American Popular Culture*. Chapel Hill: University of North Carolina Press, 2011.

Crespino, Joseph. *In Search of Another Country: Mississippi and the Conservative Counterrevolution*. Princeton, N.J.: Princeton University Press, 2007.

Dalgliesh, Elizabeth Rhodes. *The History of Alpha Chi Omega, 1885–1948*. 6th ed. Menasha, Wisc.: George Banta, 1948.

Daniel, Pete. *Lost Revolutions: The South in the 1950s*. Chapel Hill: University of North Carolina Press, 2000.

Dean, Pamela. "Women on the Hill: A History of Women at the University of North Carolina." Division of Student Affairs, University of North Carolina at Chapel Hill, 1987.

———. "Covert Curriculum: Class, Gender, and Student Culture at New South Woman's College, 1892–1910." PhD diss., University of North Carolina at Chapel Hill, 1995.

Delegard, Kirsten Marie. *Battling Miss Bolsheviki: The Origins of Female Conservatism in the United States*. Philadelphia: University of Pennsylvania Press, 2011.

Delpar, Helen. "Coeds and the 'Lords of Creation': Women Students at the University of Alabama, 1893–1930." *Alabama Review* 42 (October 1989): 292–312.

D'Emilio, John, and Estelle B. Freedman. *Intimate Matters: A History of Sexuality in America.* 3rd ed. Chicago: University of Chicago Press, 2012.

Denny, George H. "The University of Alabama Makes Provision for Women Students." *University of Alabama Index* 12, no. 4 (March 1, 1929).

Dorr, Lisa Lindquist. "Fifty Percent Moonshine and Fifty Percent Moonshine: Social Life and College Youth Culture in Alabama, 1913–1933." In *Manners and Southern History,* edited by Ted Ownby, 45–75. Oxford: University Press of Mississippi, 2007.

Douglas, Susan J. *Where the Girls Are: Growing Up Female with the Mass Media.* New York: Times Books, 1994.

Drewry, Henry N., Humphrey Doermann, and Susan H. Anderson. *Stand and Prosper: Private Black Colleges and Their Students.* Princeton, N.J.: Princeton University Press, 2001.

Durden, Robert. *The Launching of Duke University, 1924–1949.* Durham, N.C.: Duke University Press, 1993.

Dyer, Thomas G. *The University of Georgia: A Bicentennial History, 1785–1985.* Athens: University of Georgia Press, 1985.

Eagles, Charles. *Price of Defiance: James Meredith and the Integration of Ole Miss.* Chapel Hill: University of North Carolina Press, 2009.

Eisenmann, Linda. *Higher Education for Women in Postwar America, 1945–1965.* Baltimore: Johns Hopkins University Press, 2008.

Farnham, Christie Anne. *The Education of the Southern Belle: Higher Education and Student Socialization in the Antebellum South.* New York: New York University Press, 1994.

Fass, Paula. *The Damned and the Beautiful: American Youth in the 1920s.* New York: Oxford University Press, 1977.

Faust, Drew Gilpin. *Mothers of Invention: Women of the Slaveholding South in the American Civil War.* Chapel Hill: University of North Carolina Press, 1996.

Ferguson, Christelle, et al. *The History of Chi Omega.* 3 vols. Cincinnati: Chi Omega, 1928.

Fisher, Dorothy Canfield. *The Bent Twig.* New York: Grosset & Dunlap, 1915.

Foster, Gaines. *Ghosts of the Confederacy: Defeat, the Lost Cause, and the Emergence of the New South, 1865–1913.* New York: Oxford University Press, 1987.

Foucault, Michel. *Discipline and Punish: The Birth of the Prison.* Translated by Alan Sheridan. New York: Pantheon Books, 1977.

Freeman, Margaret L. "To Seek the Good, the True, and the Beautiful: White Greek-Letter Sororities in the U.S. South and the Shaping of American Ladyhood, 1915–1975." PhD diss., College of William and Mary, 2011.

———. "'Inequality for All and Mint Juleps, Too: White Social Sororities and 'Freedom of Association' in the United States." In *The Right Side of the Sixties: Reexamining Conservatism's Decade of Transformation,* edited by Laura Jane Gifford and Daniel K. Williams, 41–59. New York: Palgrave Macmillan, 2012.

———. "A Sunny Southerner or a Beautiful Alien? The Life and Writings of Julia Magruder." *Magazine of Albemarle County History* 71 (2013): 32–59.

Freeman, Susan K. *Sex Goes to School: Girls and Sex Education before the 1960s.* Urbana:
University of Illinois Press, 2008.

Gilmore, Glenda. *Gender and Jim Crow: Women and the Politics of White Supremacy in
North Carolina, 1896–1920.* Chapel Hill: University of North Carolina Press, 1996.

Godson, Susan, Ludwell H. Johnson, Richard B. Sherman, Thad W. Tate, and Helen C.
Walker. *The College of William and Mary: A History,* vol. 2. Williamsburg, Va.: King
and Queen Press, 1993.

Goodin, Peggy. *Take Care of My Little Girl.* 1950. Reprint, New York: Berkeley Medallion
Books, 1960.

Gordon, Linda. *Pitied but not Entitled: Single Mothers and the History of Welfare, 1890–
1935.* Cambridge, Mass.: Harvard University Press, 1994.

Greene, Gael. *Sex and the College Girl. New York: Dial Press, 1964.*

Gregory, James N. *The Southern Diaspora: How the Great Migration of Black and White
Southerners Transformed America.* Chapel Hill: University of North Carolina Press,
2005.

Hale, Grace. *Making Whiteness: The Culture of Segregation in the South, 1890–1940.* New
York: Random House, 1998.

Hall, Jacquelyn Dowd. *Revolt against Chivalry: Jesse Daniel Ames and the Women's Campaign against Lynching.* New York: Columbia University Press, 1979.

Haller, Margaret Paddock. *History of Delta Delta Delta, 1888–1988.* Dallas, Tex.: Taylor,
1988.

Handler, Lisa. "In the Fraternal Sisterhood: Sororities as Gender Strategy." *Gender and Society* 9, no. 2 (1995): 236–55.

Hartmann, Susan. *The Home Front and Beyond: American Women in the 1940s.* Boston:
Twayne, 1982.

Hegarty, Marilyn E. *Victory Girls, Khaki Wackies, and Patriotutes: The Regulation of Female
Sexuality during World War II.* New York: New York University Press, 2008.

Hoge, Dean R., Cynthia L. Luna, and David K. Miller. "Trends in College Students' Values
between 1952 and 1979: A Return of the Fifties?" *Sociology of Education* 54, no. 4 (October 1981): 263–74.

Hollis, Daniel Walker. *University of South Carolina,* vol. 2, *College to University.* Columbia:
University of South Carolina Press, 1956.

Hormel, Olive Dean. *Co-Ed.* New York: Charles Scribner & Sons, 1926.

Horowitz, Helen Lefkowitz. *Alma Mater: Design and Experience in the Women's Colleges
from Their Nineteenth-Century Beginnings to the 1930's.* New York: Alfred A. Knopf,
1984.

James, Anthony. "The Defenders of Tradition: College Social Fraternities, Race, and Gender, 1945–1980." PhD diss., University of Mississippi, 1998.

———. "Political Parties: College Social Fraternities, Manhood, and the Defense of Southern Traditionalism, 1945–1960." In *White Masculinities in the Recent South,* edited by
Trent Watts, 63–84. Baton Rouge: Louisiana State University Press, 2008.

Janney, Caroline. *Burying the Dead but not the Past: Ladies Memorial Associations and the Lost Cause*. Chapel Hill: University of North Carolina Press, 2008.

Johnson, David K. *The Lavender Scare: The Cold War Persecution of Gays and Lesbians in the Federal Government*. Chicago: University of Chicago Press, 2004.

Johnson, Joan M. *Southern Ladies, New Women: Race, Region, and Club Women in South Carolina, 1890–1930*. Gainesville: University Press of Florida, 2004.

Johnston, Angus. "The United States National Student Association: Democracy, Activism, and the Idea of the Student, 1947–1978." PhD diss., City University of New York, 2009.

Jones, Anne Goodwyn. *Tomorrow Is Another Day: The Woman Writer in the South*. Baton Rouge: Louisiana State University Press, 1981.

Kammen, Michael. *Mystic Chords of Memory: The Transformation of Tradition in American Culture*. New York: Alfred A. Knopf, 1991.

Kempker, Erin M. *Big Sister: Feminism, Conservatism, and Conspiracy in the Heartland*. Urbana: University of Illinois Press, 2018.

Kinsey, Alfred. *Sexual Behavior in the Human Female*. Philadelphia: W. B. Saunders, 1953.

Kreig, Shirley Kresan. *The History of Zeta Tau Alpha, 1898–1928*. Menasha, Wisc.: George Banta, 1928.

Kruse, Kevin. *White Flight: Atlanta and the Making of Modern Conservatism*. Princeton, N.J.: Princeton University Press, 2005.

Ladd-Taylor, Molly. *Mother-Work: Women, Child-Welfare and the State, 1890–1930*. Urbana: University of Illinois Press, 1994.

Lamb, Annadell Craig. *The History of Phi Mu*. Atlanta, GA: Phi Mu Fraternity, 1982.

Lassiter, Matthew. "De Jure/De Facto Segregation: The Long Shadow of a National Myth." In *The Myth of Southern Exceptionalism*, edited by Matthew Lassiter and Joseph Crespino, 25–47. New York: Oxford University Press, 2010.

———. *The Silent Majority: Suburban Politics in the Sunbelt South*. Princeton, N.J.: Princeton University Press, 2006.

Lassiter, Matthew, and Joseph Crespino, eds. *The Myth of Southern Exceptionalism*. New York: Oxford University Press, 2010.

Lears, T. J. Jackson. *No Place of Grace: Antimodernism and Transformation of American Culture, 1880–1920*. New York: Pantheon, 1981.

Lee, Alfred McClung. *Fraternities without Brotherhood*. Boston: Beacon, 1955.

Leloudis, James L. *Schooling the New South: Pedagogy, Self, and Society in North Carolina, 1800–1920*. Chapel Hill: University of North Carolina Press, 1996.

Levere, William Collin, ed. *Leading Greeks*. Evanston, Ill., n.p., 1915.

Lewis, George. *The White South and the Red Menace: Segregationists, Anticommunism, and Massive Resistance, 1945–1965*. Gainesville: University Press of Florida, 2004.

Lindgren, James S. *Preserving the Old Dominion: Historic Preservation and Virginia Traditionalism*. Charlottesville: University Press of Virginia, 2001.

Littauer, Amanda K. *Bad Girls: Young Women, Sex, and Rebellion before the Sixties*. Chapel Hill: University of North Carolina Press, 2015.

Lowndes, Joseph E. *From the New Deal to the New Right: Race and the Southern Origins of Modern Conservatism*. New Haven, Conn.: Yale University Press, 2008.

Lumpkin, Katherine Du Pre. *Making of a Southerner*. New York: Alfred A. Knopf, 1947.

MacLean, Nancy. "Neo-Confederacy versus the New Deal: The Regional Utopia of the Modern American Right." In *The Myth of Southern Exceptionalism*, edited by Matthew Lassiter and Joseph Crespino, 308–29. New York: Oxford University Press, 2010.

Marchalonis, Shirley. *College Girls: A Century in Fiction*. New Brunswick, N.J.: Rutgers University Press, 1996.

Martin, Ida Shaw. *The Sorority Handbook*. 2nd ed. Boston: self-published, 1907.

———. *The Sorority Handbook*. 6th ed. Menasha, Wisc.: George Banta, 1919.

———. *The Sorority Handbook*. 8th ed. Boston: self-published, 1923.

Mathews, Donald G., and Jane Sherron De Hart. *Sex, Gender, and the Politics of ERA: A State and the Nation*. New York: Oxford University Press, 1990.

Mathews, Lois K. *The Dean of Women*. New York: Houghton Mifflin, 1915.

May, Elaine Tyler. *Homeward Bound: American Families in the Cold War Era*. Rev. ed. New York: Basic Books, 1999.

May, Gary. *Bending toward Justice: The Voting Rights Act and the Transformation of American Democracy*. New York: Basic Books, 2013.

McCandless, Amy Thompson. "Pedagogy and the Pedestal: The Impact of Traditional Views of Women's Place on the Curricula of Southern Colleges in the Early Twentieth Century." *Journal of Thought* 20, no. 3 (Fall 1985): 263–78.

———. "Preserving the Pedestal: Restrictions on Social Life at Southern Colleges for Women, 1920–1940." *History of Higher Education Annual* 7 (1987): 45–60.

———. *The Past in the Present: Women's Higher Education in the Twentieth-Century American South*. Tuscaloosa: University of Alabama Press, 1999.

McComb, Mary C. *The Great Depression and the Middle Class: Experts, Collegiate Youth and Business Ideology, 1929–1941*. New York: Routledge, 2006.

McEnnany, Laura. *Civil Defense Begins at Home: Militarization Meets Everyday Life in the Fifties*. Princeton, N.J.: Princeton University Press, 2000.

McGirr, Lisa. *Suburban Warriors: The Origins of the New American Right*. Princeton, N.J.: Princeton University Press, 2001.

McPherson, Tara. *Reconstructing Dixie: Race, Gender, and Nostalgia in the Imagined South*. Durham, N.C.: Duke University Press, 2003.

McRae, Elizabeth Gillespie. *Mothers of Massive Resistance: White Women and the Politics of White Supremacy*. New York: Oxford University Press, 2018.

Mettler, Suzanne. *Soldiers to Citizens: The G.I. Bill and the Making of the Greatest Generation*. New York: Oxford University Press, 2005.

Meyer, Leisa D. *Creating G.I. Jane: Sexuality and Power in the Women's Army Corps during World War II*. New York: Columbia University Press, 1996.

Meyerowitz, Joanne. "The Liberal 1950s? Reinterpreting Postwar U.S. Sexual Culture." In *Gender and the Long Postwar: Reconsiderations of the United States and the Two Germanys, 1945–1989*, edited by Karen Hagemann and Sonya Michel, 297–319. Baltimore: Johns Hopkins University and Woodrow Wilson Center Press, 2014.

Mink, Gwendolyn. *The Wages of Motherhood: Inequality in the Welfare State, 1917–1942*. Ithaca, N.Y.: Cornell University Press, 1995.

Moran, Jeffrey. *Teaching Sex: The Shaping of Adolescence in the 20th Century*. Cambridge, Mass.: Harvard University Press, 2000.

Morgan, Francesca. *Women and Patriotism in Jim Crow America*. Chapel Hill: University of North Carolina Press, 2005.

Morse, Genevieve Forbes. *A History of Kappa Delta Sorority, 1897–1972*. 2 vols. Springfield, Mo.: Kappa Delta, 1972.

Mowry, Duane. "Fraternities and Sororities in State-Supported Institutions of Learning." *Educational Review* 42 (December 1911).

Mueller, Kate Hevner. *Educating Women for a Changing World*. Minneapolis: University of Minnesota Press, 1954.

Muncy, Robyn. *Creating a Female Dominion in American Reform, 1890–1935*. New York: Oxford University Press, 1991.

Newcomer, Mabel. *A Century of Higher Education for American Women*. 1959; reprint, Washington, D.C.: Zenger, 1975.

Nickerson, Michelle. *Mothers of Conservatism: Women and the Postwar Right*. Princeton, N.J.: Princeton University Press, 2014.

Nidiffer, Jana. *Pioneering Deans of Women: More than Wise and Pious Matrons*. New York: Teachers' College Press, 2000.

Osterweis, Rollin G. *The Myth of the Lost Cause, 1865–1900*. Hamden, Conn.: Archon, 1973.

Page, Thomas Nelson. "Social Life in Old Virginia." In Page, *The Old South: Essays Social and Political*. New York: Charles Scribner's Sons, 1908.

Palmer, Gordon D. "The Higher Education of Young Women." *University of Alabama Index* 7, no. 8 (June 1924).

Paris, Leslie. "The Adventures of Peanut and Bo: Summer Camps and Early-Twentieth-Century American Girlhood." *Journal of Women's History* 12, no. 4 (Winter 2001): 47–76.

Parrish, Laura. "'When Mary Entered with Her Brother William': Women Students at the College of William and Mary, 1918–1945." MA thesis, College of William and Mary, 1988.

Patrick, Ben M. "The Front Line: Materials for a Study of Leadership in College and After." Thesis, Duke University, 1942.

Patterson, James T. *Brown v. Board of Education: A Civil Rights Milestone and Its Troubled Legacy*. New York: Oxford University Press, 2001.

Peiss, Kathy. *Cheap Amusements: Working Women and Leisure in Turn-of-the-Century New York*. Philadelphia: Temple University Press, 1986.

Peril, Lynn. *College Girls: Bluestockings, Sex Kittens, and Coeds, Then and Now*. New York: W. W. Norton, 2006.

Perlstein, Rick. *Before the Storm: Barry Goldwater and the Unmaking of the American Consensus*. New York: Hill & Wang, 2001.

Petigny, Alan. *The Permissive Society: America, 1941–1965*. New York: Cambridge University Press, 2009.

Petrina, Stephen. "Luella Cole, Sydney Pressey, and Educational Psychoanalysis, 1921–1931." *History of Education Quarterly* 44, no. 4 (2004): 524–53.

Post, Emily. *Etiquette, the Blue Book of Social Usage*. Rev. ed. New York: Funk & Wagnalls, 1955.

Pratt, Robert A. "The Rhetoric of Hate: The Demosthenian Literary Society and Its Opposition to the Desegregation of the University of Georgia, 1950–1964." *Georgia Historical Quarterly* 90, no. 2 (Summer 2006): 236–59.

———. "The Long Journey from LaGrange to Atlanta: Horace Ward and the Desegregation of the University of Georgia." In *Higher Education and the Civil Rights Movement: White Supremacy, Black Southerners, and College Campuses*, edited by Peter Wallenstein. Gainesville: University Press of Florida, 2008.

Pressey, Louella Cole. *Some College Students and Their Problems*. Columbus: Ohio State University Press, 1929.

Priddy, Bessie Leach. *A Detailed Record of Delta Delta Delta, 1881–1931*. Menasha, Wisc.: Banta, 1932.

Reed, Thomas Walter. *History of the University of Georgia*. Athens: University of Georgia, ca. 1949.

Reumann, Miriam. *American Sexual Character*. Berkeley: University of California Press, 2005.

Robbins, Alexandra. *Pledged: The Secret Life of Sororities*. New York: Hyperion, 2004.

Roberts, Blain. *Pageants, Parlors, and Pretty Women: Race and Beauty in the Twentieth-Century South*. Chapel Hill: University of North Carolina Press, 2014.

Roberts, Diane. "Living in *Southern Living*." In *Dixie Debates: Perspectives on Southern Cultures*, edited by Richard H. Kind and Helen Taylor, 85–97. New York: New York University Press, 1996.

Robson, John. *Baird's Manual of American College Fraternities*. 18th ed. Menasha, Wisc.: Banta, 1968.

Rolph, Stephanie. "Courting Conservatism: White Resistance and the Ideology of Race in the 1960s." In *The Right Side of the Sixties: Reexamining Conservatism's Decade of Transformation*, edited by Laura Gifford and Daniel Williams, 21–39. New York: Palgrave Macmillan, 2012.

Ross, Lawrence, Jr. *The Divine Nine: The History of African American Fraternities and Sororities*. New York: Kensington, 2000.

Rotskoff, Lori. *Love on the Rocks: Men, Women, and Alcohol in Post–World War II America*. Chapel Hill: University of North Carolina Press, 2002.

Ruoff, John C. "Southern Womanhood, 1865–1920: An Intellectual and Cultural Study." PhD diss., University of Illinois at Urbana-Champaign, 1976.

Sartorius, Kelly. *Deans of Women and the Feminist Movement: Emily Taylor's Activism*. New York: Palgrave Macmillan, 2014.

Schneider, Gregory L. *Cadres for Conservatism: Young Americans for Freedom and the Rise of the Contemporary Right*. New York: New York University Press, 1999.

Schrecker, Ellen. *Many Are the Crimes: McCarthyism in America*. Boston: Little, Brown, 1998.

Schulman, Bruce J. *The Seventies: The Great Shift in American Culture*. New York: Free Press, 2001.

Schwartz, Eugene G., ed. *American Students Organize: Founding the National Student Association after World War II: An Anthology and Sourcebook*. Westport, Conn.: American Council on Education/Praeger, 2006.

Schwartz, Robert A. "Reconceptualizing the Leadership Roles of Women in Higher Education: A Brief History on the Importance of Deans of Women." *Journal of Higher Education* 68, no. 5 (1997): 502–22.

———. "The Rise and Demise of Deans of Men." *Review of Higher Education* 26, no. 2 (2002): 217–39.

Scott, Anne Firor. *The Southern Lady: From Pedestal to Politics, 1830–1930*. Chicago: University of Chicago Press, 1970.

Shepardson, Francis W. *Baird's Manual of American College Fraternities*. 10th ed. Menasha, Wisc.: Banta, 1927.

———. *Baird's Manual of American College Fraternities*. 13th ed. Menasha, Wisc.: Banta, 1935. Siddons, Anne Rivers. *Heartbreak Hotel*. 1976. Reprint, New York: Pocket Books, 2007.

Silber, Nina. *The Romance of Reunion: Northerners and the South, 1865–1900*. Chapel Hill: University of North Carolina Press, 1993.

Simmons, Christina. "Companionate Marriage and the Lesbian Threat." *Frontiers* 4, no. 3 (1979): 54–59.

———. *Making Marriage Modern: Women's Sexuality from the Progressive Era to World War II*. New York: Oxford University Press, 2009.

Simmons, LaKisha. *Crescent City Girls: The Lives of Young Black Girls in Segregated New Orleans*. Chapel Hill: University of North Carolina Press, 2015.

Smith-Rosenberg, Carroll. "The New Woman as Androgyne: Social Disorder and Gender Crisis, 1870–1936." In Smith-Rosenberg, *Disorderly Conduct: Visions of Gender in Victorian America*, 245–96. New York: Oxford University Press, 1985.

Snider, William D. *Light on the Hill: A History of the University of North Carolina at Chapel Hill*. Chapel Hill: University of North Carolina Press, 1992.

Solomon, Barbara Miller. *In the Company of Educated Women: A History of Women and Higher Education in America*. New Haven, Conn.: Yale University Press, 1985.

Sparks, Robbie Smith. "A Handbook of the Alabama Polytechnic Institute." MS thesis, Alabama Polytechnic Institute, 1935.

Stansell, Christine. *City of Women: Sex and Class in New York, 1789–1860*. New York: Alfred A. Knopf, 1986.

Stein, Edward V. *The Stranger Inside You*. Philadelphia: Westminster, 1965.

Steinem, Gloria. "The Moral Disarmament of Betty Co-Ed." *Esquire*, September 1962, 243–48.

Stinson, Suzanne. *Years Remembered of Sigma Sigma Sigma: The First Fifty-Five Years, 1898–1953*. Menasha, Wisc.: Sigma Sigma Sigma, 1953.

Stombler, Mindy. "'Buddies' or 'Slutties': The Collective Sexual Reputation of Fraternity Little Sisters." *Gender and Society* 8, no. 3 (September 1994): 297–323.

Straus, Robert, and Selden Daskam Bacon. *Drinking in College*. Yale Center for Alcohol Studies. New Haven, Conn.: Yale University Press, 1953.

Strout, Shirley Kreson. *The History of Zeta Tau Alpha, 1898–1948*. Menasha, Wisc.: Banta, 1956.

Susman, Warren. "'Personality' and the Making of Twentieth-Century Culture." In Susman, *Culture as History: The Transformation of American Society in the Twentieth Century*. New York: Pantheon, 1984.

Syrett, Nicholas L. *The Company He Keeps: A History of White College Fraternities*. Chapel Hill: University of North Carolina Press, 2009.

Teters, Kristopher A. "Albert Burton Moore and Alabama's Centennial Commemoration of the Civil War: The Rhetoric of Race, Romance, and Reunion." *Alabama Review* 66, no. 2 (April 2013): 122–52.

Theusen, Sarah. "Taking the Vows of Southern Liberalism: Guion and Guy Johnson and the Evolution of an Intellectual Partnership." *North Carolina Historical Review* 74, no. 3 (1997): 284–324.

Turk, Diana B. *Bound by a Mighty Vow: Sisterhood and Women's Fraternities, 1870–1920*. New York: New York University Press, 2004.

Turner, Jeffrey A. *Sitting In and Speaking Out: Student Movements in the American South, 1960–1970*. Athens: University of Georgia Press, 2010.

United Daughters of the Confederacy. *Minutes of the Fourth Annual Meeting of the United Daughters of the Confederacy*. Nashville: Foster & Webb, 1898.

Wall, Wendy L. *Inventing the "American Way": The Politics of Consensus from the New Deal to the Civil Rights Movement*. New York: Oxford University Press, 2008.

Wallenstein, Peter, ed. *Higher Education and the Civil Rights Movement: White Supremacy, Black Southerners, and College Campuses*. Gainesville: University Press of Florida, 2008.

Waller, Willard. "The Rating and Dating Complex." *American Sociological Review* 2, no. 5 (1937): 727–34.

Ward, Jason Morgan. *Defending White Democracy: The Making of a Segregationist Movement and the Remaking of Racial Politics, 1936–1965*. Chapel Hill: University of North Carolina Press, 2011.

Ware, Susan. *Holding Their Own: American Women in the 1930s*. Boston: Twayne, 1982.

Weimann, Jeanne Madeline. *The Fair Women*. Chicago: Academy Chicago, 1981.

West, Elizabeth Cassidy. *The University of South Carolina*. Charleston, S.C.: Arcadia, 2006.

Wheeler, Marjorie Spruill. *New Women of the New South: The Leaders of the Woman Suffrage Movement in the Southern States*. New York: Oxford University Press, 1990.

White, Betty. *I Lived This Story*. New York: Doubleday, Doran, 1930.

White, Lynn, Jr. "New Yardsticks for Women's Education." *Journal of the American Association of University Women* 41, no. 1 (Fall 1947).

Whitney, Mary E. "Women and the University." Charlottesville: University of Virginia, 1969.

Wiebe, Robert. *The Search for Order, 1877–1920*. New York: Hill & Wang, 1967.

Wilkerson, Isabel. *The Warmth of Other Suns: The Epic Story of America's Great Migration*. New York: Random House, 2010.

Williams, Daniel K. *God's Own Party: The Making of the Christian Right*. New York: Oxford University Press, 2010.

Williamson, Joel. *A Rage for Order: Race Relations in the Post-Emancipation South*. New York: Oxford University Press, 1986.

Wilson, Charles Reagan. *Baptized in Blood: The Religion of the Lost Cause*. Athens: University of Georgia Press, 1980.

———. *Judgment and Grace in Dixie: Southern Faiths from Faulkner to Elvis*. Athens: University of Georgia Press, 1995.

Wiltse, Jeff. *Contested Waters: A Social History of Swimming Pools in America*. Chapel Hill: University of North Carolina Press, 2007.

Winchell, Meghan K. *Good Girls, Good Food, Good Fun: The Story of USO Hostesses during World War II*. Chapel Hill: University of North Carolina Press, 2008.

Winterer, Caroline. *The Culture of Classicism: Ancient Greece and Rome in American Intellectual Life, 1780–1910*. Baltimore: Johns Hopkins University Press, 2002.

Wolf, Suzanne Rau. *The University of Alabama, a Pictorial History*. Tuscaloosa: University of Alabama Press, 1983.

Woodward, Comer Vann. *The Strange Career of Jim Crow*. 1955. Reprint, New York: Oxford University Press, 2002.

Wyatt-Brown, Bertram. *Southern Honor: Ethics and Behavior in the Old South*. New York: Oxford University Press, 1982.

Yuhl, Stephanie J. *A Golden Haze of Memory: The Making of Historic Charleston*. Chapel Hill: University of North Carolina Press, 2005.

INDEX

CPSIA information can be obtained
at www.ICGtesting.com
Printed in the USA
LVHW031712060221
678577LV00001B/53